MADAM COMMISSIONER

Former IPS officer Meeran Chadha Borwankar is a recipient of the President of India Police Medal for Distinguished Services, the Police Medal for Meritorious Services and the Distinguished Leadership Award from the University of Minnesota. She specializes in institution building, criminal investigation as well as law and governance. Meeran holds a PhD in organizational management and a Bachelor of Law (LLB) degree from the University of Pune. A Hubert H. Humphrey Fellow of the University of Minnesota, she writes extensively for national and international journals and newspapers. Currently Meeran is on the boards of several academic institutions and serves as Independent External Monitor for the Union Bank of India and National Aluminium Company Ltd. She is the author of *Leaves of Life* and *Inspector Chougule.*

Praise for *Madam Commissioner*

'A great fighter who accepts no nonsense and is willing to call a spade a spade ... [Meeran Chadha Borwankar's] reputation as an honest, competent and fair-minded police officer preceded her wherever she was posted. She made a mark as Pune's Commissioner of Police'
Julio Ribeiro, *Tribune*

'The first female police officer to boldly take on the system'
Shobhaa Dé, *Week*

'What an extraordinary story' **Cyrus Broacha, *Cyrus Says***

'Interesting, informative and explosive' ***Global Governance News***

'Looks back at [Meeran Chadha Borwankar's] thirty-six years in service, recounts the changes and what more needs to be done' ***Hindu***

'Gripping ... vivid and inspiring ... a must-read for those who care for law enforcement, women empowerment and inclusiveness, as well as for other stakeholders of the criminal justice system who wish to bring about change and strengthen the rule of law' ***Indian Express***

'Takes the readers through thirty-six years of [Meeran Chadha Borwankar's] illustrious service from the day she entered the Lal Bahadur Shastri National Academy of Administration in Mussoorie, the challenges she faced as a lady IPS officer when it came to promotions, her brush with corruption at the highest political levels, her stints as chief of the famed Mumbai police's crime branch and how she oversaw the hanging of Ajmal Kasab' ***Rediff.com***

'Enthralling ... There is never a dull moment as Borwankar narrates the gripping stories of her career ... A riveting account of how a woman storms a male bastion, relying on a solid work ethic and an uncompromising value system. It leaves an indelible mark on policing in India, inspiring a whole generation of women. This is a story of grit and glory' ***Tribune***

MADAM COMMISSIONER

The Extraordinary Life of an

INDIAN POLICE CHIEF

MEERAN CHADHA BORWANKAR

PAN

First published 2023 by Pan
an imprint of Pan Macmillan Publishing India Private Limited
707 Kailash Building
26 K. G. Marg, New Delhi 110001
www.panmacmillan.co.in

Pan Macmillan, The Smithson, 6 Briset Street, Farringdon, London EC1M 5NR
Associated companies throughout the world
www.panmacmillan.com

ISBN 978-81-19300-04-4

5 7 9 8 6

Typeset in Arno Pro by R. Ajith Kumar, New Delhi
Printed in India by Gopsons Papers Pvt. Ltd., Noida

To my mother Shunny Chadha, a complete realist and lifelong teacher
And my father O. P. Chadha, an honest cop and ambitious parent

CONTENTS

PREFACE

While writing *Madam Commissioner,* I often wondered about the genre of my book. What could we call it? Why am I writing it and for whom? Let me be upfront about it.

This book is a record of the professional journey of a woman officer in a male-dominated police domain; it is a collage of diverse, interesting, exciting experiences. A legal treatise it is not. Through my story, I want to reach out to those who care about policing and recognize that women can and do play a significant role in law enforcement. It is also for those interested in a fair, transparent and just society.

I joined the Indian Police Service in 1981 when there were hardly any women in uniform and our very relevance was questioned. Nevertheless, I was determined to don the 'khaki'. I had opted for the Indian Audits and Accounts Service (IA&AS) in 1980 and soon realized that I had neither any aptitude nor liking for accounting. My heart was set on my father's police uniform, on a life outdoors in police jeeps, with the wind blowing through my hair. Not in an office full of files. As a young girl, it did not occur to me that even a police station came with an abundance of investigation files!

Soon after, I switched to the police services, a career that I would enjoy to the hilt. I must admit that I had a few doubts initially about my capacity to handle public order issues, but I learnt along the way. As for crime investigation, I had no qualms. To my mind it is problem-solving, and I relished the challenges that crime-fighting posed. Whether it is handling public order or detecting crime, both involve teamwork. I was fortunate to have police and prison officers, forensic experts and prosecutors coming together to form positive, healthy teams.

This is what my book reflects – not the journey of a lone ranger, but a group of which I was an integral part for thirty-six years. The many events in the book I have described as faithfully as my memory has permitted. However, some inaccuracies are bound to creep in when tracing a long professional journey.

My two earlier books are also related to my career, but they were written specifically for the youth. In *Leaves of Life,* I note some interesting episodes from my career, sharing the lessons learnt and distilling action points for my readers. *Inspector Chougule,* on the other hand, is an assortment of simple police stories. Both my books were very well received, and it encouraged me to take up a writing project of greater scope – the memoir of an Indian police chief. I hope my readers find it as interesting as I found my journey as a policewoman. I also hope that it encourages a few to don the uniform or to take interest in the working of police and in the criminal justice system that we so often criticize but do not build strong pressure on state and central governments to invest in; and that we accept the responsibility of being active partners in maintaining the 'Rule of Law' in our country instead of being mere spectators.

If I can make my readers seriously consider and act on their role in creating a robust criminal justice system in India, sharing of my journey would have served its purpose. Nelson Mandela famously said: 'There is no passion to be found playing small – in settling for a life that is less than the one you are capable of living.' I exhort all my readers to live up to their full potential. In my own career, I have always tried to do so.

Meeran Chadha Borwankar
September 2023

1

I AM BALD

'Life isn't about finding yourself. Life is about creating yourself.'

– GEORGE BERNARD SHAW

It was quite dark by the time we left Mussoorie. The bus was full of young officers, both men and women, who had just finished training at the Lal Bahadur Shastri National Academy of Administration (LBSNAA). Having spent three months studying the Foundation Course, which all Civil Services trainees are required to complete, we were parting ways to undergo further training at the academies associated with our respective services. My destination was Hyderabad's National Police Academy as I was going to train for the Indian Police Service.

We rode our bus from Mussoorie to Dehradun in complete silence, feeling the wind in our faces. All of us were tired, physically and emotionally, as we bid our goodbyes, knowing that some of us may never meet again. A sombre air hung like another traveller in the bus. The pale yellow lights inside added to the gloom of our partings. We felt the cold in our bones.

The bus halted for some time at Dehradun and there was a change of driver. The new one was young and flamboyant. He jumped into the driver's seat in Amitabh Bachchan 'eshtyle'. It was late 1981 and the film star had conquered the world with his exuberance and charisma. Some of it had rubbed off on youngsters waiting to conquer the world, just like their hero. The new driver certainly gave me that impression.

Wrapping a shawl around his shoulders with panache, he took off at a speed that made me extremely uncomfortable. But it got a roar of approval from some others in the bus: '*Yeh hui na baat* – that's the way to go!' And the foot on the escalator pressed down further.

The road being empty at that late hour, the driver kept speeding with abandon. But he had underestimated the weight of the luggage that seventy of us had put on the roof. The moment the road curved, the driver lost control of the bus. Sitting immediately behind him, I could see the bus swerving left, then right at a dangerously high speed, until it collided against the boundary wall of a house with a loud thud. In a flash I saw the driver jump out. Then an iron rod fell on my head and I lost consciousness.

When I came to, I slowly tried to regain focus and found myself bleeding profusely. It was dark and there were shrieks and clamour all around. Someone was saying loudly that no one should panic. I realized I could not stand up as the rod I thought had dropped on me was in fact a portion of the iron shelf for storing baggage above the seats. A few of the male officers were breaking the bus windows open, while others rushed out through the badly mangled doors, assisting each other along the way. With great difficulty and some help, I managed to get out through the window next to my seat. Barely able to stand, I could tell that the head injury had soaked me in blood. I felt numb.

Our attempts to flag down vehicles to take me to a hospital failed. After a few minutes which felt like hours, a truck responded to our frantic waves and stopped. The truck driver's companion not only helped me climb up to the driver's cabin but also offered his towel to put on my bleeding head injury. How thankful I was!

Dropping me off at a roadside dispensary, the truck and its crew continued on their way. And I found myself gazing at a sleepy doctor in a white coat. Or was it a compounder, or a male nurse? I had no idea. I felt dizzy and weak but noticed that he looked grave. Without uttering a single word, he cut off a huge chunk of my hair and began stitching the head wound. Too dazed to protest, I was focused on feeling grateful for having got some medical help at last. Its quality did not matter to me at that time of complete distress and exhaustion. Later, a head scan in Delhi revealed that there was no internal injury. It was a huge relief, except that I had a big bald patch on my beautiful head.

And that is how I landed up for the first phase of police training at the National Civil Defence College (NCDC) in Nagpur – wearing a massive head scarf to cover the hairless patch, thereby piquing the curiosity of many who were to train with me as part of the 1981 batch of the Indian Police Service. Many of them were not aware of my narrow escape in Dehradun. Lady luck was by my side that fateful night, or this story would have been very different. I would not be around to relate it to you.

2

GANESHI

'A hundred times every day I remind myself that my inner and outer life depend on the labours of other men, living and dead, and that I must exert myself in order to give in the same measure as I have received and am still receiving.'

– ALBERT EINSTEIN, *The World as I See It*

'The Director at the National Police Academy in Hyderabad is very tough and the Assistant Director Outdoors is a demon. They removed two trainees of the 1980 batch from the service.' Such were the warnings we received during the first two weeks of training at the National Civil Defence College in Nagpur. Anticipating a tough regime ahead and averse to taking any risks, we started running and exercising vigorously. As I had recently suffered a head injury, I was a little weak but determined not to get 'dismissed'.

A fortnight later, upon reaching Hyderabad, I noted with extreme distress that I was the only female officer in my batch. It was December 1981. I had expected very few women officers, as the IPS had yet to become popular with those of my gender, but to find that I was the sole woman among seventy-odd male officer trainees was most disheartening. I had a sinking feeling and it took me a few days to adjust to this unpleasant reality. In fact many well-wishers, including my own family, had advised me not to resign from the 1980 batch of the Indian Audit and Accounts Service. We were six female officers under training at Yarrows in Shimla, and life had been fun. But I had absolutely no proclivity for accounts. Switching to the Indian Police Service was therefore a conscious and intuitive decision.

My first impression of the police academy was its vast, barren and rocky expanse of over around 275 acres. Earlier situated in Mount Abu and known as the Central Police Training College, it was renamed National Police Academy in 1967. Subsequently, in 1974, it became the Sardar Vallabhbhai Patel National Police Academy (SVPNPA) – in honour of the Iron Man of India – and was moved to Hyderabad in 1975. It took many batches of officers to adorn the institute with greenery through regular '*shramdaan*' that involved digging ditches and planting trees which today attract more than a hundred species of birds. But the academy of 1981 looked sombre and austere, yet towering and magnificent.

The room I was allotted on the first floor of the Police Officers' Mess was very stark and bare, and it intensified my loneliness. As I unpacked, I remember feeling very homesick. The first time I went down to the ground floor for dinner, I found some of my fellow trainees hanging around rather nervously. The massive dining hall looked grand and imposing. Bright, sparkling chandeliers hung from the ceiling; mementoes and trophies were displayed all around. Paintings on the walls showed gigantic forts, surrounded by cannons and uniformed officers of the gravest demeanour either on horseback or standing firm. I was truly overawed and felt very small and insignificant.

Suddenly, a smart police officer in an all-white PT[1] uniform sauntered into the hall. In an impressively loud voice, he announced that the officer trainees, generally addressed as probationers, needed to present themselves outside the officers' mess at 5:30 the next morning. We gasped, surprised by his unexpected appearance and the order delivered in a measured tone and with great authority. But before we could react or utter a word, he clicked his heels and left as smartly as he had arrived. His white uniform was at odds with the time of the day, but it had made him conspicuous, allowing him to hold everyone's attention.

This was to be the gruelling routine of my training year: 5:30 a.m. to about 7:00 in the evening, police bugles demarcating the day at stipulated hours. The early mornings were devoted to outdoor activities of various kinds, followed by indoor classes in which we were mainly taught law, forensics and management. Post lunch it was time to return to the open parade ground.

In the evenings, we had to play all sorts of games. Being a probationer at the academy meant that we would be inducted into the police force only after successful completion of our training. It felt as if the sword of Damocles was constantly hanging over our heads. The instructors did not miss any opportunity to remind us of the two probationers of the 1980 batch who had been sent home by the director. We speculated about the reasons and came up with a multitude of them that left us feeling suitably scared.

Back in my room, I was, however, lucky to have a lady attendant, Ganeshi, to help me with my daily chores. In her mid-forties, she was the wife of a male attendant at the academy, and her son was part of the staff too. They would wake us up with hot tea at dawn, tidy up our rooms after we left for the grounds, prepare our police uniforms and generally help us in sundry ways. They were permanent features in the corridors of the police officers' mess.

Ganeshi had a broad, brown face with 'no nonsense' writ large on it. She parted her henna-dyed hair in the middle. Being from Rajasthan, she would wear her sari with an '*ulta pallu*' (to me it looked like the pallu had been placed on the wrong side). She had a slightly nasal voice and was always chewing tobacco or *supari*. Her shiny nose ring was a prominent part of her persona. Ganeshi gave the distinct impression of having 'seen the world' and was always straightforward, to the point and matter of fact. Her walk was as measured as her talk.

She was very good at her job, which she would do slowly, at her own pace. I never saw her getting ruffled. Her unfailing punctuality amazed me. She would fetch my uniform from the male washers of the academy, prepare it with the blue line yard and the single star that my rank warranted. She would place uniform belts of different kinds on my desk, and my parade shoes, uniform shoes and sneakers in a straight line on the floor beside my bed. Every day she would discreetly wait outside my room as I got ready – long before sunrise. Thanks to Ganeshi's conscientiousness about her job, the state of my uniform never ticked off my instructors – not once during that long, arduous year in Hyderabad. The uniform is a matter of pride for us, a sacrosanct item within the police, paramilitary and military forces.

While I was grappling with the tough outdoor routine of the academy and learning to survive, I received a strange message. It said that I should cut my hair short. Baffled, I tried to find out why I had received this instruction and was told that it had been recommended by a senior lady police officer. I do not have very long hair but I like my mane. I also liked to wear it open during festivals and functions. In any case, I do not enjoy accepting illogical instructions, and this definitely seemed like one to me. So I argued against it but was informed that short hair would help me change into different uniforms faster during a day's training. Mind you, so far I had never been late in getting ready.

After about forty minutes of morning yoga and obstacle crossing (PT) in an all-white uniform, we would change into khaki for parade practice or weapons drills. While I used to wear a ponytail for yoga and PT exercises, I was expected to tie my hair in a bun for the parade. Someone in the top echelons had felt that changing uniforms and tying one's hair were difficult tasks to be accomplished during our ten-minute break, so I was expected to follow the instruction. My sprightly reply was that I would do so if I ever got late. The rapid switch from white to khaki and a quick hairdo within ten minutes soon became effortless, and I was happy to retain my long hair. The issue was never discussed again.

For this I must give credit to Ganeshi, who prepared my uniform with great care. I never had to look for anything. She would bring everything I needed to the changing room, from hair pins to my fully starched khaki attire, and wait outside to collect the used clothes, rush them to the washer men, pick them up on time and get them ready again. This routine continued for a year at the Hyderabad police academy – while for me it was a blessing, I wonder if Ganeshi ever felt bored.

Every morning I would ask her, 'How many days of training left, Ganeshi?' I had hung a calendar in my otherwise bare room, and would strike off every passing day. Though only a third-standard graduate, Ganeshi would either count the days for me or just smile at my daily morning query. She was a big silent support during that crucial year in which I underwent the toughest of trainings while experiencing serious bouts of homesickness.

Since she said very little, Ganeshi's only piece of advice during the first month after my arrival surprised me. 'Madam, please maintain distance from the men; do not get close to any of the male officers,' she said in her quiet, composed tone. I was taken aback. She continued in all seriousness and told me of two instances where women trainees had become intimate with their fellow probationers and subsequently 'suffered'. She mentioned that a particular lady officer's closeness to a married male officer from the previous batch had caused quite a furore. Other trainees who frowned upon this relationship had informed the officer's wife. She arrived at the academy and swiftly 'put an end to the affair'. In her own simple way, Ganeshi was warning me against personal upheavals that one could bring upon themselves in the secluded, emotionally starved environment of the academy.

I think my husband's visits to Hyderabad put Ganeshi at ease and she never brought up this topic again. She went about her job quietly, taking on the care of some of the male trainees too. The salary from the only lady officer was understandably not enough. Her workload increased significantly, yet she was always there for me.

The barely educated Ganeshi, who possessed great common sense and was meticulous to a tee, was the highlight of my first hard and lonely year as a police trainee. May she rest in peace.

3

AN INTERLOPER

'Conscience is the light of the Soul that burns within the chambers of our psychological heart. It is as real as life is. It raises the voice in protest whenever anything is thought of or done contrary to the righteousness.'

– DR A. P. J. ABDUL KALAM

I do not eat meat. So I represented the vegetarians in the food committee of the officers' mess, with RJ as the overall in-charge. He had undergone the Foundation Course in Mussoorie and played chess with my husband on occasion. A bespectacled guy with a receding hairline, he already looked like a middle-aged man instead of a young IPS officer.

We were hardly a month old in the academy when one day he approached me with a strange offer. 'Let's live together,' he said. I was shocked, but thinking that he probably didn't communicate well in English, ignored the proposition and got busy with my training.

On a Sunday afternoon, he knocked on the door of my room in the officers' mess. Half asleep, I asked what he needed

– Sunday afternoon siestas have always been very precious to me. He replied that he wanted to discuss the menu for the mess dining hall. Grudgingly I opened the door. This time he spoke in very clear terms. 'Your husband is away and my wife is in Rajasthan. Let's live together.' Even more taken aback than before, my yearning for an afternoon nap vanished in an instant, as did the misgiving about RJ's English proficiency. I banged the door in his face and immediately reported the incident to the joint director of the academy. He took serious note of it and RJ was given a strict warning. I have a feeling that it was mentioned in his annual appraisal too, but I can't be sure as these reports are confidential.

The episode soon became common knowledge within my batch, and some probationers voiced their opinion against my having approached the joint director. They thought it could have been handled internally 'at our level'. I am told that there were heated discussions among some batchmates. But I paid no heed as it was a very serious matter so far as I was concerned. I was the only lady officer in the batch and my security was of paramount importance to me. Once again, I got busy with my gruelling routine.

Every day during the outdoor training, I felt like I would faint. But I did not once miss it out of fear that I would never be able to return to the training if I suddenly skipped a day. With aching bodies and tired minds, most of us would sleep through the indoor classes, relying upon the front benchers to hold the fort and keep the lecturers engaged. Sometimes we were caught napping and pulled up for it, but the tradition of snoozing during classes continued. I am told that the teaching faculty at the Hyderabad academy are yet to succeed in breaking the probationers' classroom-napping habit.

Training at the National Police Academy ends with a grand show in the form of a 'passing out parade'. A chief guest of national renown is invited for the occasion. In our case it was the vice president of India. During the strenuous parade practice for the final day, I received a message that the academy doctor wanted to see me. I was surprised, as I was not suffering from any ailment, nor had I sought this appointment. Nevertheless, I went to see him in his office, which was across the road from the main academy building. After ushering me in, the worthy doctor looked up very seriously and asked if he could discuss a sensitive issue. I was intrigued. He said that RJ – of the 'let's live together' – had pleaded with him to request me not to mention 'the incident' to his wife, who was going to attend the passing out parade. I had almost forgotten the unpleasant episode and had no intention of talking about it with anyone. I told the doctor as much and left his office.

The closing parade was a grand success, after which we all left for a year of 'on-the-job training' in different states. About five years down the line, I came to know that RJ had been dismissed from the Indian Police Service as he was involved in a serious case of corruption in Rajasthan. He had supposedly re-joined the state service he had a lien on, having served there earlier. I don't think he deserved to be in the civil services at all. Good that he was thrown out early from the IPS, and unfortunate that the state service had to suffer such a goon. I still wonder why some of my batchmates were unhappy that I reported RJ's conduct to the authorities. Any guesses? As for me, I find reassurance in William Penn's words: 'Right is right even if everyone is against it and wrong is wrong even if everyone is for it.'

4

MY USTAD

'Treat a person as he is, and he will remain as he is. Treat him as he could be, and he will become what he should be.'

– JIMMY JOHNSON, former Dallas Cowboys head coach and two-time Super Bowl champion

'Women have steadier hands!' The ustad's words still ring in my ears.

In all police training institutions across the country, the most popular yet the most dreaded beings are our physical training instructors, who are known in the academies as 'ustads'. We love them, hate them, talk of them even post-retirement, and bond with each other reminiscing about the squads we formed under various ustads. We still recall how they harassed us, cajoled us, tested our limits, encouraged us to perform – the list is endless. To this day most of us will instinctively salute our ustads if we chance upon them anywhere.

My ustad in the National Police Academy was a sober specimen, quiet but very firm. I did not see him smile or laugh even once during the whole year. Though not very tall, Yadav

Ustad was a stout, hardy man. He used to call me 'Meera saab'. While an officer of the Indian Police Service starts from middle-leadership position, ustads are generally field-level officers of sub inspector or inspector rank. They have the difficult task of training officers who are senior to them in rank but novices in terms of service. Since most trainees are not physically fit when they join, ustads have the onerous task of shaping us to the highest level of fitness. They do so through persuasion but shout at us when it doesn't work. One of their tasks is to successfully teach us how to bellow or deliver orders in a high, authoritative voice, so that we can in turn command our men and women in uniform on the parade grounds and in situations involving public disorder. And this was not an annual event. We had regular sessions with our ustads wherein we were trained to convey orders. Yadav Ustad would shout at me from one corner of the academy parade ground, '*Meera saab, pet se avaaj nikalkiye, yahan tak pahuche avaaj.*' (Meera saab, bring your voice out from your belly so that it reaches this end of the ground.) In this way, my sweet 'feminine' voice was slowly transformed into a hoarse but powerful variety that I used with considerable success while commanding parades and managing law-and-order disturbances later in my career.

Yadav Ustad would teach us yoga in a low, quiet tone during the first morning session and raise the decibels while instructing us for parade afterwards. He would be as sleepy and sluggish as us through the afternoon classes as he taught us how to assemble and dismantle weapons like revolvers, rifles, and various automatic and semi-automatic weapons. I do not know how we managed to remain awake during those 'dry weapon drills'. We were encouraged to handle different kinds of weapons and to understand the way in which each part functioned. The academy took great care to ensure that we knew the weapons thoroughly before using them in real firing sessions, for which all of us would have to be fully alert. Ustad would then switch to his strict, non-smiling avatar, not allowing even the smallest deviation from the standing operation protocol. As a result, we never floundered and the rules of the firing range were respected to the hilt.

Some events remain etched in one's mind. Two such incidents took place during our outdoor training. I had been firing from a very basic air gun since childhood, as we had one at home. My father, who was a member of the Punjab police and later served in the Border Security Force, had brought one home for his children. I was quite good at firing, though did so intermittently.

After a number of dry firing sessions in the academy, we were finally taken to the firing range on the outskirts. It was a wide, rocky and barren patch with red flags all over to warn passersby of possible dangers. Gravely, the Assistant Director Outdoors explained to us the perils of laxity. In any case, we were so overawed by the atmosphere of the firing range that none dared to smile. The sights and sounds of the instructors' test firing and consequent booing put the fear of God in us. It took me some time to feel at ease. The air gun we had at home suddenly felt like a toy.

One day when I scored particularly well during a firing session at the academy, one of my jealous batchmates taunted me, 'Oh Meera, it was a fluke. Why don't you go back and repeat this grand performance of yours?' The others laughed, even though laughter was forbidden on the firing range. I squirmed. Yadav Ustad heard it and roared: 'Sir, I have been observing women officers at the firing range for many years. They have consistently performed better than men. Women have steadier hands.' There was a stunned silence and the officer had nowhere to hide. Firing practice resumed in all seriousness. The words 'women having steadier hands' have stayed with me ever since.

I must admit that Yadav Ustad had to work really hard to bring me to the level of fitness that the Indian Police Service demands. I did my bit by being consistent with my outdoor training, daily fear of fainting notwithstanding. Gradually I improved and my stamina increased.

Rope climbing, however, proved to be a tough challenge. During this exercise, one's body weight is felt more on the arms than on the legs and, initially, I found this very difficult to tackle, as my legs were much stronger than my arms. My hands would bleed from friction with the rough rope. But with my ustad's encouragement, I progressed slowly and steadily using both arms and legs until I could climb up the entire length of the rope.

There was a tennis ground next to the area where the ropes had been hung from thirty-foot-tall iron poles. During our outdoor schedule, faculty or other senior officers would be playing tennis while also keeping a discreet watch on us. But whenever the bugle was blown for the morning's flag hoisting or the evening's retreat, all of us – including those playing tennis – would stop and stand still until the flag was hoisted or folded up. It is a solemn tradition in all uniformed services.

This is when the second episode took place. One evening I had climbed to the top of the rope when the bugle started blowing. Yadav Ustad, who was standing nearby, shouted at the top of his voice, 'Meera saab, stay where you are at the top!' This meant I would have to keep hanging from the rope for nearly three minutes. It was a very long time to be in that awkward and precarious position. But it also meant that senior officers playing tennis looked up due to the ustad's sudden roar and saw that I had successfully scaled the top of the rope. In a flash I understood that he had facilitated a proud display of his pupil's achievement. I hung on for dear life and for the ustad who had helped me arrive at this position with his hard work and perseverance.

It is unfortunate that ustads in many police training institutes are corrupt today and indulge in favouritism. The issue plagues most state police academies, whereas training institutes need to select the best trainers, for they are the ones who shape police officers of the future. As former president A. P. J. Abdul Kalam once said, 'I believe there is no other profession in the world that is more important to society than that of a teacher.'

5

THE TOUGH POLICE TRAINING

'I hated every minute of training, but I said, 'Don't quit. Suffer now and live the rest of your life as a champion.'

– MUHAMMAD ALI

You will know well by now that I found the training regimen at the National Police Academy very tough. Especially the outdoor part. For years, the extent and proportion of physical training for police officers have been a topic of debate. But the jury is still out. During the 1980s, around 60 per cent of the total training period was devoted to outdoor training. The rest of the time, barring a few field visits, was spent in the classroom learning police-related subjects. Even though the year felt exceptionally long to me, the diverseness of the training was interesting and challenging.

Inspection of a crime scene, picking up forensic cues like fingerprints and footprints and appreciation of medical evidence were all part of our training. We visited police stations in Hyderabad to understand how they functioned. Once we were taken to a hospital, where a postmortem was to be conducted as it was crucial for ascertaining the cause of a death. Most of us had not seen a dead body before, and we tensed up when told that the lady had died of 100 per cent burns.

To the disappointment of my colleagues, I did not faint on seeing a dead body that was burnt to a crisp. I had steeled myself beforehand, knowing I would have to deal with innumerable murders and fatal accidents as a police officer. I had also told myself that policing means getting justice for the victims, and therefore, visiting such gory crime scenes is an integral part of police duties. This self-talk allowed me to witness the scene with aplomb as I took my first baby steps towards crime investigation.

While practical sessions and field visits were fascinating, indoor classes failed to engage us. I can confirm that all the exams I passed at the academy were through rote learning. This is unfortunate because soon after our basic training, we hold responsible posts and are supposed to lead crime investigations with sound knowledge of the law and police procedures. Citizens look up to us and have high expectations from direct officers of the Indian Police Service.

One of my failures during the outdoor training haunted me for a long time. I could not pass the swimming exam. As a youngster I had wanted to learn swimming. My brothers would not hear of it, though, and convinced my father against it. My mother supported them. The Jalandhar army club had a good pool, but my family's objection was to the swimsuit! However, no one took issue with my horse riding on the grounds of the Punjab Armed Police, as I was well covered in my khaki 'breeches'. So, while I passed the riding test with flying colours at the academy, I flunked swimming.

There was another reason for this glorious performance of mine. At the time, the national academy in Hyderabad did not have its own swimming pool and, once a week, we were taken to the Ritz in town so that we could swim in the hotel pool. Being the only woman in the batch, I felt conscious in my swimsuit, and the swimming coach only made things worse. He would not come anywhere near me, shouting all his instructions from a distance. Passing the exam thus remained a distant dream. I learnt to enjoy swimming much later during my posting in Aurangabad, where the coach at the Rama International hotel had no such inhibitions and helped me conquer my fear.

As for horse riding, I was confident – maybe a little more than I should have been. I did not have to learn the beginner's regimen of walking the horse or familiarizing myself with the trot, canter and gallop. I loved to canter my horse. Once while riding, I was singing a song from the recently released movie *Umrao Jaan*, when the horse showed its displeasure and started to gallop at breakneck speed down the riding ground, then across the football ground, and stopped only as it got caught in the goalpost net. The horse's sudden speed and anger had taken me by surprise but I sat tight in the saddle until the animal had exhausted itself. I'd had a similar experience earlier at the BSF ground in Fazilka and become used to the unpredictable temper of our horses. I had long concluded that police horses respect only the hostler constables who look after them daily and find our guest appearances annoying.

Another incident that amuses me to date is our 'jungle survival night'. All of us probationers were taken deep into a thick, dark forest in the interiors of Andhra Pradesh and left with basic survival items such as dal, rice, matchboxes and a few utensils. We were expected to fend for ourselves until the faculty decided to come pick us up.

It took us some time to adjust to the jungle. We went around in small groups, marvelling at the vegetation, identifying trees and collecting firewood for cooking at night. But as dusk fell and visibility became poor, we started going back to our campsite in groups. Soon it became pitch dark, and the same trees we were just appreciating started spooking us. One could hear the sounds of strange insects. The probationers who were joking about the jungle during the day had gone quiet now. The fact that we were together kept us sane.

Some of my batchmates thought I could cook, so they brought their dal and rice to me, seeking instructions on what to do with the ingredients. I had never cooked using firewood. And my 'khichdi' turned out to be as bad as theirs, if not worse. But somehow we made it through that eerie night and, subsequently, many equally gruelling rock climbing sessions in the harsh Hyderabad summer. These outdoor regimes would entail running with rucksacks on our backs, long walks with rifles, obstacle jumping, rope climbing, scaling rocks, unarmed combat and much else, so that by the time we left the academy, we were fully confident of our muscle powers. There was, however, a big question mark when it came to our proficiency in law and legal procedures.

In retrospect, I feel that there should have been more 'service' content in our training. And that there is a need for closer collaboration among police training institutes, the academia and our citizens. While more academic and field research on the criminal justice system is warranted, interaction with citizens during basic police training will make us sensitive to their concerns – especially those of the deprived and underprivileged sections.

The first report of the National Police Commission (1977) mentions, 'The basic and fundamental problem regarding the police today is how to make them function as an efficient and impartial law enforcement agency ... guided by the objectives of service to the public at large ...'[1]

We are still groping in the dark!

6
NEW LEARNINGS IN NASHIK

'The problem with gender is that it prescribes how we should be rather than recognizing how we are.'

– CHIMAMANDA NGOZI ADICHIE,
We Should All Be Feminists, 2014.

After completing my training in Hyderabad and the army attachment in Poonch, Jammu, I proceeded to Tikkanpur, Gwalior, for two weeks of training with the Border Security Forces. For me the most interesting bit was learning to drive two- and three-ton trucks. I would practise making the figure of eight while driving these heavy vehicles, despite the double clutch of those days. I was so fascinated by the BSF trucks that I would wear a khaki 'dangari' so as to be considered a part of the motor transport section. As a teenager I had been driving both two- and four-wheelers. My family would often receive complaints about my fast driving. I think it was so mainly because very few girls drove any vehicle at all in the 1970s. Driving BSF trucks was a novel and exhilarating experience for me. My eyes sparkle at the thought even today. I was also indulged by the staff as they knew that my father had been a BSF commandant; they felt proud that I had made it to the Indian Police Service. Nearly everyone knew my father by name and that made me extremely happy.

State-specific police training followed at the Police Training College (PTC) in Nashik. The district has an interesting mythological background. Nashik got its name because it is here that Laxman cut off Ravana's sister Surpanaka's nose. Lord Rama is said to have lived in the Panchavati area during his *vanvas,* while legend has it that the sage Agastya did his *tapasya* here.[1] Anjaneri near Nashik is known as the birthplace of Hanuman.

The river Godavari originates in Trimbakeshwar in Nashik, which is also home to one of the twelve *jyotirlingas*. Formerly known as Gulshanabad, it is historically, mythologically, socially and culturally a very important area. The third-largest district in Maharashtra in terms of population, it hosts the massive Sinhastha Kumbh Mela once every twelve years. Nashik's terrain is lush and mountainous; important rivers like the Vaitarana, Bhima, Girana, Kashyapi and Darana flow through it, contributing to the region's diverse vegetation.

At the verdant police training college in Nashik, the emphasis was once again on the outdoors. The prosecutors teaching us law had not bothered to update their knowledge. The faculty at Hyderabad were way ahead of them in that respect, and I realized their value after coming to PTC Nashik. The famous class of 1983 (Maharashtra Sub-Inspectors) was trained with me. Being very fit themselves, they would often urge me to run fast. The hierarchy of uniform applies even on the police training college ground. Since I was from the IPS, I was supposed to lead our daily morning runs. But I could run only as fast as my body allowed.

Being junior in rank, they could not overtake me, so, in a low tone, they would say, 'Madam, phast,' bringing a smile to my face and a scowl on the instructors'.

This was also my first brush with the notoriously heavy monsoons of Maharashtra. The rule at PTC was that you must be on the ground even if it was raining, which gave me a serious bout of sinusitis. But I kept it to myself as I did not want to hear any gendered remarks. When Arvind Inamdar, our highly strict principal, ordered us one morning to run for nine kilometres up to the *Pandav lanies* (caves) with rifles and report for indoor classes immediately thereafter, I again kept quiet, despite boils forming on my feet. I am sure other officers went through a tough time too. The intention of the faculty was to prepare us for the hard life of a police officer, a career we had all chosen for ourselves.

After three months, I reported for on-the-job training at the Nashik police headquarters. An IPS officer trains for two long years and this was the last leg. A detailed programme had been drawn up. I was attached to a police outpost, police station, subdivision, the police headquarters, prison, the district magistrate, public prosecutor, sessions judge and others. These associations provide a trainee with a comprehensive understanding of the way in which different departments and functionaries operate in the field.

During the training days and later as Assistant Superintendent of Police (ASP) at Nashik in 1983–84, I felt that the senior superintendent of police, Ashok Ankola, was quite uncomfortable with me. A tall man with a very impressive personality, he had his own views about the relevance of women in police but did not voice them out loud. He preferred me sitting with his wife during social gatherings, which I did not mind. I found the wives of police officers welcoming and ready to share their household tips with me. I enjoyed these occasional sessions about housekeeping and cooking. Conversations about clothes were rare as the sari was the norm for married women in those days and designers were yet to appear on the scene. Life was simple.

The Ankola family was entirely non-vegetarian, while I do not eat meat. Mrs Ankola would send vegetarian food for me along with a *dibba* for her husband during our district tours. The wives of policemen, from constables to the director general of police, have strongly supported me throughout my career.

There were very few women in the police during the early eighties, and officers in Nashik were both uneasy with and unsure of my 'standing'. I also happened to be from Punjab with hardly any knowledge of either the language or culture of Maharashtra. But I would try to speak the local language and read newspapers to improve my Marathi. Police officers would explain the documentation work to me diligently either in Hindi or Marathi. It involved registration of the First Information Report, recording of the spot *panchnama* (scene of crime) documents related to search and arrest, miscellaneous investigation papers, drafting of the charge sheet, etc. I am told that there was a debate on how I would accompany my colleagues for police raids. Owing to my rank, I was supposed to occupy the front passenger seat in the jeep, while the 'all-powerful' inspector-in-charge was expected to sit in the back. This was not acceptable to a few at the Bhadrakali police station in Nashik. But Inspector Asaram Shinde accepted the protocol graciously and advised the staff to not make an issue of it. After some time, they overcame their hesitations in taking me along for nighttime raids on illicit liquor dens, gambling and prostitution raids.

In retrospect, I feel sad that in those days we used to arrest sex workers as offenders, not understanding that most of them were selling their bodies either due to utter poverty or because they had been forced into the profession by deceit. The reality and magnitude of human trafficking and that sex workers were usually victims of exploitation dawned on us much later. For this I would credit all the NGOs working for the cause of women.

Over the course of my internship with the senior SP, I had a very interesting early encounter. One day the District Special Branch (DSB) officer came to carry out his usual morning briefing for Mr Ankola and informed us of a serious law-and-order problem expected to unfold the next day. A particular political party had supposedly paid ₹100 to each member of a group of local slum dwellers for throwing stones during an ongoing agitation. Without even looking up from the file, the senior SP thundered, 'Distribute rice bags to the same group!' The agitation did take place but there was no stone-throwing.

Another time, I was sent to the small town of Kalwan, where a local group had called for a *bandh*. The senior SP instructed me to draft a '*bandobast*' order and ensure it was ready by the time he reached the place. I held discussions with police officers, studied the ground situation and available manpower, evaluated the likelihood of violence, before ultimately deploying police personnel.

The arrival of the senior SP was announced on the wireless set and we rushed to receive him. The six-foot-tall officer got down from his car, looked around and, in a mighty voice, ordered the policemen to 'fall in', which in police parlance means 'gather'. He shouted a few more orders that the men obeyed without question. There was a sudden surge of positive energy among them. This is when I realized that even though I had worked hard to draft and organize the bandobast, I did not possess the personality of a police officer. Disheartened, I worried if I would ever be able to do justice to my job.

There were two additional superintendents of police in Nashik district. One exclusively looked after the Malegaon sub-division while the rest of the district was the other one's responsibility. Malegaon is a communal hotspot – one of the most sensitive areas in Maharashtra. I would visit it occasionally to understand the dynamics between Hindus and Muslims. Communal tension during festival season was common and there were frequent altercations that threatened the town's peace. These would have immediate repercussions all over the state. The Additional SP in charge, S. M. Mushrif, was a young, energetic officer who responded very quickly to even the smallest incident of communal friction.

However, I interacted more regularly with the additional SP posted in Nashik, as I was based there. He was always slow and measured in his responses. The junior officers humoured him and took their own decisions or consulted the senior SP, Mr Ankola, when it came to important decision-making. Watching the two additional SPs at work, I concluded that the government is quite a mixed bag. It is tolerant of snails who sit on powerful chairs, making no contribution to governance. Weeding them out is very difficult unless they commit a grave blunder. But being snails, they are averse to taking any risks and thus the chances of them committing bloopers remain minimal. Since these officers hate change and are loath to take bold initiatives, they debilitate the system slowly and silently. Resolute, motivated officers carry the load of these snails throughout their careers.

Governments in India are clever in the way they use good officers strategically, as was the case with the additional SP in Malegaon, but they are unable to shake off the snails. Both officers in this instance would get the same pay packet and their promotions were simultaneous. And yet they were so different in the speed and quality of their performance.

Corruption was also spreading through the police force like a virus. The idealism of a young, independent India was giving way to a cynical, materialistic one. The determination to provide honest, selfless service was waning. And our democracy was not even forty years old yet.

In the words of Netaji Subhas Chandra Bose, 'Men, money and material cannot by themselves bring victory or freedom. We must have the motive-power that will inspire us to brave deeds and heroic exploits.'

7

MOM-COP

'Most women work one shift at the office or factory and a "second shift" at home.'

– ARLIE RUSSELL HOCHSCHILD

After Nashik, I was posted as Assistant Superintendent of Police at the Gadhinglaj division, with headquarters in Kolhapur. Located in western Maharashtra, the city runs along the banks of the Panchganga river and is surrounded by the Sahyadri mountain ranges. Legend has it that the goddess Mahalakshmi killed a demon named Kolhasur who used to oppress the locals. The demon's dying wish was that the place should be named after him. And that is how the region came to be known as Kolhapur. About 387 kilometres from Mumbai, it is famous for its Mahalakshmi temple, forts, 'Kolhapuri chappals' and unique local jewellery, especially a particular style of necklace called 'Kolhapuri saaj'.[1] The residents of Kolhapur have deep faith in the goddess Mahalakshmi.

Gadhinglaj division consisted of rural and far-flung police stations bordering Belgaum and certain other parts of Karnataka.

I had to tour frequently in police jeeps, which had become rather uncomfortable as I was expecting my first child at the time. Nevertheless, I continued to visit crime scenes, including a few gory ones, and also inspect police stations as mandated by the police manual.

By the sixth month of my pregnancy, I had to switch from uniform to sari. I remember being quite embarrassed while inspecting in a sari a parade at the Radhanagari police station. All the police officers had turned up in their full formal uniform except me, the inspecting officer.

I continued working until the eighth month of my pregnancy and then proceeded to my parents' place on maternity leave. First by car from Kolhapur to Pune, then by train from Pune to Delhi, and finally by car again to Chandigarh (where my parents still lived) for the delivery. It went smoothly, although the baby arrived twenty days earlier than expected.

The wives of senior officers would often wonder how I would manage a child, my home and my hectic travelling job. I honestly had no idea but was lucky to have been blessed with youthful energy and enthusiasm. I often advise young girls not to fret about future difficulties. It is my experience that one does find a way when faced with adversity. Earlier, during my civil services interview at the Union Public Service Commission, the same question about balancing home and work had been posed to me. My reply was: 'I will cross the bridge when I come to it.' This policy has enabled me to keep worry and stress at bay.

Bringing up my child simultaneously with a touring job was definitely challenging. Not having any role models, I either invented my own processes or followed my gut instincts. Police station inspections with night halts meant that our troupe included the infant, his maid and two baskets full of baby stuff.

My driver Chougule would often double up as my cranky child's personal jester and amuse him thoroughly. I learnt from someone that he had made a bet with an officer at the police control room that I would have a boy!

Our team may have been very professional and prompt when it came to investigating crimes, but handling law-and-order issues was tough during this phase. Once, while still pregnant, I had to order a lathi charge against a riotous mob. Another time I had to keep handkerchiefs in the pockets of my police shirt as I was a lactating mother who was not able to nurse her child during the day or harvest her breast milk, as is possible today. This time, too, I was on a public-order duty facing a hostile mob.

While all my batchmates had been promoted to district police chief rank (Superintendents of Police) in 1986, I agreed to be Additional Superintendent and continue in Kolhapur as it involved fewer responsibilities, the other reason being that my husband was also posted in Kolhapur and it suited the family. I have made these compromises throughout my career as I did not want to miss out on enjoying the many different facets of my life. Performing the role of a homemaker, cooking for my children and organizing their birthday parties have all been highly pleasurable activities for me – not to mention spending my annual leave with family in Chandigarh and later in Delhi. My husband has also been a great support in bringing up our boys.

While learning to adjust as a young mother-cop in Kolhapur, I was shaken by an incident involving the death of a young man in police custody. I remember it vividly. The senior SP was not at the headquarters and I was heading the police force in his absence. Fearing strong disciplinary action and citizen backlash, the police station staff had initially concealed the facts. However, the news leaked out and spread like wildfire. Understandably, there was an outrage, as agitating citizens took to the roads.

I rushed to the police station, making my way slowly and cautiously through a very aggressive crowd. I remember women beating their chests and lying down in front of the police station. The situation was indeed quite grave. On-the-spot enquiry revealed that the boy had been brought to the police station by the detection staff at night and beaten black and blue all over. There was absolutely no justification for this. It was, without a doubt, an inhuman act that led to an irreparable loss.

I immediately suspended the delinquent officers, and a criminal case of murder was registered against them. This drastic action conveyed to the protesting citizens that the administration was as appalled by the policemen's violence as they were. Kolhapur went into mourning. Shops were shut down and the roads soon became empty and forlorn. All of us grieved for the loss of a young life.

While the session judge of Kolhapur guided me through this truly unfortunate incident, the young IPS officer K. L. Prasad stood by me during the turmoil that came to be known as '*Pandav Prakaran*'. The case later got prosecuted in the court. It strengthened my belief that a district is best governed if all departments work together as one team. It also showed me the underbelly of my department, where some of us exploit our uniform to violate the basic human rights of citizens. These sadists need to be weeded out at the earliest. They harass and torture poor and marginalized citizens but bend over backwards to please the powerful. This breed exists at all strata of police hierarchy but more so at the field level.

Another incident that marked my tenure in Kolhapur was the rape of an eight-year-old girl in a Maruti car by a local industrialist, once again leading to extensive agitations in the city. This case drove home the importance of the police's sensitivity in handling cases, especially those concerning women and children, and of a healthy rapport between citizens and law-enforcing agencies.

On another note, I believe in undertaking night rounds as they convey to the district police that senior officers are part of the team. Otherwise, the general impression is that IPS officers are soft and comfort-loving. During one of my night rounds in Kolhapur, I found the outer gate of a bungalow wide open. Deciding to investigate, I got down from my police car and knocked on the door. It was a new-moon night and the surroundings were pitch-dark. An old lady opened a window tentatively and seemed taken aback to see a uniformed person at the gate. On hearing the reason for my call, she opened the door and walked with me to the wooden gate that opened to her garden and locked it quietly. The next day I received a call from a senior police officer, who informed me that the lady was his mother-in-law – a widow. She had been living alone for some years and was pleasantly surprised by my nighttime visit in uniform. She told him that she felt secure in the knowledge that police officers – even women officers – carry out night patrols. This was a reaffirmation that police presence and visibility are helpful and particularly appreciated by senior citizens.

My Kolhapur stint convinced me about the need for continued and sustained collaboration between the police and our community. As Robert Peel famously said, 'The police are the public and the public are the police; the police being only members of the public who are paid to give full time attention to duties which are incumbent on every citizen in the interests of community welfare and existence.'

8

THE LONG ROAD TO JUSTICE

'Don't tell your daughters not to go out; tell your sons and men to behave.'

I was tired. The previous night's patrol had taken its toll. On reaching my office, I asked for a hot cup of tea and surreptitiously took off my uniform shoes under the huge teak table. Sipping the energizing beverage, I began to plan my day when the office orderly mentioned that two people were urgently seeking an interview with me. This was quite rare in Kolhapur as I reserved one hour each evening for citizens to meet me without having to make an appointment. We had given this arrangement due publicity too. As a result, there would be a number of visitors to see me about police-related issues between 4 p.m. and 5 p.m., and hardly anyone would show up without an appointment through the rest of the day.

Thinking that it could be something serious, I asked them to be ushered in. Two soberly dressed men walked in and sat down. With no exchange of pleasantries, one of them, wearing a deep frown on his face, began to tell me about the rape of a child inside a Maruti car. His Marathi was too fast and I could barely understand his words. Totally confused, I asked if it was his daughter who had been raped.

At this, the gentleman broke down. That's when the truth and gravity of the issue dawned on me. I asked someone to get him a glass of water and began making enquiries of the person accompanying him, only to realize that he was in no better state. After a few minutes of complete silence, the first gentleman mustered strength and resumed speaking. I learnt that his eight-year-old daughter had left for her private tuitions around eight in the morning. Afterwards she came home crying and told her parents that she had been forced by a person into a car on her way back. From her descriptions, it became clear to the parents that she had been sexually assaulted by the person who had pushed her into the car. The child was too young to understand or explain that she had been raped, but the parents were in no doubt. Crestfallen, the father, an officer with the government of Maharashtra, had then rushed to my office in a very quiet part of Kolhapur.

The father's words shook me to the core. Forgetting my fatigue, I asked for the officer looking after the local crime branch. He was known to be quite dynamic and his office was nearby. Realizing that the incident might fall under the purview of the Shahupuri police station as per the description of the parked car, I contacted the inspector and sought his presence too. Both reached my office within the next twenty minutes.

The father, more composed now, repeated to the police officers what his daughter had told him. This time he mentioned an important detail: his daughter had described the car as a 'red Maruti'. He added that he had visited the spot before coming to my office and collected some information about the car. The inspector of Shahupuri police station, Manohar V. Katamble, looked grave and advised the father and his friend to accompany him so that they could lodge a formal complaint. All three left my office.

The crime branch inspector, Nandkumar P. Chavan, also known as Chandu Chavan, stayed behind and discussed the complaint in detail with me. He was as surprised and distressed as I was and wanted to concentrate on tracing the car while the Shahupuri inspector registered the complaint. Chandu Chavan was a man of medium height, with a pleasant mustachioed face. He was married to the daughter of a powerful local politician. I knew that behind this childlike visage and happy-go-lucky facade was an officer seeking tough challenges. He always seemed in a hurry and it reflected in the superfast way in which he spoke. He was young, with an I-don't-give-two-hoots attitude. By contrast, Inspector Katamble was gracefully grey, measured in his responses and respectful of authority. He looked like a college professor. I was sure that between the two they would be able to detect the case.

In the 1980s, the Indian economy was yet to be liberalized. Fiat and Ambassador cars ruled the roads in those days. Maruti Udyog had been launched in 1981 but many of its cars had yet to reach small towns like Kolhapur.

Inspector Chavan left my office with a determined look on his face. And I was left wondering if such a grievous incident could take place in a car, in broad daylight, in the town that revered goddess Mahalakshmi!

At Shahupuri Police station, the father mentioned in his official complaint that his eight-year-old daughter was a student in the fourth standard. On 24 September 1986, she had left home at around 8:15 a.m. for tuitions in the same colony where she lived with her parents. While she was on her way back around 9:15 a.m., an unknown person had caught hold of her hand and told her that he needed help with fixing some wires in his Maruti car parked close by. As she went near the car, the accused pushed her inside and tried to rape her. After the child came home weeping and narrated the incident to her father, the mother examined the girl's undergarments and private parts. She noticed something sticky on her daughter's clothes and knickers – it was semen. There was some redness on her vagina. The girl was able to describe the assailant to her parents, who went numb with shock. After the father recovered, he drove his scooter – his daughter riding pillion –to the spot where the incident had taken place. Finding no car there, they came home, unsure of what to do next. The mother gave her child a bath and sent her to school.

Unable to allay his distress, the father returned to the spot and started talking to anyone he could find there. A college student who lived nearby told him that she had seen a chocolate-coloured Maruti in the morning and the licence plate may have read MGR-942, but she couldn't recollect exactly. That's when the father decided to speak to me and arrived at my office thereafter in a highly disturbed state of mind.

Inspector Katamble, after recording the father's complaint, visited the exact spot with him and drew up a panchnama. Talking to the young child, he told me later, was the toughest part. Thinking that the girl may get overawed by his uniform, the inspector had donned plainclothes. Then he acted as if he was visiting their home for a cup of tea, eliciting as much information as possible from mother and child. The mother told him that the girl had complained of pain after returning from school and they had consulted their family doctor. Later, the inspector drove the father and the child to the civil hospital for a medical examination.

In the meanwhile, Inspector Chavan, who was conducting a parallel investigation, rang me up to say that he had identified a few school-going kids who had seen the parked car. Its red colour made it conspicuous and they even remembered some of the digits on its licence plate. Chavan immediately proceeded to the local road transport office and looked up the numbers allotted to red Maruti cars. He soon zeroed down on a car that was registered in the name of one Parashuram Jadhav.

Wasting no time, Chavan drove to the address against which Jadhav's car had been registered at the RTO. To his disappointment, he learnt that Parashuram Jadhav had sold his car sometime back but the transfer of the vehicle had not yet been formalized. Nonetheless, on the hunch that the story could be a lie, Chavan brought Jadhav to his office. Jadhav was afraid that he was getting entangled in something serious, so to prove his point, he offered to lead Chavan and his team to the person who had bought his car.

Without wasting a minute, the Crime Branch staff hastily got into their jeep and set off. Jadhav navigated them to Shirol, a small town about thirteen kilometres from Kolhapur, where they finally stopped at a factory. He introduced the officer to the owner, Rajendra Jawanmal Gandhi. A man in his mid-thirties, Gandhi was from a respected family in Kolhapur.

Taking a seat in Gandhi's impressive factory office, Inspector Chavan started the rapid-fire questioning he was known for. 'Who is your driver?' 'Where is he from?' 'Did you know where he was this morning?' 'And where was your car earlier today?' While waiting for Gandhi to call his driver, the inspector noticed that the man had become nervous. Jadhav, on the other hand, was his talkative self, and even revealed the name of Gandhi's driver. Inspector Chavan asked the driver about his whereabouts that morning. He replied that he had left his house around 9 a.m. to report for duty at Gandhi's house. At around 10:30 he had driven his boss to the factory. Before that, he did not have access to the car, which he had found parked at Gandhi's house. He had no idea where the car was around 9 a.m. I was told that the driver was literally trembling. Chavan was known to have that kind of effect.

All this while, the wily inspector had noticed that Gandhi was perspiring profusely. He asked Jadhav and the driver to let him talk to Gandhi alone. After they left the room, he asked Gandhi about his coordinates between eight and nine in the morning. Gandhi claimed to have been in the factory at that time, so the inspector shot back with the driver's testimony that he had driven Gandhi to the factory around 10:30. A few more unsatisfactory replies to his questions convinced Chavan that there was something terribly wrong about this 'respectable gentleman'. He asked Gandhi to climb into the police jeep and started for Shahupuri police station, after asking Gandhi's driver to follow in the Maruti car along with Parshuram Jadhav.

An intense round of interrogation ensued. Gandhi's movements since morning were traced minute by minute and cross-verified. Inspectors Katamble and Chavan confronted and cross-questioned him until he broke down and confessed to the heinous crime. He was arrested the same evening – on 24 September 1986 – and sent for the medical examination mandatory in rape cases.

Next morning, the news of an eight-year-old girl's rape inside a Maruti car made it to the front page of local and state newspapers, causing tremendous commotion in the city. The police control room reported to me that angry citizens were agitating on the streets, while some had already reached Shahupuri police station.

I spent the whole day meeting delegations of local citizens – women in particular – who kept repeating that they were scared of sending their children to school and for tuition classes. As the media was yet to report Rajendra Gandhi's late-evening arrest, it took all my energy to convince them that the accused had already been apprehended and they need not be afraid. But the protests went on unabated and we had to deploy reserve staff from the police headquarters to control the outraged crowds.

Inspector Katamble, meanwhile, continued with his investigation, tracking down witnesses and recording their statements. We had not yet received the child's medical examination report. Surprisingly a government doctor at the civil hospital called up the victim's father, asking to meet him, who in turn asked for my advice. Finding the conduct of the medical officer very suspicious, I recommended the father against meeting him.

In such sensitive cases, the medical certificate is provided immediately, so the delay seemed odd to me. On the third day since the incident, citizens took out a huge *morcha* outside the civil hospital, demanding the medical report and insisting that it be handed over to the Additional Superintendent of Police, that is, me. The police control room was monitoring the agitation and keeping me informed. I decided to go to the civil hospital as tempers were running high and could lead to serious public order issues.

On my arrival, the agitators gheraoed me and demanded to know why the doctor had not submitted his medical report and what the police were doing about it. They relented only after the civil surgeon – the hospital chief – agreed to hand over the report to me. Despite the agitators' insistence that I open the medical report on the spot and read it publicly, I refused to do so. Making my way out of the hospital with great difficulty, I returned to my office with the sealed envelope safe in my custody.

On perusing it I found, to my utter surprise, that the certificate described a few minor injuries but there was no mention that the child had been raped. I immediately understood why the medical officer had wanted to meet the victim's father. The rich and influential accused, in all probability, would have reached him before the police did. Disturbed by the doctor's conduct and the delay with the report, we decided to form a panel of doctors to re-examine the victim. This is a rare practice, but I felt the case warranted it as it was unlikely that an eight-year-old child would tell a lie or falsely implicate someone. Besides, I had serious doubts about the veracity of the medical report. I was also aware that the compromised report, coupled with the delay in its submission, would agitate citizens further. They had been protesting continuously and I had experienced their anger first-hand at the civil hospital. With the civil surgeon's help, we shortlisted three doctors for the panel: Dr Naganonkar, a gynaecologist; Dr Kudakar; and Dr (Mrs) Maladkar.

The next day, the newspapers prominently reported the negative report and the subsequent formation of a fresh panel of doctors. The protests carried on. I have rarely seen the kind of public anger that this episode evoked in Kolhapur. Finally, the Maharashtra government's health department suspended the offending medical officer as well as the civil surgeon in charge of the hospital.

Around the same time, the panel of doctors re-examined the child victim and certified the 'tear of hymen at 3 o'clock position' and rape-positive. Curiously the government doctor who had examined the girl initially and submitted a rape-negative report came forward with a revised opinion, asserting that she had been raped. Rape cases are, to a large extent, dependent on the veracity of the complaint and the medical certificate. In this instance, nobody disputed the child's statement, but contradictory medical opinions could irrevocably damage the case.

Due to the fast movement of Kolhapur police officers and the arrest of Rajendra Gandhi, we could regain the trust of the citizens as well as the parents of the victim. Our investigation was further strengthened when the girl identified the accused before a magistrate during the Test Identification Parade (TIP). Until then, some people had remained unconvinced owing to the Gandhi family's reputation. And to think that his daughter was the same age as the victim!

Over the course of the investigation, Inspector Katamble had collected the accused and the victim's items of clothing and sent them for a forensic examination. With the help of experts, he had also picked up semen stains on the car seat. The forensic report we received showed that the semen on the child's knickers and dress, on the seat of the car and the accused's trousers was that of Rajendra Gandhi. This greatly helped our case. Inspector Chavan had also identified some witnesses who had seen the Maruti car and the accused at the scene. On completing the investigation, Katamble filed a charge sheet in the court against the accused on 24 October 1986 for offences punishable under sections 376 and 342 of the Indian Penal Code.

Rajendra Gandhi being a wealthy businessman, engaged a good lawyer and applied for bail. It was rejected by the Additional Session Judge initially, but four days later he was released on bail. At the time of granting him bail, the court had directed him to stay out of the territories of Kolhapur and Shiroli, the site of his factory, for a period of twenty-five days. This was to ensure that he did not interfere with investigation and because anger against

Gandhi was still brewing and a breach of peace seemed likely. On 3 January 1987, the case was transferred to the Court of Sessions at Kolhapur for trial.

On 2 February, Rajendra Gandhi moved a criminal application in Bombay High Court for the transfer of his case from Kolhapur. He mentioned that justice would be unattainable as the citizens of Kolhapur were against him. After a long delay, it was dismissed on 30 November. Determined not to give up, he then moved the Supreme Court on 11 December against the Bombay High Court's order dismissing his earlier petition. This petition too was heard and dismissed by the Supreme Court on 11 April 1988.

Thereafter, Gandhi engaged R. D. Ovalekar, an experienced attorney from Mumbai, as his defence lawyer. On 14 July, charges under section 376 of the IPC were framed against Rajendra Gandhi and his plea of not guilty was recorded. The case was then adjourned to 14 September for hearing.

In the first week of August, Ovalekar expressed his reluctance to appear in the case, owing to some threats he had received. So, Gandhi approached a few other lawyers with his brief, but no one was willing to take the case.[1] Now once again he approached Bombay High Court to get the case transferred out of Kolhapur. The court noted:

> There was lot of agitation at Kolhapur. While the accused was in custody his house was also stormed by a mob consisting of large number of persons from Kolhapur. Similarly, morchas were taken to the Civil Hospital, Kolhapur, and to the office of one Mr J. J. Bardeskar, an Advocate from Kolhapur, who had appeared for the accused for moving for bail. Morchas were also taken to the Bar Association at the District Court, Kolhapur ... all this was reflected in newspapers.[2]

Citizens had formed a 'Nagrik Kruti Samiti', a social action group that would pursue and monitor the case until it reached the Supreme Court. P. D. Hankare, a social activist, led this movement, funding it often out of his own pocket.

The Bombay High Court, taking note of the public agitation, declared: 'It is the fundamental right of the petitioner under Article 22(1) of the Constitution of India to be defended by a Counsel of his choice ...', and considered it 'expedient for the ends of justice to transfer this case from the Sessions Court at Kolhapur to the Sessions Court at Greater Bombay'. The special public prosecutor wanted to challenge the transfer at the Supreme Court, but the High Court refused permission to do so as no new legal argument had been made, 'hence the prayer for leave to appeal to the Supreme Court is rejected'.[3]

The Nagrik Kruti Samiti nevertheless filed a public interest litigation in the Supreme Court. The state of Maharashtra too opposed the transfer of the criminal case to Mumbai. Their contention was that it sent the wrong signal to rape victims who rarely come forward to lodge their cases, and that it would be difficult for witnesses to go to Mumbai for court hearings. On 28 February 1989, the Supreme Court acceded, transferring the case to the neighbouring Satara District Sessions Court. A special order was passed that required both lawyers to be present on 17 March to start the trial that ultimately began on 5 May 1989, more than two and a half years after the rape.

Understanding the sensitivity of the case, we had sought the appointment of a special prosecutor for the trial. The Government of Maharashtra's Home Department agreed and an experienced lawyer from Pune, Uday Singh A. Jadhavrao, was appointed. During the trial, the prosecution received a serious jolt as the young victim failed to recognize the culprit in court. More than two years since the incident, Rajendra Gandhi, who did not have a beard when he had committed the crime, had grown one to confuse the child in the courtroom. Multiple medical opinions further weakened the prosecution's case.

Meanwhile, I had been transferred to Mumbai as a Deputy Commissioner of Police. Unaware of the latest developments in the trial, I was surprised to receive a call from the special prosecutor. He expressed his desire to examine me in court because the victim's father had approached me first after coming to know of the rape. The special prosecutor felt that my testimony would give credence to the genuineness of the complaint, which had recently suffered a setback.

It so happened that the date on which I was supposed to appear in court coincided with my elder son's first day in school. It was a real *dharam sankat* for me. I fretted about it for a week, unsure what to prioritize. In the end my strong urge to get justice for the victim won. My husband stood in for me and took our crying son to school while I travelled from Mumbai to Satara in order to depose in court.

Inspector Katamble, a seasoned officer and stickler for documentation, had conducted a thorough investigation, which was ably presented in court by the equally competent special prosecutor Uday Singh A. Jadhavrao. The Satara sessions judge convicted Rajendra Gandhi on 6 October 1989. He was sentenced to seven years' rigorous imprisonment with a fine of ₹5,000 under section 376 of the IPC and six months' rigorous imprisonment under the Bombay Children Act with a fine of ₹500. The Maruti car was 'ordered to be forfeited and confiscated to the State'.[4]

Many years later, while travelling by the 'Deccan Queen' from Mumbai to Pune, I found myself sitting next to the district and sessions judge who had convicted Rajendra Gandhi. He had recognized me. After some hesitation I asked him something that had always intrigued me: How could he convict Rajendra Gandhi when the child had failed to recognize him in court? His reply was clear and simple: 'The child was very natural in giving evidence. If she had recognized the accused after nearly three years, I would have concluded that she had been tutored by the police and the prosecutor.'

The High Court, however, reversed the conviction of rape after an appeal but upheld the conviction under the Bombay Children Act, enhancing the fine amount to ₹40,000. The accused was ultimately convicted for a minor offence under section 354 of the IPC, i.e., 'outraging the modesty of a women', and sentenced to thirty-three days' imprisonment, which he had already undergone. The Protection of Children from Sexual Offences (POCSO) Act would be enacted much later in 2012.

This reduction in sentence and the dismissal of the rape case angered the citizens of Kolhapur once again. The Nagrik Kruti Samiti had been meticulously keeping track of the case in the Bombay High Court. The convener of the Samiti, P. D. Hankare, met me in Mumbai and shared his distress. He requested the state government to file an appeal in the Supreme Court. I checked with the Law and Judiciary Department and was told that they would do so 'in due course', though the public prosecutor in the high court had stated that the matter was 'not fit for appeal'. I was shocked, but persisted with the department so they would approach the Supreme Court at the earliest. I was also disturbed by a comment from Hankare that the victim's family had lost interest in the case. On cross-checking, I was told that Rajendra Gandhi had deposited the fine of ₹40,000 as per the court order and ₹25,000 had already been withdrawn by the victim's father.

Around this time, Hankare filed a PIL in the Supreme Court against the reduction of sentence by the Bombay High Court. While admitting it, the court asked the Government of Maharashtra about its reasons for not filing an appeal. Publicly shamed, the state did so on 29 April 1997, as did Rajendra Gandhi, who wanted the Bombay High Court's conviction under section 354 to be set aside.

The case came up for hearing after eleven long years in the Supreme Court which finally set aside the high court's verdict. It allowed the state's appeal and converted the conviction of Rajendra Jawanmal Gandhi under section 354 to a conviction under section 376/511 (attempt to commit rape), sentencing him to five years in prison on 11 September. It upheld the conviction and sentencing of the accused under section 57 of the Bombay Children Act along with the fine of ₹40,000. It took eleven long years, but the child victim did eventually receive justice.

The Supreme Court in its verdict, however, made the following negative observations about the Nagrik Kruti Samiti-led citizens' agitation:

> We agree with the High Court that a great harm had been caused to the girl by unnecessary publicity and taking out 'morcha' by the public ... A trial by press, electronic media or public agitation is very antithesis of rule of law. It can well lead to miscarriage of justice.[5]

This observation of the court was later criticized by the legal luminary Upendra Baxi, who lauded the Samiti's efforts:

> ... a social action group whose fierce exertions made it difficult for the State not to appeal against the High Court's verdict. The

> Supreme Court makes the success of peoples' movement against rape into its very failure! ... If, indeed, as the Court asserts that the crime of rape is a 'crime against the whole society', there seems no justified ground in disallowing people's participation in the administration of criminal justice in ways which enhance prosecutorial vigour and accountability.[6]

A few centuries ago, in another part of the world, Benjamin Franklin had said, 'Justice will not be served until those who are unaffected are as outraged as those who are.'

It had been a long and arduous legal battle for justice and the Supreme Court of India was conscious of it. While sentencing Rajendra Gandhi on 11 September 1997, it mentioned in its final order:

> The question of imposition of sentence after lapse of 11 years of the offence troubled our mind a great deal ... the message is loud and clear that no person who commits or attempts to commit rape shall escape punishment.

9

BOMBAY PORT THEFTS

'When everything seems to be going against you, remember that the airplane takes off against the wind, not with it.'

– HENRY FORD

'Oh, cargo thefts are uncontrollable, so are the port thieves. I am surprised that you have been given this charge,' said the senior office heading the Anti-Corruption Bureau of Maharashtra. I had gone to meet him for the customary 'calling on', having recently taken over as Deputy Commissioner Ports, Mumbai.

Earlier that day I had received a brisk phone call from the Mumbai police control room officer, who wanted to check if the 'DCP Port Zone' had reported for duty. On receiving an affirmative reply, he informed me that I was to go on a night round in the city. It was January 1987 and this was my first day on duty in the metropolis.

From the rural environments of Kolhapur, I had been transferred to the concrete jungle of Mumbai. Certain locals raised their voices against this transfer, but my DIG,

P. S. Narayanaswamy, sagaciously advised me not to pay any attention, and instead take over at Mumbai, however inconvenient it might be for me personally.

It was my good fortune that the first night round went peacefully. My new driver, Chintaman Jadhav, and the wireless operator Raosaheb R. Pande, sitting next to him in the front passenger seat, were completely unknown to me. But police culture was not. I knew how to be comfortable even in the unfamiliar and spent my time listening to the control room instruct officers on the wireless and admiring the well-lit roads of Mumbai, which looked very broad at night. Such was my welcome to the country's foremost harbour.

The centuries-old Bombay Port began to be developed at great speed after its transfer to the East India Company by the royal charter in 1668. The opening of the Suez Canal in 1869 revolutionized the city's maritime trade. It shifted the import and export trade from India's east coast to the west and the Bombay Port became the principal 'Gateway of India'. The present-day autonomous Bombay Port Trust (BPT) was set up in 1873 for administering its affairs.[1] The construction of a customs house, a warehouse, dry docks, among other facilities, began thereafter, with jetties and more warehouses accruing as the years went by.

During the late 1980s, Bombay Port was a bustle of terminals, transit sheds, jetties, warehouses and support infrastructure. Being an integral part of the city, several Bollywood movies have revolved around the port, its porters, crimes and rampant corruption. Many small-time port criminals later graduated into dreaded 'dons', about whom legendary stories abound – some real, others embellished into folklore.

It took me some time to understand the widespread power and influence of organized criminal gangs operating in the dark alleys of the harbour, plotting their well-planned port thefts. All I could see were massive containers and gigantic consignments everywhere, and my nose only picked up the sharp, pungent smell of chemicals in the air. This odour became more prominent at night and I came to associate it with my night patrols. I even developed a strange liking for it. It reminds me of my hard work and youthful energy which I had in abundance in the 1980s.

The port handled around fifty million tons of cargo in those days. There was such an overflow of import and export that the union government had to start constructing the Nhava Sheva Port in Navi Mumbai. It became operational in 1989. Most container traffic now flows through the Jawaharlal Nehru Port Trust (JNPT, Nhava Sheva), while the once-teeming Bombay Port wears a forlorn, deserted look.

I soon realized that the nefarious links among port officers, security staff, local police, customs officials and insurance companies were very deeply entrenched. And in the beginning, they did not take me seriously, busy as I was familiarizing myself with police officers and the geography of the zone. The port had three police stations: Yellow Gate, Sewree and Wadala. I had heard and read of organized crime, but here I was faced with organized thefts worth crores. In the late eighties, there was a dangerous and illegal parallel government within Bombay Port with its own rules and regulations. I had first-hand experience of it when I started receiving threatening calls at night, interspersed with silent calls with eerie sounds in the background.

This mafia, very early in my tenure as DCP, organized a front-page news piece in a local English daily that I had failed in my mission to control port thefts, for which I had been specially brought from Kolhapur. Highly embarrassed and agitated, I decided to meet the commissioner of police, D. S. Soman, and explain my efforts towards curbing these thefts.

I reached the impressive regal building which houses the police commissioner's office in Crawford Market, dreading a talking-to from the boss. He was known to be a man of few words and extremely intolerant of corrupt practices which were slowly creeping into the state police ecosystem. His head buried in a file, the commissioner asked me to take a seat. Then he picked up the local daily from a side table and said in a matter-of-fact voice, 'When I read it, I thought to myself, the young lady has started working in earnest.' The commissioner had clearly understood that the article had been orchestrated. What can be more motivating for a young officer than a supportive boss during challenging circumstances. I left the commissioner's office in a happy daze.

The Chief Vigilance Officer of the Bombay Port Trust, S. S. Puri, was a Maharashtra cadre officer of the Indian Police Service. He took a keen interest in explaining to me the way the port mafia operated, offering suggestions on how to break the nexus. Later in his career he became the chief of Special Investigation Team (SIT) that investigated the internationally notorious Telagi stamp paper scam. Mr Puri came across as a man of class. An old-timer, he believed that integrity was paramount, and any compromise on that score was totally unacceptable to him. A stickler for rules, all officers of the port trust, including me, were in awe of him.

A few months after starting my new assignment, I found that the crime inspector from Yellow Gate police station was involved in a massive port theft. He had detected the case and identified the criminals. But the case papers showed that the investigation had suddenly stopped thereafter. As a result, the stolen consignment had not been recovered. To my queries he had no answer. Shaken by his brazen misconduct, I approached the commissioner of police with a written report. After studying it, he suspended the officer. This sent shockwaves across the port trust and the police. In Mumbai, crime inspectors tend to be quite powerful, perhaps even more so than the senior inspectors in charge of police stations. This one action of mine made the police officers realize that I meant business.

The Chief Security Officer of BPT supported me in weeding out the 'criminals' from among his staff. The Port Users Forum started becoming active and sharing information. In about a year's time, the number of port thefts came down to an extent that I started wondering if the police stations had started a 'non-registration' operation. So, I kept up my frequent night rounds and surprise checks. During one such visit, I found Yellow Gate police station staff in a panic as a drug addict who had been arrested by them had broken an electric bulb and eaten the shards while in lock-up. He had gone into 'withdrawal' without any access to drugs and felt overwhelmed.

Another time, while passing through the port, we came across a young thief with a bag containing stolen goods. In our enthusiasm, my wireless operator Pande and I got down from the car and chased him. Terrified on finding two uniformed officers after him, the boy jumped down to the jetty. A police constable standing nearby used his presence of mind and quickly jumped after the thief in full uniform to save him. I heaved a sigh of relief when the boy was brought back. If either the addict mentioned earlier or the young port thief had died, we would have been held responsible for their deaths.

Around this time, a local pharmaceuticals company reported a theft of two expensive imported consignments that had been stored in port sheds. We checked with our informants and also in areas known for trading in stolen goods. Police crime prevention staff regularly visited what was known as the '*chor bazaar*'. In fact, we had cultivated informants who would study the market and tip us off about the scarcity of particular goods, such as chemicals, ball bearings, etc., and their possible planned thefts. We would thereafter mount special surveillance on imported containers carrying those scarce items. However, in these two cases, both consignments had been stolen within a short span of time. The Yellow Gate police station took it as a challenge and one case was soon detected by Inspector Suresh Walishetty, an officer reputed for his detective skills. And the owner of the company himself brought us information about the whereabouts of the second stolen consignment, which we recovered by conducting a raid. The pilfered consignments were worth crores.

While investigating another case, to my utter distress I found a constable in my office involved in a container theft. Each container carries a seal with a specific number. In this instance and in many others, port thieves opened containers en route to different sheds, took out expensive goods and replaced the seal. The theft would be detected only several days later when the container was opened at its destination. As a result, it would be difficult to determine whether these were cases of fraudulence/short consignments on the international exporters' part or theft on the ship or at Bombay Port. Criminal gangs at the port were taking full advantage of these loopholes and, this time, my young office constable had joined hands with them. But by then our well-oiled system of informants had started showing results in neutralizing organized crime syndicates. After the crime inspector, this was the second 'casualty' within our ranks.

The police commissioner who had supported me through the media campaign against me did not bat an eyelid before discharging the constable straightaway since his probation period had not yet ended. Such quick disciplinary actions can have exemplary results.

Talking of ethics, it must be noted that even criminals have their own. One morning, I woke up early to a call from the mafia gangster Varadarajan Mudaliar's right-hand man. He introduced himself as Kuku and informed me that my police car driver had approached him with a demand of ₹2,000. 'What should I do?' he asked. Taken aback, I replied, 'Beat him up with your shoes.' 'I expected this from you,' he told me and hung up.

I immediately checked with the officer heading the Motor Transport (MT) section of the Bombay Police and learnt that my regular driver Jadhav had been granted emergency leave and a new driver had been allotted to my car as a temporary arrangement. He had not even spent a day driving my vehicle before deciding to make the most of his newfound opportunities. Such criminals in uniform have unfortunately increased in number, giving our profession a bad name.

Another morning I received a call from the chairman of the BPT, S. Ramamoorthi, who said he wanted to see me. So far, I had seen him at a few meetings in the conference hall at the port trust. This would be my first visit to his office at Ballard Pier. What a huge and awe-inspiring chamber he had! Wood-framed portraits of past chairmen and other luminaries hung on the walls transported the viewer back in time. Mr Ramamoorthi received me warmly and congratulated me on my success in controlling port thefts. I was pleasantly surprised, in particular when he quoted a few statistics with regards to past port thefts and compared them to the recent numbers. But his next question threw me into utter confusion. 'What can we do for you?' he asked me, in all seriousness. Thanking him for his compliments, I sought time to come back with a reply to his unexpected generous offer. He gave me a benign smile and time to think it over. I left his office walking on cloud nine.

Mulling over what to ask him for, I went to meet the CVO, Mr Puri. He was quite amused by my reaction and reminded me that though the DCP Port was the ex officio head of the department of BPT, the official chamber of the DCP did not do justice to the title. It was a small room next to the lift on the fourth floor of the main BPT building. The office staff had a hall to themselves about a hundred metres away. It was a golden suggestion that I embraced with enthusiasm.

The chairman was informed of my wish for a respectable chamber. And it was soon allotted to me and my staff – a well-done-up, fully air-conditioned space at par with the offices of other HODs at the port trust. It was a wonderful example of a senior motivating a junior officer through appreciation and concrete action.

Thus, I shifted to my freshly painted office in Ballard Pier. While I could not believe my luck, the office staff soon started complaining that the AC was making them catch colds and causing pain in their joints! Those were pre-liberalization days. Life was relatively simple and the commercial capital had yet to develop a fancy for modern technology like air conditioners. Sitting in the cool room, sheltered from the city's humidity, I felt that my productivity had gone up. Though I must admit it was the hustle-bustle of the port and its chemical smells that really motivated me to give my best.

Later I was told that due to my innumerable rounds after hours, a rumour had spread, both among the dock thieves and law enforcers, that I strapped my two-year-old son to my back and patrolled the port on a motorcycle at night!

10

MY CHARRED CAR

'You can conquer almost any fear if you will only make up your mind to do so. For remember, fear doesn't exist anywhere except in the mind.'

– DALE CARNEGIE

It was Dussehra and there were festivities all around. We had made a *toran* of marigold for the front door of my official residence at Byculla. My Police drivers Dilip Veerkar and Chintaman Jadhav had brought flowers, sweets and a coconut. In accordance with Maharashtra Police tradition, we performed a puja for my car and weapon (a 9mm pistol issued to me by the Naigaon police headquarters). The coconut was broken in half and *prasad* was distributed. It was a sober ceremony. Though Dussehra is celebrated peacefully in Mumbai, police patrolling is intensified on the day. So immediately after the puja, we hit the road.

The evening rally led by the Shiv Sena – Maharashtra's most well-known regional political party – in Shivaji Park, Dadar, is a prominent event in Mumbai. It would attract massive crowds that came to listen to the party founder, Bala Saheb Thackeray, whose bold, satirical, humorous speeches would enthrall the audience. The rally is also a show of the Shiv Sena's strength and continues to serve this purpose, though Bala Saheb is no more.

There was a change of guard at the top and a new commissioner had taken over. I had spent more than a year with the Bombay Police by then and would often wonder how I would handle violent law-and-order situations. The port was infested with organized crime but there had been no protests or agitations. Compared to other deputy commissioners, I was short and thin. By contrast, they looked impressive and awe-inspiring in their well-creased uniforms, and suitably grim too.

I had not realized that the opportunity to test my nerves was waiting round the corner. During a mid-morning patrol on Dussehra, I suddenly heard the police control room directing various police vans to Kamathipura, where a serious riot had erupted. I was listening to the wireless network in my car. The DCP Zone II informed the control room officer that he had reached the spot as it was his jurisdiction. Soon the control room reported more violence followed by police firing. A little later the wireless broadcast reported that the commissioner of police who had joined recently had been gheraoed by local citizens. The control room officer thereafter started directing all police officers in the vicinity to rush to Kamathipura as the situation had gone out of control. I left for the site immediately.

On the way, while driving down Mohammed Ali Road, I noticed a few traffic branch officers on duty. I enquired if they were aware of the riot in Kamathipura, and they replied in the negative – the traffic wireless channel is different from the zonal ones. I informed them that the commissioner was facing a violent mob and advised them to follow my car in their jeep.

As we entered Kamathipura, we found big crowds on both sides of the streets. Seeing my vehicle with its amber beacon light, many citizens rushed towards us. I alighted from my car. The angry crowd informed me that a police officer wearing dark glasses had come to the site in his car earlier and opened fire from his revolver, killing a young Hindu boy on the spot. They were anguished that the officer did not even get down; he had fired through the window of his official vehicle. I could see that these people were distraught and aggressive. One of them read my name on the nameplate on my uniform and shouted, 'Borwankar, where were you when the trainee sub-inspector Gokhale was killed on this street last year? What are you going to do now that another young Hindu boy has been killed?' I realized that the riot had acquired a communal tone and the officer who had fired at the boy was the DCP Zone II – a Muslim officer.

In an effort to pacify everyone around me, I assured them that there would be a government inquiry into the incident. Yet our twenty-minute-long discussion, which felt like hours to me, was getting us nowhere. Instead, the crowd was growing more belligerent. I looked around for the traffic branch officers who had followed me. But not one of them was in sight. The only guy standing next to me was my bodyguard, who looked very worried.

Standing amidst the seething crowd, I realized that we were in a precarious situation. So, I veered the heated discussion towards the commissioner of police who had been gheraoed at the other end of the locality and asserted that I should be allowed to reach him. The crowd did not budge. 'Answer us here and now' was their refrain. I knew of the young officer who had been shot dead a year earlier in the same area and that a criminal case had been registered. The crowd now demanded to know about the progress of the case, but it was information I did not have. The atmosphere was intensifying by the minute when a few from the crowd suddenly said I should proceed towards the commissioner.

My antennas were on full alert. There were only two of us now, as the traffic officers seemed to have disappeared. I gauged that proceeding ahead could be dangerous. I was also conscious of the 9mm pistol in my holster and the possibility that someone could snatch it while I passed through the crowd. Therefore, instead of accepting the offer, I stood firm. Suppressing my inner turmoil, I said that I would not proceed until the crowd parted to make way for me. A few people agreed that they should let 'the officer' pass, but many others refused. It was a spontaneous gathering of angry citizens and I could see that there was no single leader. Their noisy debate on the right course of action went on for another ten minutes, after which, fortunately, a consensus was reached that I should be allowed to make my way to the commissioner.

As the crowd parted, albeit grudgingly, I walked down the road for about 500 metres and came across the commissioner in a by-lane to my left. He and the additional commissioner stood near a police van, surrounded by a frenzied mob. As I approached him, the new police commissioner asked me in a very irritated tone, 'Have they sent *you* to help us?' I was appalled and humiliated by his reaction. The additional commissioner noticed this and changed the topic immediately. He asked me to use the wireless device in his vehicle and seek more reinforcements from the control room.

As I was walking towards his car, I heard the loud blaring of a police siren. Many of us rushed to the main road to find that the crowd had overturned my police car after forcing the driver out. The vehicle was ablaze, its siren going off at full blast. My terrified driver stood next to it, looking helpless. It was the same car for which we had performed the puja in the morning. I went numb with shock.

Various items, including my briefcase, had been thrown out of the car. It was half burnt. I picked it up, handed it to my bodyguard and went on to ask for more manpower from the police control room. The reinforcements arrived soon. I could hear on the wireless set the control room officer informing the motor transport division of the Bombay Police, 'The crowd has burnt port madam's car. Please send a vehicle for her.' By the time the situation was brought under control, another vehicle had arrived for me.

I was shaken by the day's events, especially my car getting charred to a crisp, not to mention the commissioner's debasing remark. It was distressing that the traffic police officers had vanished from the scene of the riot. Incidentally they were tall, smart and very impressive-looking – model male police officers, one would think! My five-foot-four-inch frame had to stand the ground and face the ferocious mob to the best of my ability. It dawned on me that my complex about my height was a pointless mental hurdle. It was by way of this unfortunate violent incident that I finally overcame this problem. I also realized that mere brawn is not enough when it comes to handling violent and sensitive public order issues.

It was quite late by the time I reached home that eventful Dussehra night. Tired to the last bone in my body, I opened my half-burnt briefcase to find that my three-year-old son's photograph was untouched by the fire.

Later, during a government-ordered inquiry, the traffic police officers denied having fled the spot. The inquiry officer, Ravi Budhiraja, had called me to his office, where I found them waiting outside. Just before I entered his office to record my statement, one of the officers came forward and told me sheepishly, 'You are like our sister; we did *not* desert you.'

11

THE TURNING OF THE TIDE

'Time and tide wait for no man.'

– GEOFFREY CHAUCER

I was on a public order bandobast duty along with other Bombay Police officers when suddenly senior police officers' transfers were announced on the police wireless network. Generally, such orders are issued through an internal daily bulletin called 'Police Notice' or faxed or sent in the form of individual letters. The DCP Zone 1 standing next to me looked up and said out loud, 'They have given Zone 4 to *you*?' Stung by his comment, I instinctively retorted, 'Why Not?' The truth is that I was equally surprised as it was the toughest zone in Mumbai during the 1980s, infested with violent organized criminal gangs notorious for cold-blooded murders. It also included Dharavi, Asia's biggest slum. Besides, an IPS officer who had recently been posted there had not yet completed his tenure. So, the news of my transfer was sudden and surprising indeed.

I moved to the new zone after bidding a sad and earnest goodbye to the port. I had learnt a lot during my posting there, battling organized crime for the first time in my young career. To this day I miss my night rounds of the port and feel nostalgic whenever I pick up the familiar smells of pharmaceuticals and other goods stacked in sheds and warehouses.

Zone 4 had no particular smell except that of the sweat of men and women toiling in densely populated shanties and slums. I went on rounds in the areas under the jurisdiction of nine police stations and noted their distinct characteristics. Dharavi, Deonar and Govandi had mixed populations (with most residents below the poverty line) belonging to diverse religions. Matunga was mainly Tamil, Dadar was Maharashtrian and Mahim had a significant Muslim population. Chembur, a refugee settlement after Partition, was now a mix of Hindus, Muslims, Sindhis and Buddhists. Antop Hill had resettlement camps and a huge government residential colony. The Rashtriya Chemicals and Fertilizers (RCF) and Bhabha Atomic Research Centre (BARC) police stations catered to the respective institutions and their residential colonies.

Besides having a high crime rate, this zone saw a multitude of incidents needing police intervention because of Sion Hospital, officially known as the Lokmanya Tilak Municipal General Hospital. As very few government hospitals in Mumbai conduct postmortems, most cases of unnatural deaths ended up here. While citizens are usually aware of the documentation required for investigation, they are mostly oblivious that, by law, the police have to conduct inquiries into accidents and unnatural deaths and there is a great deal of paperwork involved. Sub-inspectors and head constables record statements of persons known to or last seen with the deceased in cases of unnatural or accidental deaths. It is a legal requirement as there is a possibility that such a death could have happened due to a crime.

After a few months of settling in, reviewing crime statistics, having discussions with officers and making repeated visits to police stations, I realized that Dharavi was not as crime-infested as I had feared. The living conditions, however, were so appalling that after every visit to a scene of crime inside the slum I would come up with a new definition of hell. There would be children playing in the gutters, pigs roaming free, men and women cramped together in tiny shanties, some of which somehow had two storeys. The local inspector Shivajirao Babar and his team were excellent at their job. I could see that they were more burdened with petty disputes, called non-cognizable cases, and application enquiries than serious crime. Such cases – water disputes, quarrelling neighbours, fist fights between adults, petty fights among children, etc. – do not exactly require police intervention. So, I decided to bring in two reputed social service institutions: Nirmala Niketan and the Tata Institute of Social Sciences. Their senior students were placed here as interns who would settle these minor issues under the direction of local police officers. The faculty regularly supervised their work, mainly the coordination between citizens and the police. To my surprise, the feedback was that the policemen were more eager to talk to the faculty and students than the citizens, using the opportunity to discuss their family issues and generally decompress. Recent studies have shown that police officers have serious physical, emotional and mental health issues – understandable as their daily shifts often extend up to fourteen hours.

The Mahim police station area had simmering Hindu–Muslim tensions throughout my tenure as Deputy Commissioner. We had to resort to firing thrice to disperse communities confronting one another on the streets. The local corporator was said to provoke these tensions, though he was sugary sweet in his behaviour with me. At a time when we were facing frequent violent public order issues, a widely circulated local newspaper suddenly came up with a front-page story that an unauthorized religious structure was coming up near Mahim Creek and that the police were turning a blind eye to it.

The Additional Commissioner of Police summoned me to his chamber the same day and conveyed the commissioner's directive that the construction must stop and police security should be provided when the illegal under-construction structure was to be demolished by the Bombay Municipal Corporation. I was advised to take it up with corporation authorities. The Add. CP said it was urgent and promised to provide additional manpower but advised total confidentiality. A cheerful person and a great motivator, that day he looked quite grim. Arriving back at my office, I called the ACP Mahim Division, Senior Inspector and Inspector (Crime) Mahim Police Station and apprised them of the commissioner's order. The next day we invited a senior officer from the Brihanmumbai Municipal Corporation and discussed the issue. He had already received instructions from his seniors to demolish the illegal structure.

While we were confident that the operation would be successful, keeping it confidential was a big challenge. I had not seen the structure and decided to go take a look. Since my visit could alert people and the police, I went there not in my uniform, but wearing a salwar-kameez, with a dupatta covering my head and part of my face. I also decided not to use my beacon-flashing police car and instead rode pillion on the scooter of the inspector from the crime division. We observed that the unlawful structure was visible during low tide, but it could not be seen when the tide was high. This too was discussed in detail with the BMC officer, who calculated the low tide timings for the day of the demolition. It being early morning was a big relief. He promised total confidentiality and that he would bring along his best team so as to finish off the task before people in the neighbourhood woke up and become aware of it.

I made three more trips in disguise to chalk out the bandobast for carrying out the demolition. All my training with respect to drafting outer and inner cordons, making preventive arrests, etc., came in handy, but one thing that I believe in strongly was not possible – direct communication with the staff. We shared this sensitive information with as few people as possible.

A formal confidential report was sent to the Commissioner of Police seeking extra manpower 'to remove hutments near Hinduja hospital'. Being aware of the actual operation, he did not raise eyebrows at our request or at the large number of officers requisitioned by us. On D-day, a well-equipped BMC demolition squad reported at my office, which was located above Matunga police station. So did officers and personnel from other zones. The best officers from my zone had been deployed in the troublesome localities of Mahim. Most of them were in civil clothes as we did not want to raise any alarm. Without announcing a curfew, we informally prevented local people from gathering in one place.

After these painstaking preparations, to our utter horror we learnt that the corporation had wrongly calculated the low tide timing. The unauthorized structure, therefore, was not visible. I could not believe my eyes, which could see only water in the morning twilight. Feeling extremely stressed, we decided not to move re-enforcement staff and officers to Mahim until the tide turned. The enterprising Matunga senior inspector and the assistant commissioner organized breakfast for everyone and encouraged the personnel to play cards so that they would not speculate about the reasons for the delay in their deployment.

Police officers in full uniform playing cards while on duty, right under my nose, was an unbearable sight. But I had no choice.

As soon as the structure came into view, the BMC team got into action and demolished it. The bandobast staff, in the meanwhile, had been brought to Mahim and strategically deployed. By the time the local residents noticed the unusual police presence, the mission had been accomplished. Preventive arrests made the previous night meant that anti-social elements who could have created problems were in police custody and not on the streets.

Since the structure was unlawful, citizens could not make an issue of its demolition. Had the construction already been completed, demolishing it would have been very difficult despite its illegal status. In our country, such illegal constructions are everywhere. Instead of asking for their removal, people take to the streets in protest if the administration tries to demolish them.

As they say, a stitch in time saves nine. In our case, with the local media reporting about the unauthorized construction, the police commissioner taking a firm decision and the BMC team completing the task successfully, many possible conflicts and riots were preempted. It also averted a slew of future litigations that would have inevitably been filed against the demolition of the illegal structure. The case taught me another crucial lesson: it is very important to calculate tide timings accurately! I have since closely followed the words of Harriet Beecher Stowe: 'Never give up, for that is just the place and time that the tide will turn.'

12

A DARK AND VIOLENT NIGHT

'Ahimsa is the highest duty. Even if we cannot practise it in full, we must try to understand its spirit and refrain as far as is humanly possible from violence.'

– MAHATMA GANDHI

Two years later, on Dussehra, we were on bandobast duty once again. The annual Shiv Sena rally was to take place in Shivaji Park, Dadar, in Zone 4, which fell within my jurisdiction. To date it is considered one of the most sensitive rallies in Mumbai as it draws large, boisterous crowds. By now I had become a little more confident when it came to handling violence and public order situations. But this time a riot broke out in my area which was in a league all its own.

We had planned the deployment of police officers at Shivaji Park meticulously and picked up local antisocial elements the previous night. The special branch had been monitoring the situation and the police commissioner was himself supervising our preparedness. Party workers being very fond of their charismatic leader Bal Thackeray, we knew they would come in full strength to listen to his speech, which usually guaranteed ardour, wit and sarcasm in equal measure.

During the morning briefing, the police control room informed us of an early morning caste-related riot in the neighbouring area of Thane that we did not take seriously. And we could not have made a worse mistake!

As expected, the evening's event at Shivaji Park was well attended. Bala Saheb was at his fiery best and the eager crowd lapped up his every word. It was at the fag end of the programme, when the customary thanksgiving was ongoing, that I heard of a stabbing incident in a Muslim locality in nearby Mahim. Sensing that it could take a communal turn as the Dadar crowd consisted mainly of Hindus, I rushed to the scene. Other senior officers stayed put and supervised the crowd's dispersal. It was quite late by then.

Even the biggest police deployments at such huge public rallies look minuscule compared to the crowds. A uniformed team that looks sizeable on paper tends to get lost in a sea of people – in such situations one simply has to trust that citizens will remain peaceful. In our profession, dispersing crowds are considered risky; they can turn violent in an instant and destroy public property. Sheer numbers give them a false sense of safety and solidarity, and many lose their sense of proportion. One of our senior officers would often consult astrologers whenever such large events were organized in Mumbai!

While at Mahim, I received information on the police wireless network that there was a serious riot in Chembur, which came under my purview. I decided to proceed towards it and directed the assistant commissioners of both Mahim and Matunga divisions to go straight to Chembur. On the way, I heard a constable on the wireless channel shouting *'Zone 4 madam na lawkar pathva ethe firing suru jhale ahe.'* (Send Zone 4 madam immediately; they've started firing here.) He repeated his distress call twice, literally crying out loud the second time. I also heard the control room dispatching police vans to the spot.

Realizing the gravity of the situation, I decided to take more policemen along and asked the staff of Machimar Chowki in Sion to join me in their jeep. As usual, my escort vehicle, with an officer and a handful of constables, was following me. Since the Eastern Express Highway was totally blocked by trucks full of crowds returning from Shivaji Park, we reached the scene of the riot through the wrong side.

Night had set in. The highway was pitch dark as the rioters had managed to deactivate the electric poles. Molotov cocktails, petrol and gasoline balls, stones, bottles were raining down, and the policemen who had reached the spot earlier were ducking inside their vehicles. As I got down from my car, I too had to duck on the far side of the highway, out of the reach of the fireballs. The ACPs following me in their jeeps came forward to inform me that the road was in fact not in our zone. The left side of the road and the highway came under the jurisdiction of Nehru Nagar police station in Zone 5, but the right side was part of Chembur. Patil, who was ACP Mahim, was a very experienced officer who had opened fire twice earlier and was definitely not a coward. In his usual brisk tone, he told me that we should leave the place immediately.

But I simply could not bring myself to and refused. Now that the car beacon had declared my presence, going back was not an option. With 'missiles' flying all around, I was pondering what to do when a Shiv Sena leader from one of the trucks approached me. He had an imposing presence and a large entourage of young men surrounding him. His first words to me were, '*Madam, aplaya policena bangdya daya; bagha kase jaun basle ahet gadyan madhe.*' (Madam, you should ask your policemen to wear bangles; see how they are sitting and ducking in their vehicles.)

It soon dawned on us that the morning's caste riot in Thane had travelled to Mumbai, causing this violent disturbance. Some of the hutment dwellers on both sides of the road belonged to a particular caste and had thrown stones at the trucks carrying the Shiv Sainiks, who represented the other caste in the Thane riot. They had also put big boulders on the road to stop the Sainiks from going back to Thane. The trucks had no choice but to stop, so the Shiv Sainiks got down to retaliate, leading to another deadly riot.

I asked the leader – who I later came to know was Anand Dighe, a firebrand from Thane – to control his men while I got my men out of the vans. The control room had, in the meanwhile, relayed that the ACP Chembur and senior officers of Nehru Nagar police station had reached their respective areas and were trying to control the stone- and missile-throwing slum dwellers along the highway. Pounding on the doors of police vans with my official baton, I exhorted the policemen to come out. My personal security staff was with me. With helmets on our heads and megaphones in hand, we went from one police van to the other. Slowly and sheepishly, the policemen started alighting.

Suddenly I saw a very skinny constable tumbling to the ground in front of me. I was shocked but had too much on my mind to now take a pause. He was instead rushed to the hospital by some of the policemen. We found out later that upon seeing the violent crowds he had fired sixteen rounds in the air from his rifle. Whether he fainted from stress and exhaustion or feigned the whole thing, we will never know.

A few metres from us, other officers were using their megaphones and advising the hutment dwellers to stop pelting stones and firing missiles. Since there was no compliance despite warnings delivered through my megaphone, I ordered my men to fire tear gas towards the hutments. I knew that tear gas would not be effective as the violent crowd was far and scattered but I still wanted to follow the protocol for crowd control. In the deep darkness we could see the tear gas smoke rising, but the area being huge and open, the grenades were understandably of not much use. The gas guns, however, made impressive loud sounds. After a lull, the stone-pelting started again. With another warning on the megaphone, I ordered one round of rifle fire. My gunner and other officers kept sounding warnings through their megaphones that we would continue to fire if the stone-throwing didn't stop.

I also requested the Shiv Sena leader to move the trucks. He refused to do so until the boulders ahead were removed by 'those who had placed them'. By then hundreds of Shiv Sainiks were on the highway, itching to teach the hutment dwellers 'a lesson for life'. I did my best to discourage them, but to no avail. The two ACPs had, however, managed to stop the stone-pelting. Electricity had still not been restored and we were operating in the dim light emanating from the headlights of our vehicles.

To my great relief, another zonal DCP, K. P. Raghuvanshi, sent to the spot by the control room, had just reached. Having worked in Thane earlier, he knew Anand Dighe and was able to persuade him to move the trucks and his men. Policemen and

Shiv Saniks jointly lifted the boulders and cleared the highway.

As they left shouting slogans, we picked up our megaphones again to call out to the injured so that we could take them to hospitals. Initially there was no response but slowly hutment dwellers, including a few women, came forward and were taken to nearby hospitals in police vans.

Post midnight, when the additional commissioner in charge of law and order arrived at the spot, the situation was well under control. Looking at me, he asked, 'Where is DCP Zone 5?' and it suddenly struck me that all this time I had not been in my own zone and had in fact ordered tear gas and firing while standing on the highway. Yet I did not for a moment feel that I had done anything wrong. The situation had called for someone to take charge without delay and I had followed the standing operating procedure for crowd control. The caste riot was a serious incident and we had all responded to the best of our ability. Some of the officers had opened fire only to control violent mobs. I too had ordered one round. Unfortunately, four people, at different points, had been killed in the firing, one of them a sixteen-year-old girl. Many, including policemen, were injured and had been rushed to emergency wards.

Later, when the commissioner took stock of the situation, it was found that around seventy rounds had been fired during the riot. The next day most of the officers reported that I had ordered them to open fire. This is a common occurrence: officers start firing in a challenging situation and then try to place the responsibility on the senior officers at the scene. I learnt that the commissioner had lost his cool and asked each officer to 'take responsibility for the firing as the DCP Zone 4 could not possibly have been at so many places at the same time over a stretch of one kilometre.'

I was told that the Nehru Nagar senior inspector was the only one who took full responsibility. Others may have fired in self-defence or in a panic, like the policeman who fainted in front of me, but did not want to own up to their actions. The commissioner, V. K. Saraf, and the additional commissioner, G. N. Ubale, made them do so.

The commissioner was also very upset that officers from Zones 4 and 5 had responded to the riot while the DCP Zone 5 was missing. When he was asked to explain his absence, the six-foot-tall DCP insisted that he 'could not find the spot'. He was transferred out of Mumbai the next day.

One officer brought a few empty rounds a week after the riot, claiming that he was too disturbed to report earlier that he too had opened fire.

A judicial inquiry was ordered by the government. We spent days and nights preparing the necessary documents. Those were very grim days as Chembur was still simmering with wrath over those four deaths. The cremations of the deceased were a public order challenge as huge crowds would accompany each dead body. But the officers and staff rose to the occasion and worked ceaselessly for a week, never stopping to take a break. I stayed in the Rashtriya Chemical Fertilizer colony guest house until things settled down.

One surprising and pertinent observation of the Mumbai Police special branch was that the ACP Chembur Division was at the hutments for about half an hour just before the riot. How could he then not anticipate the mood of the hutment dwellers and gauge the possibility of violence? Why did he leave the area ten minutes prior to the commotion growing into a full-scale riot? He belonged to the same caste as that of the hutment dwellers. Could it be that he was aware of the planned violence and had decided to keep quiet? Did he silently consent to retaliation for the morning incident in Thane where this particular caste had been the victim? Were his caste loyalties stronger than his faithfulness to the uniform? I did not have any answers then. Nor do I have them now. But I believe that religion and caste superseding a police officer's professionalism can be extremely harmful for our country. And that citizens and the media need to take serious interest in policing.

About a year later, I was called for my deposition by the judicial commission. It was to take place before a retired judge of the Bombay High Court who was looking into the riots. Most of the citizens and junior officers had been examined by then. My statement and its cross-examination by the commission were turning out to be a long affair. The whole riot was spread over a one-kilometre stretch. Though I was aware of what had happened in front of me, I was oblivious to the events further on the Eastern Express Highway or in the hutments on the two sides of the road.

It was a strong possibility that officers would contradict one another before the commission. So, we had prepared hard. I had seen the maps created by the Chembur and Nehru Nagar police stations, with special reference to the exact spots where police firing had occurred. We had taken photographs too. The broken bulbs, tube lights, fireballs, Molotov bombs, bottles and stones scattered on the highway vividly conveyed the ferocity of the mob violence. Tragically, the Nehru Nagar senior inspector who had fired from a close range during the riot had, in the meantime, committed suicide.

I narrated the incident as I had observed it to the commission: my attempts to move the Shiv Sainiks and their trucks from the highway; warnings to the mob from the hutments against stone-pelting and firing Molotov cocktails; ordering tear gas and one round of firing. The commission listened to me patiently and said in reponse that many citizens had indeed deposed that 'a lady police officer had warned us on her megaphone. Later she asked the injured to come out and sent them to hospitals.'

The cross-examination followed. As I narrated the sequence of events to the best of my knowledge and memory, I do not think I either contradicted myself or other police officers. That night, rendered jet-black without electricity, with two large hostile groups throwing stones and missiles, convinced the judicial commission of the need for police firing, which it justified in its final report.

On the last day of my gruelling examination, just as I was leaving the stand, the judge remarked, 'Officer, if I had a medal with me, I would have given it to you today.'

13

THE BDD CHAWL RIOT

'But sir, I did not order the police firing,' I reiterated.

As Deputy Commissioner of Police, Mumbai, I was destined to handle public order issues so many times that I had lost my fear of facing and tackling violent crowds. I understood that those of us in uniform are generally so few in number, making us indistinguishable in large crowds that are extremely difficult to manage, especially if hostile. And that our own uniformed officers can be highly unpredictable in their response. I have seen them running away from violent riots, deserting their colleagues and seniors. I have witnessed their panic and overreaction to mob fury. I have witnessed our senior officers not reporting or misreporting their locations to avoid going to spots of violence. This is the underbelly of the police that sometimes comes to the fore during grave and violent public disorder incidents.

That said, on most occasions police officers do assess the situation rationally and respond with professionalism, highly conscious of their responsibility. One heartening fact is that gender is inconsequential when it comes to handling public order clashes: women have shown as much courage as men and stood their ground. Shirkers and cowards in uniform can be found among all genders.

During my Mumbai tenure as DCP, I sometimes found myself responding to public order issues outside my jurisdiction. The Bombay Development Department (BDD) chawls riot in Worli is one such case. This department was established in 1920. It was responsible for providing land for housing and for the construction of about 50,000 tenements on reclaimed land. Out of around 200 BDD chawls, 121 chawls are in Worli.[1]

I had just reached home one evening and was not feeling well when my wireless operator Munde informed me of a riot in the Worli BDD chawls. He said that the control room officer had asked the DCP Zone 4 to rush to the spot and handle the situation. So I asked him to find out from the control room if the DCP Zone 3 was on the scene, as it was his jurisdiction. He reported affirmatively. I then sought the location of the night round DCP and was informed that he too had reached the chawls. As I was a bit indisposed, I advised the wireless operator to check with the control room officer as to who had instructed him to direct me to the scene of the riot, given that it was not in my zone. The reply was, '*Varishtan che adesh ahet.*' (These are instructions from seniors.) Asking further questions would have amounted to insubordination and all such wireless conversations can be heard by everyone tuned into the channel. I changed into my uniform and left for Worli.

As was typical with Mumbai riots, the BDD chawls were enveloped in darkness, miscreants having cut off electricity. From a distance, one could vaguely make out young men throwing missiles at each other from rooftops. Most of the stones and bottles, instead of landing on the opposite buildings, were dropping to the ground, making loud, crashing noises. I had no idea of the area's geography or chawl building plans. A few police vans had already reached, and the staff had got down. There were some officers too, but they seemed as clueless as I was. All we could make out was that some groups hostile to each other had got on the top of the 'chawls' and unleashed a violent ruckus.

A quick discussion with the policemen revealed that no one was familiar with the area and had been sent by the police control room from nearby locations. Therefore I decided to follow the standard operating procedure taught to us during our training. We started warning the boys on our megaphones to stop pelting stones. They were quiet for a while, but resumed throwing their missiles and fireballs soon enough. It was pitch dark with shady figures on the roofs and us on the ground in our uniforms, mulling over our next move. I asked the police vans to be parked in a way that the headlights would throw some light in the direction of the chawls and enable us to find our feet. The staff took out their searchlights too.

Meanwhile, the control room informed us that serious riots were ongoing in many other chawls. Shortly after, we were told that a stone had hit a traffic inspector who was passing by in his jeep after duty hours. He had to be rushed to the hospital.

Our efforts to get the rioting boys down to the ground failed. So I checked if the police vans were carrying tear gas and was informed that it was at hand. Such vans operate under directions from the control room. As they are the first to respond when a public order issue is reported, policemen operating the vans are usually armed with helmets, lathis, tear gas guns and grenades, rifles and megaphones. I asked for a tear gas gunner and one of the men came forward. They are generally well trained for this task. I told him that as the boys were not responding, I was planning to use tear gas but I would order firing and not tear gas firing through my megaphone. The purpose was mainly to scare the boys. He understood. I asked the staff from the vans to fall in line and urgently explained that even when I yelled 'Fire!', no one was was to touch his rifle. Instead, only the tear gas gunner standing next to me would get into action. I made him raise his hand to identify himself. Since I did not know the policemen, I made them repeat my instructions to ensure there was no confusion. I also asked the officers to reiterate the orders to their men in clear and coherent Marathi. Since we were all stressed out, I did not want any accidental firing from a regular gun just because one of them had not understood me correctly. All this while, the boys were watching us from the rooftops. Thankfully we were out of earshot.

The police van staff standing in line made an impressive presence but there was no stopping the violent missiles from flying around. I once again announced that if the rioters did not get down from the roofs, I would order firing. After a repeat warning from my megaphone, I ordered 'One round fire!' in a loud and clear voice. The gas gunner fired a tear gas grenade. There was a loud blast and the boys started scampering in a panic.

Not wanting to waste any time, I asked the policemen to come with me to the chawls and make a thundering noise as we entered. They were perplexed, so I repeated 'Ho! Ho! Ho! Ho!' as an example. That day Yadav Ustad's training in controlling crowds and commanding parades came to my aid. If the officers and policemen were amused by my actions, they did not show it. They had also undergone similar crowd control training and were therefore quick to grasp and respond.

We blasted into one chawl after another and climbed up to the roofs. As expected, the boys had rushed back to their rooms in the chawls. We found nothing other than broken glass bottles and stones scattered all over. We soon returned to our original location and waited for instructions from the control room, which reported that the situation in other chawls had been brought under control as well and that a police team had opened fire. It also informed us that the additional commissioner G. N. Ubale had reached Worli police station.

Sometime later, a local Zone 3 assistant commissioner approached us. He relieved me from the spot, saying that the additional commissioner had called me to Worli police station. I thanked the policemen who had responded to my unconventional methods and left.

On entering the chamber of the Worli senior inspector, I found the additional commissioner being briefed by other police officers. I could feel the tension and stress all around. When alone, he asked me, 'Meera, why did you open fire?' I replied that I had not. 'You did – the control room informed me,' he said tersely. That's when it dawned on me that when I had ordered 'one round fire' and got a gas grenade launched, someone from the BDD chawls may have informed the control room that the police had opened fire. But I had taken the policemen on the scene into confidence and not one of them had used their rifles. The senior officer listened to my account patiently but his face betrayed no expression. In the early hours of the morning, I was instructed to go back, and I returned home thoroughly exhausted.

The next afternoon I received a phone call that I was to report to the police commissioner's office. On reaching, I found G. N. Ubale sitting next to the commissioner, V. K. Saraf. Both men looked grim. After I took a seat, Mr Ubale asked me to repeat the whole episode to the commissioner. I did as I was told and noticed them looking at each other. Then the commissioner asked me, 'Why were you there when it was not your zone?'

I filled him in about the instructions from the control room officer. And mentioned that when I asked the CRO to confirm the orders, he had said that I was being sent to the spot as per '*varishtan che adesh*'.

The commissioner looked at the control room logbook in front of him and retorted that there was no entry to that effect. I was also told the CRO was denying that he had dispatched me to the BDD chawls. I was shell-shocked and tried to explain. But the commissioner cut me short, advising me to forget about it and keep up the 'good work'.

Unfortunately, a few days later, the traffic inspector who had been hit with a stone while passing through the riotous chawls, died of his grave head injury. To date, I am not sure on whose instructions I was sent to the chawls and why the CRO denied having sent me there. I did not hear of any disciplinary action being initiated against him either.

These days most police control rooms in India have audio recording facilities. It ensures that instructions from CROs to police officers and communication between citizens and control room staff can be recorded and subsequently verified. If the Mumbai control room of the late eighties had such infrastructure, I would not have been in that awkward position, struggling to explain my presence in the thick of a riot on that dark night in Worli.

14

THE FIRST WOMAN DISTRICT POLICE CHIEF OF MAHARASHTRA

'To call woman the weaker sex is a libel. It is man's injustice to women. If by strength is meant moral power, then woman is immeasurably man's superior.'

– MAHATMA GANDHI

One morning I received a call from the office of the Director General of Police Maharashtra, V. K. Saraf, summoning me to his office. This was not normal. As the deputy commissioner of the crime branch's preventive and social security division, I was reporting to the Mumbai police commissioner, and the DG's office generally did not directly communicate with the officers of the Mumbai Police. This is the tradition to date in Maharashtra.

I reported in full regalia to the DG's office. I was apprehensive, as I had completed nearly five years in Mumbai and had been asking to be transferred to an independent district as District

Police Chief. In some states this position is called Superintendent of Police, and Senior Superintendent in others. My son was now six years old, and I felt confident about heading a district police force and looking after him simultaneously. It was customary for the director general to recommend officers to the government for postings in the state. Sadly, politicians have usurped it now and prevail upon 'establishment boards' to nominate their favourites, showing hardly any respect for merit.

Outside the DG's chamber, I sat wondering about his decision regarding my posting. Suddenly a smart constable came out and ushered me in. As I took a seat in the elegant wood-panelled office, the DG looked up. 'Young lady, have you approached the office of the chief minister for continuing in Bombay as DCP?' he thundered. I was startled for a second but quickly regaining my composure, I said that it was the opposite and politely reminded him that I had in fact approached him in the past seeking a district. 'Yes, and that's why I sent your file to the CM's office twice, recommending an independent district for you. While all our proposals have been agreed upon, your file has come back unsigned both times,' the DG informed me. He wondered aloud if I was playing games: asking his office for a district while conveying unwillingness to the CM's office. It was a thoroughly uncomplimentary remark and not at all true. I told him as respectfully as possible that I very much wanted to be the chief of an independent district.

He told me that when he had mentioned this to Sharad Pawar – the chief minister at the time – the latter had remarked, 'She is doing well in Bombay; why do you want to shift her?' The second time he broached the subject, Mr Pawar had apparently said, 'If anything goes wrong in Bombay, we are here to help her out, but what can we do if she's in a faraway district?'

Until then no woman had been made District Police Chief in Maharashtra, and it was clear that the CM was not comfortable giving me that role either. I tried to convince the DG that I did not need any help and that eleven years of service in the police force had given me enough confidence, knowledge and skills that I could take care of myself. As the Mumbai police commissioner, he had himself observed my work at close quarters. I was sure that he would be able to persuade the CM.

Imagine my surprise when one evening an inspector of the Mumbai Social Security Branch called me up. He informed that I was being transferred to Aurangabad (recently renamed as Chhatrapati Sambhaji Nagar) and that it was a very difficult district, often simmering with communal tensions. His advice was that I should refuse the appointment and offered to get my transfer cancelled. He was a well-meaning guy, but it shows how powerful our inspectors are. They have solid networks and come to know of transfer orders even before they are issued. They can get senior officers transferred out or have their transfers called off! This is the ground reality as inspectors are closer to politicians and therefore more amenable to their questionable orders than most officers of the Indian Police Service. Though, sadly, IPS officers are also catching up now.

The politician–bureaucrat–criminal nexus is well known and is no doubt a detriment to our nation and its citizens. The 1993 Vohra (Committee) Report had highlighted it. Vigilant citizens and an alert independent media have to work in a sustained manner against this problem. I believe that with liberalization business lobbies also joining the cartel, the situation has worsened. Many adverse decisions are taken in the interest of these lobbies rather than for the benefit of the common man.

After turning down the inspector's generous offer to get my transfer to Aurangabad cancelled, I readily accepted the government orders once they arrived. I had become fond of Bombay and learned a lot as the deputy commissioner of two zones and as DCP Crime (Preventive). But I had begun to stagnate.

I soon arrived in Aurangabad, with all my luggage and my six-year-old son in tow.

Most of Aurangabad district is located in the Godavari river basin. The Purna, Shivna and Kham are some of the other prominent rivers that run through the area. Two UNESCO World Heritage monuments, the Ajanta and Ellora caves, adorn the district, as do the historically significant Daulatabad Fort and Bibi ka Maqbara. Considered the tourist district of India, it attracts visitors from all over the world. Paithan, a town near Aurangabad, is famous for its colourful Paithani silk sarees. At the same time, the region has been a hotbed of intense sociopolitical activities.[1]

When I joined the district as the police chief, the Ganpati festival was round the corner and I had to straightaway begin the necessary preparations. An eleven-day-long festival, it is celebrated both privately and publicly with great enthusiasm in Maharashtra. Lord Ganesh's idol is worshipped with offerings of flowers and *durva* (strands of young grass) during morning and evening prayers. Pandals with huge idols are set up on the roads and people come out in large numbers to perform *aarti* and admire the beautiful structures.

I was aware of the district's communal history of Hindu–Muslim conflicts and was further briefed about it in detail by local officers on my arrival. It was a robust and confident team and many of the officers had handled serious riots in Aurangabad earlier. After an extensive tour of the district and familiarizing myself with the police stations and their respective officers, I decided to take a pause. And that's when it happened.

One Sunday morning I took my son to Daulatabad Fort. Situated about fifteen kilometres from Aurangabad city, it is a twelfth-century fortification that sits on a small hillock, surrounded by verdant greenery. Also known as Devagiri Fort, it offers a mesmerizing view of the city. It takes roughly 750 steps to reach the top of one of the most powerful fortresses from the medieval period. Famed for its ingenious engineering, it attracts both domestic and international tourists.

We, the mother–son duo, started climbing up to the fort, with my wireless operator a few metres behind us. He was not in uniform, and we had left the official car at the base of the hillock. After covering some distance, I noticed two boys harassing a foreign tourist. She was alone and looked frightened. Forgetting that I was not on duty nor in my police uniform, I challenged the boys in my Yadav Ustad-inspired voice. Taken aback, they looked at me and then at the girl, indecisive for a moment. My wireless operator, seeing the commotion, came rushing. He chased the boys but could not catch them. The episode had unnerved my young son, so I distracted him by narrating the stories of Shivaji's valour in conquering several Mughal forts. We resumed our trek before long, putting the unpleasant episode behind us and proceeding to have a wonderful time together.

The next morning, the incident made headlines in some of the local newspapers. Being a woman IPS officer, my posting had elicited considerable interest in Aurangabad, but this episode announced my arrival to those who were still unaware. Invitations to local programmes, festivals, meetings, and the number of citizens wishing to meet me increased tenfold! I was even invited to negotiate with a delinquent youth!

I had been visiting different police stations, interacting with policemen and involving citizens in policing work – my favourite endeavour – when one night I received a call from the police control room and learnt that a young boy, after shooting someone with his illegal weapon, had climbed to the roof of a multistorey building. He was threatening to commit suicide. The wounded person had been rushed to a nearby hospital and was reported to be in a serious condition. It was late by then. The shooter announced that he would come down only if the lady SP came to the spot and assured him that he would not be shot dead by the local police. The inspector called me up and very hesitantly asked if I would come as a huge crowd had gathered and the situation was getting tense. Donning my ever-ready uniform, I rushed out of my home.

On reaching the spot, I found that the crowd was behaving as if they were watching a scene in a film instead of acknowledging the gravity of the situation. Police officers were trying to disperse them, which they did successfully only after some impetuous altercations. It was quite dark and there were very few streetlights, allowing us only a faint idea about the locality. The air felt heavy with tension. I grabbed my megaphone from the car to talk to the boy. I had just introduced myself when, in a resounding voice, he declared that he would jump from the roof and kill himself. He had become hysterical. A few young police officers considered jumping across from the neighbouring building but the distance was too much.

I continued talking to the boy who had gone from sullen to toxic and aggressive. Occasionally he would lift his arms and walk to the edge of the roof and our hearts would stop beating. I had never counselled and negotiated with someone simultaneously and was trying my best. After about half an hour of intense dialogue, I was able to persuade the agitated boy to change his mind.

In such emergencies, every minute feels like an hour. All of us heaved sighs of relief when the youngster finally climbed down and surrendered. Police officers have to handle innumerable tricky situations such as this one through common sense and presence of mind. Perhaps it will help to introduce counselling as a subject into the basic police training programme.

A question I frequently faced in Aurangabad was why my police car did not have a pilot police jeep ahead of it and an escort vehicle following behind. The locals would tell me that my predecessors would travel with an entourage of police vehicles. My answer, that Aurangabad had returned to peace and normalcy and thus I did not require so many vehicles around me, did not satisfy many. I often wonder why we are enchanted by people who surround themselves with symbols of power.

That year, the eleven-day-long Ganesh festival concluded smoothly in Aurangabad. We had held peace committee meetings in all sensitive areas and citizens had participated with enthusiasm. The district magistrate, Pramod Mane, was a seasoned officer who guided me frequently. He had been working in Aurangabad prior to my appointment and was well acquainted with the district. In consultation with him, we detained the rabid communal elements under various preventive sections of the CrPC, sending a message that the administration did not want a repeat of earlier violent Hindu–Muslim riots. It paid off.

The final day Ganpati *visarjan* procession continued until 4:30 a.m. the next day. All district police officers were on their feet. We celebrated the peaceful passage of the pageant by playing badminton in the police recreation hall at five in the morning after the visarjan of the last idol. I played a few fast strokes before calling it a day. Both the political and police leadership must have felt relieved that Aurangabad 'did not burn'. In Maharashtra, if you can ensure a peaceful Ganpati festival in a communal district, you have truly passed the test. I think I had too!

15

A DIRECT BRUSH WITH CORRUPTION

'Power does not corrupt. It is fools who get into a position of power that corrupt power.'

– GEORGE BERNARD SHAW

Being the divisional headquarters of the Marathwada region of Maharashtra, Aurangabad is overseen by a senior IAS officer in the role of a divisional commissioner, while a deputy inspector general of police (DIG) looks after the police range. The post was later upgraded to inspector general of police (IG). About eight months after my taking over as the police chief, the district was bifurcated: Aurangabad city was converted into a commissionerate and the rest of the district became Aurangabad (Rural) – this separation prevails even today.

One day the DIG who supervised the range police administration sent a notice that he would be visiting my office. He was a senior IPS officer who had come to some disrepute in the past. I had found him erratic at times but generally cordial. Once he had an argument with his wife. In a fit of anger, he overdosed on some medicine and fainted. His wife rang me up, frantically requesting for medical help but extremely apprehensive about the news leaking out. We had to ensure the urgent arrival of a local doctor and that the episode would not reach the media. It was an unpleasant domestic issue and we treated it as that.

As the DIG's visit entails a review of the district police's operations, we got busy updating our crime records and listing out our recent initiatives. It took a fortnight of intensive work. All local officers, in their impressive uniforms, were present in my office when the DIG arrived. After the reception, he took a seat in my chamber. As per tradition, one by one the local police officers apprised the visiting supervisor of their duties and achievements. From one such officer, the DIG demanded money in a cagey manner, saying, 'Your cousin has not come to see me in a long time ...' The officer responded to him warily until their conversation turned into a heated argument. All the while I was sitting next to the DIG, understanding the conversation only in bits and pieces. I finally got it when the officer said, 'I have sold my wife's *mangalsutra* and yet you are not satisfied.' Now all limits of propriety had been breached, and I confronted the DIG about his intentions. Tersely he replied, 'It happens everywhere, just not in front of you.' I was stunned. Corruption among senior police officers had become common by the late eighties but I didn't know it could be *this* blatant. I went red with anger. The DIG left my office in a huff.

Immediately after his departure, I dictated a confidential letter describing the entire incident and had it dispatched to the Director General of Police through a constable. The next morning, the DG called me up to ask if the DIG had said those things in jest. 'Maybe he was joking?' the DG suggested tentatively. I had no such illusions and told him that it was humiliating to witness a senior officer ask one of my officers for money in my presence. And that I expected strong action to be taken against him.

The following day, a senior police officer arrived in Aurangabad to conduct a preliminary inquiry and submitted a report corroborating my letter. Years later he told me that the sub-inspector from whom the DIG had demanded money had cynically wondered if he, a junior officer, was being made into a sacrificial goat by three IPS officers! The inquiry officer, the DIG and I were all from the elite service.

Until he was transferred out of Aurangabad, the DIG would harass me at the slightest opportunity, issuing memos, seeking explanations every single day on one pretext or the other. Thankfully, the top leadership of the Maharashtra Police was honest in those days and I knew I had nothing to fear. I replied to every single memo. My instruction to my personal assistant was that the memos should be shown to me only during morning hours and replied to on the same day. I did not want to read them in the evenings and carry the unpleasantness into the night. This was how I kept my sanity. I wanted my time at home with my son to be peaceful and enjoyable.

After the DIG's transfer based on the premilitary inquiry report, a detailed inquiry by the Anti-Corruption Bureau followed. I am told it was conducted by one of the DIG's batchmates. I am not sure what happened exactly but the officer's career chart trajectory never went up.

A corrupt senior police officer rang me up one day, soon after it became known that I had written to the DG about the DIG's demand for money. He congratulated me profusely, calling me '*Jhansi ki rani*'. A few honest officers suggested that I should not have written the letter as it might land me in trouble. Most police officers, however, preferred to remain silent.

16

THE JALGAON SEX SCANDAL

'A woman with a voice is by definition a strong woman. But the search to find that voice can be remarkably difficult.'

– MELINDA GATES

Late one afternoon, when I was working as a superintendent with the Criminal Investigation Department in Pune, I got a call from the Director General of Police, Shivajirao Baravkar. I had joined the organization on transfer from Aurangabad and after availing maternity leave. I was too junior for the topmost police officers of the state to contact me directly, so I felt surprised. Hierarchies are strict in our uniformed profession. There were officers at the Pune headquarters who were three levels above me in the CID, and yet he had called me!

Getting straight to the point, the DG ordered me to leave for Jalgaon immediately, though I must admit that his tone was polite and even. He enquired about my younger son – just one year old then – and suggested that I take him along, adding that if I had a maid looking after the child, she should accompany us too. I kept wondering about these detailed personal instructions coming directly from the DG, oblivious that he could foresee me spending the next one year in Jalgaon, while I was blissfully blind to the fact.

Jalgaon district was earlier a part of the Khandesh region of central India. According to some sources, it gets its name from the Khandava forest in the Mahabharata. The rock temples and caves in neighbouring Nashik and Ajanta reveal that during the first three centuries CE, Khandesh was governed by rulers who patronized Buddhism. Much later, in the eighteenth century, it was captured by British troops from the Holkars. After the formation of Maharashtra in 1960, Jalgaon became a district.[1] It is nicknamed 'Banana City' as the region contributes approximately two-thirds of Maharashtra's banana production.[2]

The DG was in a rush to send me to Jalgaon as a sensational case of human trafficking, rape and sexual exploitation had been exposed there in July 1994. Young girls, many of them minors, had allegedly been tricked, drugged, tortured and raped by local politicians and criminals. It was speculated that more than a hundred girls had been exploited in this way over five years.

This series of rapes that came to be known as the 'Jalgaon sex scandal' shook the state of Maharashtra, soon making headlines in national newspapers and catching the attention of the international media too.

By the time I reached Jalgaon, the atmosphere in the city was already grim. There were agitations and *dharnas* led in particular by large numbers of women. The Maharashtra government sent two senior lady officers of the IAS who, after their initial inquiry, concluded that the media reports were indeed true. An article in *India Today* stated, '... after the appointment of a three-member committee – Nashik Divisional Commissioner Leena Mehendale, Chandra Iyengar, Secretary, Women and Child

Welfare Department, and Meera Borwanker, superintendent of police, CID, Pune – to help probe the scandal, victims have eventually begun to come forward to tell their stories'.[3]

While the two lady bureaucrats left Jalgaon after their inquiry, I was tasked to supervise the investigation. But supervise what? There were no FIRs, no formal complainants, and yet the town was on fire.

The additional director general of the state CID in Pune, Arvind Inamdar, had also rushed to Jalgaon. He held a number of meetings with local citizens and police officers. While the media cried itself hoarse and rumours continued to fly about, getting the victims to come out with formal complaints was proving impossible. In the meanwhile, the main suspects had managed to run away.

Subhadra Bhombe was the only woman assistant sub-inspector in the district at the time and knew the town thoroughly. It was with her help that I was trying to reach out to the victims. Since we could not find any complainant in the first few days, Subhadra would go around the city with women constables. They approached schools, colleges, residential colonies, contacting girls who were suspected to have been exploited, advising them to register police complaints. Later, the DG's office in Mumbai started deputing more women police officers from neighbouring districts to Jalgaon. They would come by turns to assist our team in identifying victims and afterwards with the investigation as well.

Mr Inamdar, who was supervising the case, advised me to leave the city and stay in a nondescript old bungalow belonging to the Maharashtra State Electricity Board. He felt that the victims were not coming forward as I was staying in the guest house within the police headquarters. It made sense as most victims in such cases are very apprehensive about their identity leaking out.

Thus, I was on the move again, with my younger son and our bag and baggage, to a decrepit old house on the outskirts of the city. It may have worn a deserted look, but the bungalow was open and airy, with lots of trees and green fields around. It was easily approachable by road. The plaster on the walls was peeling off and there were patches of moss in the very basic toilet. The floor was a cold pale green. The rickety wooden windows and doors completed the dilapidated look. But it was livable and I hoped that this move would encourage the victims to come out and meet me.

My wish came true. Slowly the girls started approaching us. Most of them would cry while recounting their exploitation but they refused to register cases. They would play with my son for hours, eat with us, sometimes laughing, often crying, and generally in a disturbed frame of mind. A few of them were eventually ready to lodge formal complaints, but their families would not agree. The girls' futures – especially their marriage prospects – weighed heavily on the minds of the parents who would refuse to listen to us.

One day I received a letter from a girl from Jalana, a nearby district town. She wrote that the police were bound to come across her nude photos and videos as she was a victim of the gang's sexual exploitation. But she was now married, so she did not want the police to visit her. She threatened to commit suicide if we made an approach. I realized that we were treading on a very delicate path.

By this time, we had recorded FIRs against the three main accused: Pandit Omkar Sapkale, a sitting municipal councillor of Jalgaon; Raju Tadvai, another sitting municipal councillor;

and Sanjay Pawar, the son of a former Maharashtra MLA. As soon as the scandal had become public, they had gone on a spree, destroying videos they had recorded and burning nude photographs of the girls they had persecuted. However, the local police had recovered stark-naked photographs of two girls. We identified and located these girls and approached them discreetly. They explained to me how they had been trapped and blackmailed, but refused to register complaints.

In the meanwhile, special squads had been formed to arrest the accused. CID officers and the district police scoured all of Jalgaon district and literally dug them up from their hideouts in nearby villages and towns. But Pandit Sapkale was able to elude the police. Since he was one of the kingpins, the media and the public was not going to spare us for our failure to arrest him. Fortunately, we received a specific tip that he was in Gujarat, and a team of police officers was rushed there. They arrested Sapkale at a railway station just as he was about to board a train at Bardoli.

The gang's modus operandi included securing admission into local colleges to get access to the female students. Rich and politically powerful as they were, by promising marriage to young, gullible girls, the men would develop sexual relationships with them, photograph them in the nude or stealthily record videos of them having intercourse. This material would thereafter be used for blackmail. It was also suspected that these videos were being sold in neighbouring districts. The gang was using room 206 at Jalgaon's Tirupati hotel on a long-term lease. A concealed video camera in the room quietly recorded the activities.

Once compromised, the gang would then force the victims to have sex with their friends. Too scared to confide in their parents, this is how the girls would get sucked into a vicious cycle of exploitation. After a while, three such college-going girls finally lodged complaints with us. They described meeting the gang members at their colleges, how the men would impress them by attending college functions as chief guests and flaunting their political and financial power. Many young girls got taken in by their 'charm' and entered into physical relations that were now proving so very costly and damaging.

The gang also exploited the powerful positions they occupied within the city's administration. One girl's complaint stated that about six months earlier, her family had received an exorbitant electricity bill, even though they lived in a hutment. Her mother sent her to their municipal councillor to get it corrected. Finding the girl alone, he invited her inside his flat and raped her.

Another complainant mentioned that she needed money for her mother's surgery. On the pretext of helping her, the accused municipal councillor raped her. Finding her vulnerable as a divorced woman, he continued to exploit her for months.

While various women police officers such as Bharati Kurade, Sandhya Pawar, Savita Turekar, Smita Pathak, Pratibha Joshi, Varsha Ghevare and their staff identified and spoke to girls who were victims of the sex racket, inspectors Narayan L. Shinde and A. B. Rokade, head constable Pravin N. More and other officers of the state CID recorded their statements and dealt with the paperwork. Some officers were of the strong opinion that the girls would not support court prosecution and that our efforts would go to waste. Nevertheless, we continued with our efforts and registered twenty cases under various sections of Indian Penal Code, twelve of which involved rape. Other cases were about threatening witnesses, destroying evidence, etc.

The investigation was made difficult by the delays in the registration of the rape cases, which is generally fatal to prosecution. The reasons for such delays have to be very convincing. Most of the victims were educated, so their decision to hide the incidents from their parents or not reporting them to the police immediately thereafter, weakened our cases, and we were conscious of it. The most recent rape had taken place six months prior to registration. Other cases were much older. Medical reports in most cases carried remarks like 'habituated to sex', which further dented our investigation. We were also finding it tough to trace witnesses, as they were terrified of the gang's political influence. Besides, the accused had taken adequate precautions while committing their crimes. Rape cases are typically single-witness cases, the victim being the only person to depose about the entire incident. Other witnesses can only provide circumstantial evidence, for example, having seen the accused with the victim before or after the crime. Such testimonies do not carry much weight in the courts.

During our long stay in Jalgaon, my son often suffered from bouts of 'infantile asthma'. Fortunately, Meenakshi Agarwal, the wife of an IAS officer posted in the district, would get me the homeopathic medicines he frequently needed. When bouts of loneliness would hit me hard, she would spend hours keeping me company. The distance between Pune and Jalgaon being more than 450 kilometres, it was not possible for me to visit my family frequently. Staying in Jalgaon with the child was the only option, while my elder son and husband carried on with their lives in Pune.

Since the late registration of the rape cases had hurt the prosecution, we were afraid that the accused would be granted bail and proceed to threaten the girls and their families. It was therefore proposed that all three should be detained under the National Security Act, as per section 3(2): 'acting in any manner prejudicial to the maintenance of Public order.' This stringent law requires that the case of a detenu should be put before an advisory board within three weeks for review.[4] The board's members are of the stature of high court judges.

By the time the board summoned us for the review, I had suffered a fracture in my left foot and my leg was in a plaster. I still went to Mumbai, injury notwithstanding. The board members patiently heard our justifications for the detention of the rapists under the draconian NSA and scrutinized the documents we had submitted. Looking at me, the chairman asked, 'But why have you brought only one proposal?' Feeling a strong surge of relief, I replied, 'Other proposals are under preparation, sir.' All three detention proposals against the main accused were upheld by the board, making Jalgaon a safe place for some time at least.

It was a tough investigation and the additional director general, Mr Inamdar, called one of Mumbai's leading lawyers to look through our investigation papers. This gentleman had earlier worked as a government prosecutor and was the boss's personal friend. He studied the documents in detail, feeling as unhappy about the delay in the reporting of the rapes as we were, but accepted the prosecution brief. A difficult man, he was impatient with the investigating officers who could not match up to his brilliance.

The Maharashtra government appointed a special court where the cases would be tried before a lady judge – Mridula R. Bhatkar would serve as both joint district and additional sessions judge. It was decided that the trial should take place in Pune as the atmosphere in Jalgaon was still too 'hot'. Families of the accused had started harassing the victims and their families, threatening them of dire consequences if they deposed against the gang in court. A few victims temporarily relocated to Pune or nearby towns outside Jalgaon. Some citizens had started blaming them for registering police complaints, bemoaning that henceforth no one would want to marry girls from Jalgaon. Many claimed that some of the local girls' engagements had been cancelled and the boys' families had returned the engagement rings. The town was besieged by all kinds of rumours and the sensationalist media had further vitiated the atmosphere.

We could gauge the public interest in the cases from the fact that many families in Pune volunteered to host the victims during and even before trial. Never in my career have I seen this kind of police–citizen collaboration. Besides accommodating the girls, the hosts – women from middle- and upper-middle-class families – would counsel them through their distress. Pune is known for its progressive women's movements and I got my own taste of it during the trial of the Jalgaon cases.

However, as soon as the first case came up for trial in the special court, the investigating officers started showing their displeasure towards the special prosecutor. They didn't so much mind his harsh behaviour but complained that he was very difficult even with the young judge, embarrassing her frequently. In one of my review meetings, they unanimously demanded that the special prosecutor be replaced. This was not going to be easy, as the government had announced his appointment and it had been widely publicized. He was highly competent with a well-established reputation in the state.

I conveyed this to Mr Inamdar, who was extremely unhappy about my endorsement of the investigating officers' suggestion. Since the gentleman would travel from Mumbai for every hearing, a carefully considered excuse about his inability to frequently travel to Pune was put forward. A new Pune-based special prosecutor, Uday Singh A. Jadhavrao was appointed to conduct the group cases. I had met him during the trial of

Kolhapur's Gandhi rape case, wherein he had been able to secure a conviction. He was equally seasoned and hard-working but more patient. The officers were comfortable with him, even though he would pull them up when dissatisfied with the quality of investigation. And thus, the trials continued.

A junior prosecutor named Seema Phadnis would often visit my office to read case papers and talk to those involved with the investigations. This would go on beyond office hours, but my office staff, including Pravin More, Ananat N. Narute and head constable Vaman M. Salvi, would patiently wait for her to finish. We would study the investigation papers and review the case trials until late every evening. And this continued for more than a year.

Unfortunately the accused in our first two cases were acquitted by the court. Both the girls refused to support the prosecution, going back on their complaints. Instead, they alleged that they had been forced to lodge FIRs by the police. Our sources from Jalgaon informed us that the accused had promised to pay for the marriage expenses for both victims, and that a compromise of sorts had been reached between the girls' families and the offenders. This is common in India and one of the main reasons for acquittal in rape cases.

The news of the acquittal was received very badly by senior officers in the police and the government, despite their knowing that the cases were inherently weak. One of the complainants had alleged in court that I had visited her house in a 'black coat' and forced her to lodge a police case. She was referring to my official dark blue blazer that I sometimes wore during the 1994 winter while leading investigation in Jalgaon.

The third case that came up for trial involved our youngest victim and the special prosecutor decided to examine her mother first. His logic was that if the mother stuck to her statement before the court, so would the girl. It was an unusual strategy, as generally the complainant is examined first. In view of what had transpired in the two earlier trials, he wanted to first test the future of this case and prepare us for another possible acquittal. The mother did not support the prosecution and once again we felt terribly let down.

But the young girl got extremely angry, swore at her mother and, to our total surprise, stood by the evidence in the court, which passed its first conviction order. She was the one whom the municipal councillor had raped when she had gone to him with the faulty electricity bill. Later, when the Maharashtra government offered jobs to the victims, two girls accepted them, but she, our youngest complainant, turned it down. She requested us not to contact her after the trial or ever again in the future. And we respected her wish.

In all, six rape cases emerging from the Jalgaon sex scandal were convicted. Getting to this point involved intense hard work on the part of the investigating officers: A. B. Rokade, P. K. Hire, M. B. Shahane, R. B. Korde and my staff officer Inspector N. L. Shinde, who regularly burnt the midnight oil in preparation. I had two attendants in my office, Shakuntala P. Deshmukh and Nandakumar V. Bhosle, both of whom became proficient in 'beating' frothy hot cups of coffee because our team would need them aplenty as the clock ticked on. My office staff were so deeply involved in the investigation that whenever advocates Jadhavrao or Phadnis needed any document; they could dig them out in a jiffy. In fact, Nandakumar Bhosle would often be the first to trace case files and present them triumphantly to the prosecutors. His keen wish was to be a police officer but he had to join the force as a peon as he did not meet the height criteria.

Our unit was always the last on the state CID campus to close in those days. My stenographer, Dhananjay Vaidya, who took countless dictations for the group cases, not only improved his typing speed but also became an expert investigator himself! Even today a cup of well-beaten frothy coffee reminds me of the hard work our team put in while investigating the Jalgaon and Parbhani rape cases.

During the Jalgaon trials, two more sex rackets were exposed, one of them in Parbhani and the other in Malegaon. While we took over the investigation of the Parbhani scandal, I visited Malegaon with my team to guide the investigation that was being conducted by the local police. Both cases saw convictions eventually, as complaints were registered immediately after the rapes. It is unfortunate that the accused in the Jalgaon cases were later acquitted by the Bombay High Court, and the chief reason, as anticipated, was that the victims had not registered their FIRs promptly. The media reported that thousands of women took part in a silent morcha to the Jalgaon collectorate, in protest against the acquittals, and afterwards handed over a memorandum to the district collector, asking that the accused not be allowed to enter Jalgaon. They also burned the offenders' effigies.

We learnt many lessons during the investigations into these sex scandals, the most prominent of which is the need for better communication between parents and children. Had the girls in Jalgaon talked to their mothers, their further exploitation by the accused could have been prevented. The girls had been photographed naked and forced to have sex with the accused and their friends, who used them as commodities. Afraid that there would be repercussions for not complying, the victims felt that they had no choice. One of the lady officers who had once gone to fetch a victim from her house during the investigation came back very angry. She informed us that the young girl was so rude to her mother that the officer felt like 'slapping her'. We had observed that these school- and college-going girls were rude to their parents, especially to their mothers, who were usually uneducated housewives.

In many cases, the parents came to know of their daughters' exploitation only when we informed them. Nearly all the victims said that had they confided in their parents, their further education would have been in jeopardy. It was also surprising that their teachers and professors were completely unaware of what was going on in their institutions.

We observed a communication gap between the parents and daughters in the Parbhani gangrapes too. One of the victims, who was living with her aunt, was being mistreated by her. Another one was also unhappy at home. Both the girls were minors and had been studying in the same school in Partur, a small town in Jalna district. They used to confide in each other and one day decided to run away. Theirs was a very painful case for me to understand and supervise as the girls were exploited and raped by officers of the Indian Railways, policemen and local politicians over a period of just a few days. *India Today* had this to say about it:

> ... Maharashtra Government has more to reckon with. Jalgaon is not the sole claimant to notoriety. The gang-rape of two minors in early July, at Parbhani in the neighbouring Marathwada region, has forced the state government to agree to a CID probe.
>
> What is even more embarrassing is that the alleged culprits are again linked with the ruling Congress(I). Indeed, there seems to be no end to the scandals plaguing the party. The only

> way the party can regain the confidence of the people is by holding fair trials.[5]

Initially three different cases of sexual exploitation were registered by the district and railway police.[6] Since the Maharashtra government ordered the CID to take over this scandal as well, another round of visits to the crime scenes, statement-recording and arrests got underway. Inspector Sahebrao Vyavahare took over the investigation from the district police. Both the girls had already been medically examined and their clothes sent to a forensic laboratory. The sites of the gangrapes too had been identified by the investigating officers. The minor victims were able to identify the accused during the test identification parade (TIP) held by the magistrate. There were some contradictions as the girls were young and the accused had taken them to different places to perform their criminal acts. But we could sort out the issue by recording supplementary victim statements.

After completing the investigation, we proposed a special prosecutor for the trial of this case too. The Maharashtra government agreed to and the Pune-based advocate Prakash S. Suryawanshi was given the assignment. Commuting from Pune, he diligently led the prosecution until the accused were convicted. As no special court had been appointed for this scandal, the trial dragged on for years, owing to the large number of accused – powerful politicians, police and railway officials – involved. A sessions court convicted most of the accused and the Bombay High Court upheld the judgment.

One fine evening, twenty years later, I got a phone call from a lawyer requesting me to change my stance in this case and depose in favour of the accused during the hearing of a petition they had filed in the Supreme Court. I was shocked at this 'blatantly illegal demand'. The next day, one of the victims rang me up to say that she too had been asked to deny her statement before a magistrate. Mercifully the Supreme Court upheld the convictions[7] and dismissed the review petition.[8]

I also learnt that we need many more women officers in the police. Only one lady officer in all of Jalgaon in 1994 was a mockery of our intention to provide a safe and secure environment to women. Female victims are far more comfortable with women officers, especially in sensitive cases of sexual assault and rape. By way of the Criminal Law Amendment Act, 2013, popularly known as the Nirbhaya Act, it is now mandatory for FIRs in sexual assault cases that statement of victim is to be recorded by 'women police officers/woman officer'. They need focused training and continuous updating of their legal knowledge in order to carry out high-quality investigations. India follows an Anglo-Saxon legal system that is based on the jurist William Blackstone's ratio: 'It is better that ten guilty persons escape, than that one innocent suffers.' As a consequence, defence lawyers have to find only a small loophole in the prosecution in order to get an acquittal.

Over the course of the Jalgaon and Parbhani investigations, it also became clear to me that the police and prosecutors must work as a team or convictions in rape cases will continue to be low. They are currently around 30 per cent.

Whatever convictions we got in the Jalgaon cases at the sessions court level can be attributed to the tremendous team spirit displayed by the police officers of the district, the CID officers in Pune and various teams of women officers sent from adjoining districts.

Twenty-four years later, after my retirement, I visited Jalgaon on a public speaking tour in 2018. It was to promote my first book *Leaves of Life*, written with a view of inspiring the youth. I was told that the hall of the local library where I addressed the young men and women of Jalgaon had never been used for a public event earlier. The organizers apologized for its poor acoustics, though the audience in that jampacked hall seemed happy. After the event was over, one of the organizers informed me sheepishly that the better venue originally booked for my address belonged to one of the accused in the Jalgaon sex scandal case. When he came to know of the purpose for the booking, he cancelled it, forcing the organizers to host it at the library hall.

Many private cases were filed against me and other police officers by the all-powerful criminal gang of Jalgaon. Attempts like these meant to demoralize police officers are not uncommon. One such case is still pending against us, twenty-eight years later!

17

HIGHWAY DACOITS

'Have a bias toward action – let's see something happen now. You can break that big plan into small steps and take the first step right away.'

– INDIRA GANDHI

'You have been Superintendent of Police in Aurangabad; why do you want an independent district again?' boomed a senior officer from the head office in Mumbai.

I had completed more than three years at CID, Pune. My younger son was now over three years old and I was once again keen to lead a district. When I approached the DG's office, I was told that one independent district was enough. Then came this loud query. Feeling stung, I asked politely, 'Why was this question not put to male officers who were leading two to three districts as police chiefs?' The senior officer preferred not to reply; instead my movement orders followed.

I moved from Pune to Satara, this time with both my sons. My predecessor there was Ashok Kamate, a brilliant officer whom we lost during the 26/11 terrorist attack in Mumbai. His dynamic, youthful energy could be felt all over. An outstanding officer, he had all but cleaned the district of illegal activities. Citizens and police officers held him in very high regard. Thus, my initiation was smooth and I quickly started familiarizing myself with the twenty police stations in the district.

Picturesque Satara is famous for its hill stations Mahabaleshwar and Panchgani and for sending a large number of its youth to the Indian Army. It used to be the capital of the Maratha kingdom. It is also believed that Wai in Satara district is the '*Viratnagari*', where the Pandavas lived during the thirteenth year of their exile.[1] Karad, another important town in Maharashtra, lies at the confluence of the Koyna and Krishna rivers in Satara district. It is known as the sugar bowl of the state due to its many sugar factories. The resting place (*samadhi*) of the first chief minister of Maharashtra, Yashwantrao Chavan, in Karad, is a highly respected site. For all these reasons, Satara is considered historically, politically and socially significant.

On taking over as the police chief, one of the first phone calls I received was from a lady belonging to the erstwhile royal family of the region. She had felt amused when one of the local women had come to her saying that if the 'queen' would not accede to her demand, she would 'approach the new woman superintendent of police'. It is true that women holding positions of power, especially the ones in uniform, lend a sense of empowerment to those who have suffered harassment and atrocities at the hands of men.

I was welcomed in Satara with open arms and warm hearts. I could see that the women there had high expectations from me. The media coverage of the Jalgaon sex scandal had certainly played a part. But I have always wanted to live life my way and never allowed myself to be caught in any expectations trap or be made into a role model. Such a trap rewards expected behaviour and actions, while empowering others to judge you. My independence has always been immensely important to me.

Having worked in Kolhapur district earlier, I had some idea about the culture of western Maharashtra, and touring Satara district helped me further understand it. I found Koyna Dam and its surrounding areas Mahabaleshwar, Panchgani and Wai to be lush and luxuriant. By stark contrast, talukas like Maann and Khatav were totally dry and poor. During my visits to Maann, I would feel as if I had gone back in time by a century. While in Mahabaleshwar, the natural beauty was depleting due to a regular flow of a large number of tourists from Pune and Mumbai. Tourism had led to undesirable development – more houses, hotels and motels, as well as exploitation of land causing environmental degradation. The Venna Lake chowpatty was a tourist hotspot, where visitors would come for picnics, blaring music, showing scant respect for the natural environment. British colonialists had developed the town as the summer capital of the Bombay Presidency. Now, the Raj Bhavan and a few other time-worn buildings still retain their old-world charm.

As the superintendent of a district in Maharashtra, it is mandatory to make night halts at each police station once a year and formally inspect them. I enjoyed interacting with the simple rural folk and savouring the local cuisine during these inspections. However, while at Koyna, I would often get paranoid about the security of the dam which was in the district's interior. Situated deep inside the jungles of the Western Ghats, the dam was built between 1956 and 1964 on the Koyna river to generate hydroelectricity. My surprise visits would reveal that the police there, being lonely and isolated, would become lax and frequently leave their duty points. I also found them ignorant about the threat of terrorists to such dams, or maybe it was my overimaginative mind that would conjure all kinds of terrorism-related scenarios. Fortunately for me, we had three young IPS officers who were a formidable team when it came to tackling crime and touring the district extensively. Archana Tyagi was full of positive energy, Vineet Agarwal an out-of-the-box thinker, and Nikhil Gupta a keen learner who would occasionally threaten to leave the service!

But it was not the terrorists who struck Satara during my tenure but dacoits – on the Mumbai–Bengaluru highway that passes through the district. And they did it repeatedly, causing considerable panic in the surrounding areas. Their tactic was to loot the luxury buses plying on the highway at night. The gangs would board the buses as passengers, hiding sundry weapons inside their clothes or in handbags. Buses en route to Bengaluru would reach Satara around midnight. That is when the dacoits would launch their attack on the passengers, particularly women wearing jewellery. After forcing them to part with their cash and belongings, the dacoits would get down in the '*ghat*' area of Satara. By the time the bus drivers would report the cases to the nearest police stations, the criminals would have vanished. It was the mid-nineties and mobile phones were yet to become common in India. The dacoits would thus keep getting away with their crimes, and their repeated looting created an atmosphere of terror in the area.

We responded to the problem by increasing police patrol on the highway. My staff officers took the lead. While Deepak S. Sawant was calm and measured, Sambhaji A. Patil was dynamic and energetic in the way he strategized. Both of them led from the front when dealing with serious crime. But we still could not stop the nighttime bus dacoities. That is when we decided to enrol the local community on a big scale. Police stations adjoining the highway held meetings with villagers and sought the help of young boys for night patrolling through a traditional Maharashtrian forum called '*Gram Suraksha Dal*' (Village Security Group). The response of the village youths was very encouraging – many of them agreed to patrol the portion of the highway bordering their villages. At the same time, the local crime branch made arrangements with the highway *dhabas*. It was decided that our police staff would wait with the village boys at the dhabas for information about dacoits, and be ready to apprehend them. 'Police Help Centre' boards were put up prominently outside these dhabas to increase the police's visibility. I would frequently patrol on the highway at night, waiting for lady luck to smile.

After about three months, our efforts fructified. One night, some vigilant village boys successfully chased and caught a group of dacoits after they deboarded from a bus with their loot. It was an unbelievably long chase, with criminals running through fields and rivulets and jumping across fences. I was told one of them even climbed a tree to hide himself. But the boys, thin, lean and highly motivated, just would not give up. To them the police's assignment was an interesting challenge, and they finally succeeded in catching the dacoits. To our utter shock and surprise, it turned out that the criminals had come all the way from the Malda district of West Bengal.

The modus operandi of this dreaded gang of looters was to board the Geetanjali Express – a superfast Calcutta-origin train – and get down at Dadar in Mumbai the next day. Thereafter, they would board luxury night buses headed to Belgaum or Bengaluru from the Dadar terminus. On the way they would loot passengers and return to Mumbai by getting rides on trucks plying on the highway. While we registered police complaints about these incidents, they would be well on their way to Mumbai and then to Kolkata by the same Geetanjali Express. It was perhaps a combination of our good fortune and the agility of the village boys that allowed us to catch the dacoits red-handed with looted property, and arrest and charge-sheet them in court.

After they were apprehended, I rang up the superintendent of police in Malda district to inform him of what had transpired. He congratulated our team and added that the dacoits had wreaked havoc in his district too and that he was deploying more than a hundred men to carry out night patrols in Malda.

These kinds of interstate dacoit gangs are not very common as most criminals operating in adjoining states like to come back to their states, where they remain largely passive to avoid the local police's suspicion. Many a time, they act as informants for their own state or district police while operating in neighbouring states and districts. It was quite rare for criminals to come all the way from Bengal to commit dacoities on an interstate highway running through Maharashtra.

Such habitual offenders who carry out organized crimes are the most dangerous. They have no remorse when it comes to killing someone or looting their property. These criminals getting bail poses a grave threat to society, as they resume their operations immediately after their release. The police find it very difficult to locate them for court trials as they frequently change their address. They are protected by their own lawyers, who are paid substantial sums for their services. The moment the police pick up such criminals, their lawyers approach the courts to get them out on bail. Sureties are also identified beforehand. This is standard procedure for crime syndicates.

My observation is that police officers put up a tough fight against these criminals, considering it to be one of their core responsibilities. The activities of such gangs pose a challenge to their detective minds and many find it worth their while to hound and neutralize them. It gives them a tremendous sense of achievement and satisfaction. Officers who enjoy this type of work generally opt for specialized units like the Crime Branch. However, it can be extremely dangerous if a police officer starts colluding with these gangs. Furthermore, when politicians bless criminal–police collaboration, it may as well be the end of the rule of law. Such a phenomenon is not uncommon. Active, interested citizens and a vigilant media are antidotes against such unholy alliances.

The criminal–police nexus is usually not found in rural districts. But it is a serious issue in metropolitan cities, where anonymity gives a false sense of security to officers and the stakes are really high. I did observe close police–politician tie-ups in Satara, with the latter trying to influence their vote banks through uniformed professionals. Similarly, police officers would directly approach politicians for getting a posting of their choice.

The times were certainly changing.

18

NEXUS

'If a country is to be corruption free and become a nation of beautiful minds, I strongly feel there are three key societal members who can make a difference. They are the father, the mother and the teacher.'

– DR A. P. J. ABDUL KALAM

Mid-way through my tenure as the district police chief, a direct officer of the IPS was posted in Satara city as the assistant superintendent of police. It was his first assignment since he had completed nearly two years of training. He was four months into the job and still learning the ropes when suddenly we received his transfer orders and a state service officer close to the deputy chief minister replaced him. The deputy CM was in charge of the Home department portfolio too. I was aghast as it was both extremely unfair to the young officer and unprofessional. I took it up with the Director General of Police, who got the transfer cancelled. The deputy CM was out of the country at the time. On his return, he promptly had the order reversed. Once again, I raised the issue with the DG's office, but this time they seemed helpless. I thought of going on protest leave and rang up one of my batchmates who advised me against it. In the meanwhile, the IPS officer approached me and requested that he be relieved as he did not want to make an issue of his sudden and untimely transfer. I told him that I would support him if he decided to take a stand. He reiterated that it was not his intention. He had joined the IPS after working in another government department for about five years and was aware of the ways of politicians. How sad that that this kind of injustice and unprofessionalism have become so normalized in our country that officers close to a political leadership, irrespective of their competence, will get 'prize' postings.

I have observed that capable officers are generally deployed whenever there is a crisis. Sometimes they are also used as 'window dressing' to appease citizens or to handle serious public order issues. Otherwise, politicians prefer their own men. They like to ensure that Station House Officers (SHOs) or officers in charge of police stations are people of their liking. In this regard, all political parties are the same because they all want to use field-level police officers to their advantage. Even citizens are aware of this bitter reality but are unfortunately apathetic to it. It is not that such officers are incompetent per se. It's just that they look after the interest of political leaders far more than that of citizens. The rule of law is substituted for the 'politician's law'. It becomes a game of quid pro quo. Neither politicians nor police officers consider it to be wrong. Rather, it is the norm in our country and considered a 'practical' arrangement. It has created a culture where valid disagreement and dissent are considered disobedience. This has been the bane of the nation's civil services.

Much later in life, during a meeting of the Association of Officers of the Indian Police Service (Maharashtra cadre), I spoke against the three-month extension granted to two Director General-level officers. Can you tell how many officers of the elite Indian Police supported me? Only one. And he happened to be my batchmate from 1981. While I was not personally affected by these extensions, even those directly and adversely affected preferred to remain silent. Everyone knows that extensions are 'favours' granted by politicians to officers who toe the line.

This is the undesirable culture in the civil services today. Instead of debates and discussions, showing respect for differing points of view, doing what's best for our citizens and the country, we choose to self-serve. There are honourable exceptions, no doubt. And then there are many competent civil servants who have mastered the uncanny art of getting along with politicians of all hues. I would put most SHOs in this category. Many senior police officers also take this route, though not as deftly as our SHOs. I have concluded that our field-level officers humour senior officers most of the time, take them seriously some time, but depend on politicians all the time.

I had a taste of this police–politician nexus during a riot outside District Cooperative Credit Bank in Satara city. I was at the police headquarters, writing annual appraisal reports about policemen when the control room informed me of a lathi charge. Satara being a quiet town, it came as a surprise to me and I rushed to the spot.

We had been monitoring a power tussle between two political groups that wanted to gain control of the rich local co-operative bank. The chairpersons and boards of these banks enjoy immense latitude when it comes to granting loans from the available funds. They can oblige the needy and also take out handsome amounts as commission for sanctioning the loan – under the table of course. When you have both power and money at your disposal, it can be a deadly and heady combination. Political parties therefore take a keen interest in getting hold of these institutions.

In those days, Satara's DCC Bank had a local leader as its chairman. Wanting to dislodge him, the opposition party invited a former member of parliament from Buldhana district, Anandrao Adsul, to challenge the bank's existing board. He was a labour leader and delivered a fiery speech. His supporters started pelting stones at the bank building, forcing policemen on duty to resort to lathi charge in order to disperse them.

I reached the scene to find stones scattered all over the road and policemen mildly caning curious passersby. Since the violent mob had dispersed, there was no reason to do so. I immediately asked the staff to get into their vans and report back to the headquarters. I had to use some force on my own policemen, as I could see that they were being irresponsible as a result of their heightened emotions. Had this taken place in the age of mobile phone cameras, both agitators and the Satara police would have landed themselves in serious trouble. I have seen that many times police response is not well calibrated. Police leadership tends to defend those who respond to public order issues, ignoring their overreach, as the inclination to run from the scene has become quite rampant. Over the years, the number of '*bhagodas*' in the police force has only increased. As mentioned in earlier chapters, it is a very serious issue facing us today. So while those who withstand violent mobs and do not desert the site of action are appreciated, they may still overreact due to the anxiety generated by a crisis situation.

But the Satara policemen wielding lathis were in a different league. There had never seen a serious riot in the city and, in this particular one, a number of policemen had been injured in the stone-throwing. They had been taken to the civil hospital immediately. Witnessing some policemen suffer from bleeding injuries had angered their colleagues.

The local inspector, in the meanwhile, took the ex-MP to the police headquarters, where I found him sitting in his spotless white kurta–pajama. The officer informed me that eleven policemen had been injured in the stone-pelting and were receiving treatment at the civil hospital. The political leader responsible for inciting the crowd was neither from Satara nor any adjoining district. He had travelled all the way from Buldhana – about 550 kilometres away – and set off a riot with his provocative speech. He deserved no sympathy as far as I was concerned. Touching his spotless kurta, I informed him that he was under arrest. He could not believe it, as he belonged to the ruling party in the state. What he did believe was that he and his party men were above the law. And here was a police officer, a woman at that, placing him under arrest. He may have been shell-shocked, but I was going strictly by the book. We had been taught that a police officer has to touch the person they intend to arrest and I was simply following the rules to a tee.

Sensing that there could be trouble later, I suggested that all injured policemen be photographed and the state Home Department and DG office in Mumbai informed of the arrest as the gentleman had been an MP until a few weeks before the episode. In view of the injured policemen, I advised our Deputy Superintendent of Police (Home) – a law graduate – to attend court the next day along with the prosecutor to ensure that we got the rioters in police custody.

Later that night I got a call from the chief minister asking me politely not to oppose bail for the rioters. I had never received such instructions from a political leader in the past. Surprised, I asked back, 'Sir, how can I face my men if I do not seek custody of those who injured them?' I added that in such cases of violence, taking remand of rioters was essential. Going beyond official protocol, I asked the CM about what he intended to do for the injured policemen. He made some gentle remarks that he would definitely look into the matter and hung up.

The next day the prosecutor and the deputy SP showed the injured policemen's photographs to the magistrate who happened to be a woman. After patiently hearing about the riot outside DCC Bank, the court remanded the rioters to police custody.

Now I received another call. This time it was the director general of police. He was known to be an honest officer who did not take instructions from politicians, all the more so if they were corrupt. He asked me why I had opposed bail when the CM had advised against it. How could I not, I replied, when so many policemen had been injured? Besides, we needed to document the events by interrogating them. Stone-pelting in a peaceful town like Satara was an extremely disturbing event, I added.

The DG sounded very angry. At the time he was in the middle of getting several new policies favouring the police cleared by the chief minister. It irked him that I was concerned about small battles when he was fighting a war. 'You think you are the only honest officer in the department?' he shot at me. Hurt and seething with anger, I firmly pointed out to the DG that his comment was 'below the belt'. I do not remember how exactly the conversation ended but after it did, I was quite sure that my marching orders would soon follow.

They did not. Being an honest, uncorrupt officer, maybe the DG did eventually sympathize with my viewpoint. That the chief minister did not seek my transfer out of Satara was equally surprising.

Earlier the district magistrate, a quiet, competent lady officer, had been shifted before she could complete her tenure of two years. She had been taking strict action against encroachers into Mahabaleshwar forest land. I learnt that the builders lobby being quite influential, it prevailed upon the government to replace her with a pliable magistrate. Tragically, but as expected, no eyebrows were raised as citizens take no interest in governance and thus, as we have seen time and again, end up with officers who are more interested in self-service than serving the public.

In fact, once the Maharashtra government was showcasing Satara district as its site for women empowerment initiatives. The district magistrate, superintendent, assistant SP, judicial magistrate, jail superintendent at the time were all women. The Centre too had posted a lady income tax officer and another woman officer in the postal department. There were seven of us in total.

One day a local MLA from the Karad taluka constituency walked into my office and in a very harassed voice complained that there was nowhere he could have tea in Satara as all officers were women. I promptly offered him a cup. Another MLA, after the Republic Day parade, within full earshot of other officers, asked me about my impending transfer orders. 'Why are you so keen to get me out?' I retorted, to which he sheepishly replied that he had heard I would be promoted soon. It is true that having so many women in positions of power had proved beneficial for the citizens of Satara, but it was a 'nuisance' for local politicians. They were not comfortable with us as they could not ask us for favours. Many of them also missed the booze parties where they would freely mingle with officers and indulge in toxic gossip. The district had become too dry for their taste.

To their credit, the local politicians did not trouble me much. I think they were able to settle many of their issues through the ground-level inspectors. I did not have the time and energy to go into the minute details of police station operations, which I felt was the task of middle-level district police officers. Whenever I came to know that any of them had become corrupt, I would take immediate disciplinary action.

While investigating an unfortunate case of a gelatin stick blast outside Satara city, in which six people lost their lives, I heard that a young deputy SP had accepted a bribe. We were trying our best to arrest the absconding accused, when I learnt that they were gloating about paying off the officer. Enraged, I got this information verified and called the officer to my chamber. Confronted with the hard facts, he admitted to having accepted ₹30,000. I sent an urgent report to the DG through a special messenger. The officer was transferred overnight and an enquiry followed soon thereafter.

I completed my three years in Satara, having enjoyed every minute of my tenure, and sought a deputation to work in the Central Bureau of Investigation. By the time I left Maharashtra in 1999, corruption had become a serious issue at all levels of the police force, and it was fast losing sight of its responsibilities towards citizens, which is the mainstay of honest and transparent policing.

Even the rural police had tasted blood.

19

WHITE COLLAR CRIMES

'I would consider a government machinery corruption-free only if the purpose for which the machinery is set up is fulfilled, in letter and spirit with honesty, sincerity and purposefulness.'[1]

– DR A. P. J. ABDUL KALAM

From the simple and staid life of rural Maharashtra, I got thrown into the fast-paced megapolitan Mumbai, when I opted for a deputation to work in the Central Bureau of Investigation, the premier investigating agency of the country. The CBI is a Government of India organization that can be traced back to the Special Police Establishment Act formalized in 1941 to deal with cases of corruption in the War and Supply Department during World War II. Initially it investigated only central government employees. After the war, with the dissolution of the War Department, it came under the Home Department's purview in 1946 and operated as the Delhi Special Police Establishment. This arrangement continued until 1 April 1963, when the DSPE was renamed the Central Bureau of Investigation by a government resolution. Slowly the ambit of the

Bureau was expanded to include public-sector corporations and banks. A Special Crimes Division was added subsequently to deal with traditional crimes of sensitive nature, such as sensational murders, kidnappings, suspicious deaths and so on. The Supreme Court and high courts can transfer criminal cases to the CBI, if needed. Sometimes there is a public demand for the handing over of certain cases to the agency. Such matters are decided by the state and central governments as the consent of both is essential for transferrals.

In early 1999, I was allotted the Economic Offences Wing at the CBI's Mumbai head office. It investigated cases in western and southern India. Given my seniority, I should have been allotted the Anti-Corruption Branch – if not immediately on joining, then at a later stage. I learnt from a senior officer that the Delhi headquarters did not feel 'comfortable' having a lady officer in one of its crucial anti-corruption units. I also did not pursue this as I thought it would be interesting to investigate economic offences now that the economy had been liberalized.

These offences are popularly known as 'white-collar crimes'. Often they are frauds committed for obtaining unlawful advantage by wrongful means such as forgery, deceit, concealing facts, breaching trust. Forging financial instruments, providing false commercial information, insider trading all fall under this category. A common example of embezzlement is funds allocated for low-income housing being used for the personal gain of builders, contractors and government officers. Whereas money laundering is to 'layer' or deposit large amounts of illegally gained wealth into the legitimate financial system by creating a complex web of monetary transactions. The aim is to make the ill-begotten wealth look legal. Corporate frauds carried out by the Infrastructure Leasing & Financial Services and the infamous stockbroker Harshad Mehta's securities fraud are all examples of economic offences or white-collar crimes. The Central Bureau of Investigation, the Enforcement Directorate and the Serious Fraud Office of India investigate these crimes, especially if they involve international or interstate transactions. The Economic Offences Wings of state governments also investigate such cases, but they are generally of a lesser magnitude with local or inter-district ramifications.

The investigation of financial crime is complex and often prolonged, with a large volume of transactions involving numerous real or false entities and hordes of documents. My unit in Mumbai had a target of registering only nine fresh cases every year and to follow through on the old cases pending trial in courts. The Chennai unit also had similar targets and many cases pending trial. The Bureau's quality of investigation is better because officers are not rushing around performing miscellaneous duties. Here they are able to concentrate on the investigation and do a thorough job.

The CBI officers' monitoring of court trials too is more effectual than that of the state police. While attending a trial, one of our '*pairavee*' officers (sub-inspector) found the presence of a particular gentleman suspicious and intriguing. After he reported this, we started an immediate inquiry. It transpired that the highly sophisticated man was an additional sessions judge in Rajasthan. He was known to the accused and was attending the special court after taking leave from his office so he could guide the offender's defence lawyer. It was brought to the notice of the senior judicial officers and we did not see him again in the Mumbai court. Two young officers from my office were tasked to ensure that witnesses remained present in the special court and that relevant documents were produced.

Due to meticulous investigations and close court monitoring, the Bureau's percentage of conviction is much higher: roughly 65–70 per cent as compared to the state police's 50 per cent. Bureau officers may not have the resources that the city police enjoy, but they have the privilege of time which is essential for the investigation of complicated economic offences.

During my tenure at the CBI's Economic Offences Wing in Mumbai, import–export frauds were very common. Many companies would show fraudulent export of goods to claim government subsidies which had been instituted to encourage exports. The exported goods would not be what was shown on paper; for example, it turned out that in many cases of garment exports, the products exported were actually *chindies* – old clothes and fabric. On the basis of these false exports, dubious companies would avail subsidies from the government. And the so-called payments received from abroad were actually their own ill-gotten black money first sent out through 'hawala' channels and then brought back as legitimate payments by foreign importers. It was not as if everyone involved in these frauds was a typical criminal. One of the offenders was a respected retired commercial pilot living in a posh apartment in the western suburbs. Flashing his dubiously acquired wealth, he would throw lavish parties and socialize with high-ranking bureaucrats and film stars. It made me wonder if there is any limit to human greed.

Investigation into these cases involved going through the documents of the Customs department, balance sheets of companies and their subsidiaries/affiliates. Sometimes the investigations would take us overseas. Freshly arrived from Satara, it took me some time to understand the workings of the Bureau with its long-winded investigations. Fortunately, the superintendent of the Mumbai unit Virendra Singh was from the income tax department and came with sound knowledge of accounts and taxation, while the Chennai unit had Seema Agrawal, a very competent lady officer from the IPS. All of us reported to Mr Neeraj Kumar, IPS, one of the most dynamic officers I ever worked with. He later retired as Commissioner of Police in Delhi.

In due course I developed my own sources. We specifically targeted the nexus between public-sector bank officials and private companies. The former would arbitrarily grant loans to parties with doubtful credentials after taking a certain percentage as commission. This is one of the main reasons the Indian banking system is stuck with non-performing assets or NPAs. The Chennai-based Indian Bank is a classic case. The imprudent and capricious decisions made by its chairman M. Gopalakrishnan led to a loss of around ₹1,500 crore for the bank. Investigations led by our Chennai unit later led to his conviction.

While investigating the Unit Trust of India scam, I marvelled at the studious approach of its equity research cell and felt distressed that the top leadership ignored their professionally sound advice, causing its unsuspecting investors to suffer huge losses. We arrested the UTI chairman P. S. Subramanyam and his associates. So serious was the issue that the central government appointed former RBI Deputy Governor S. S. Tarapore to inquire into the dubious and damaging investments of senior UTI officials.

Working at the CBI for nearly three years was an enormous learning experience for me. It exposed me to investigations of international standards and gave me the opportunity to interact with great minds both here and internationally.

From the backwaters of the Koyna river, I had landed in a Mumbai inundated with greed and white-collar crimes. To tackle the challenges, I took to the digital world in earnest, as the analogue ways were most inadequate to deal with reams of forged papers, files and invoices. And slowly but surely, I learnt to navigate the murky waters of the financial capital.

20

THE HUBERT H. HUMPHREY FELLOWSHIP

'... the moral test of government is how that government treats those who are in the dawn of life, the children; those who are in the twilight of life, the elderly; and those who are in the shadows of life, the sick, the needy and the handicapped.'

– HUBERT H. HUMPHREY

In 1999, I applied for the Hubert H. Humphrey Fellowship. It came through in 2001 with the news that I had to join the University of Minnesota in the US by mid-August. The CBI headquarters was very happy to relieve me after we arrested several senior UTI officials in one of the fraud cases we investigated. (I was told that a powerful lobby in Delhi felt we had shaken the financial system of the country by registering the case.) I was sanctioned study leave and permitted to proceed.

The university was a good change of scene for me, even though I had been warned of Minnesota's cruel winters. Professor G. Edward Schuh was the programme in-charge at the university's Hubert H. Humphrey School of Public Affairs at the time. The

Humphrey Fellows that year had come from eight different countries, and Dr Schuh welcomed us all very warmly. He had served on President Gerald Ford's Council of Economic Advisers in the 1970s and later as Deputy Undersecretary for International Affairs and Commodity Programs at the Department of Agriculture during the Carter administration. Being very well travelled, he could relate to most of the developing countries and their issues.

During one of our interactions, I posed to him a question that had been bothering me for a while: what did he think were the reasons for India's slow economic progress. A man of few words, Prof Schuh asked for some time to reply. A few days later, he called me to his office. As he invited me to take a seat, I noticed that he looked grave with books and papers all over the room. He explained that he had been thinking about the possible answers to my question, and that the main reason for my country's slow economic growth could be because 'in India, industry does not work with academia'. Surprisingly he did not attribute our sluggish pace of progress to either socialism or corruption.

The Humphrey Fellowship Programme encourages its fellows to intern with agencies relevant to their core work. I thus interned at the local Minneapolis and St Paul Police Departments. I also visited police organizations in Seattle, San Francisco, Atlanta and Chicago. For an external internship I opted for the New York Police Department, but they declined to accept me as they were 'overwhelmed' with the investigation of the 9/11 terror attack. So instead, I interned with the Interpol in Washington, DC.

During one of my local police attachments, I had two interesting experiences. One evening a detective from the Minneapolis PD's homicide unit received a call about a gun shooting incident. The victim was a woman of colour whom he suspected of being a small-time drug peddler. When she was in a position to talk, we visited her at the hospital. While recording her statement, the detective asked her to describe the assailant. She went on to describe a white man, but the detective would refuse to believe her. An argument ensued, with the officer alleging that she was shielding a black man known to her who must have been the one responsible for the shooting. She argued back aggressively from her hospital bed. After some time, she stopped replying to the detective's questions altogether. Informing her that he would close the case as she was not cooperating, he walked out of the hospital with me in tow. The next day I found him writing a closure report for the case. I was surprised and wondered if it was not a 'hasty closure', to which he clarified that he had no option as the victim was not being cooperative. I was not sure if his senior would accept a closure on the third day after the incident, especially as a weapon had been used. But he replied with confidence: 'Yes, he will.'

This was a totally new phenomenon for me. In an attempt-to-murder case, an investigating officer in India keeps the case under investigation for ninety days. If the victim doesn't cooperate, he is advised to check other angles. It is true that our emphasis is more on paperwork than on collection of real-time scientific evidence. I have come across a few officers who wrote false case diaries, claiming to have checked the houses of suspects – without having left the office! Similarly, I have also known that some supervising officers have not taken action despite being aware of these false reports, intensifying a toxic brotherhood of silence. Overworked in urban metropolises, they justify false reports and corrupt practices by simply ignoring them. Even in cases where we are able to gather evidence, our conviction rate is less than 50 per cent.

Another time in Minneapolis, I was accompanying an officer on patrol duty late one evening. He got a call about a robbery from a store on the outskirts of the city. On reaching the spot, we found a man of colour alleging that he had been robbed by a woman police officer. The patrol officer tried talking him out of it as the storekeeper informed us that no woman police officer had visited his store. Nevertheless, the complainant, who was drunk, urged us to believe him and continued to repeat his story. When the officer asked him to get into our patrol vehicle, he did so reluctantly. Throughout the journey the police officer kept questioning him about the alleged robbery. He stuck to his version, lying down in the back seat of the car in his inebriated state. I was sitting in the front with the officer.

After we reached a police station, the officer tried to take the man in, but the police staff would not open the glass door. It was a sophisticated automatic door and could be opened only from inside. Embarrassed, the officer excused himself, walked some distance from me and prevailed upon the duty officer. Soon the door was opened. I suspect that he mentioned he was with an international police officer. After we both went in, the officer introduced me, and the two police officers began to discuss the case. All this time, the complainant was waiting inside our car. About ten minutes later, the officer signalled to me that it was time to leave. On the way back, he informed me that we were taking 'the backseat guy' to a shelter.

At the shelter, before we had a chance to discuss anything with the lady at the counter, the drunk man studied the dinner laid out on a table nearby and declared that he did not like the soup he found in the two tureens. The police officer was surprisingly tolerant and asked him to jump into the car again. We went to a second shelter where, on checking the menu, the man agreed to stay. It was very late by then, so the officer said he would decide the course of action the next day. He was of the opinion that the man was homeless and his complaint was false.

Many police stations in the twin cities of Minneapolis and St Paul are locked from inside, as the fear of guns is all-pervasive. I noticed that they were generally fortified and everyone wore body armour. But reluctance in opening the door to a fellow police officer remained a mystery to me. The various soups on the menus of homeless shelters and the way the 'homeless' person took his pick spoke of a wealthy community.

I saw signs of a well-to-do society on my visits to shelters for victims of domestic violence as well. They had good amenities and comforts.

The horrific problem of violent men abusing, beating and hurting their wives and partners is universal. That status and education could lead to less violence against women has always seemed like a myth to me. The average monthly income of an American worker is $4,245[1] and around 90 per cent of Americans are high school graduates. Yet violence against women is rampant in the country. As for India, the gross enrolment ratio in high secondary schools is around 57.4 per cent[2] and India's per capita monthly income was estimated to be $573.[3]

I interacted with a few victims of domestic violence in US shelters and found them to have undergone a loss of self-esteem and confidence, which was no different from my experience with such victims in India. I was faced with the same blank looks, sensed the same loss of purpose and listened to their concerns about the welfare of their children – another commonality with the victims I had met back home.

During my time in the US, I was attached to a civilian officer who belonged to the Community Police Unit of the Minneapolis

PD. They team up with uniformed police officers and visit blocks, hold meetings apprising residents of the crime situation in their areas. They discuss local issues and educate citizens about prevention of crime. All these activities are well documented. Churches are frequently used for hosting such events. I observed that an American police officer, though respected, is not particularly friendly. He tends to put up a stern front and his body language and posture are generally aggressive. Most of them are high school graduates and have not been to college. They tend to be in awe of universities. During my Fellowship year, we were given visiting cards which reflected the University of Minnesota affiliation as our main identity. The fact that I was from the U of M, as the university is popularly known, opened many police doors for me.

The chief of the St Paul Police Department gave me letters of introduction for visiting the Seattle and Chicago PDs. In Chicago I attended an interfaith meeting organized by the local police. What I liked most about it was that the facilitator was a civilian. Unlike meetings held by the police in India, where we talk and citizens listen passively, the facilitator gave each person equal opportunity to put their ideas across. The discussion was professionally facilitated and getting an expert outsider to conduct an interfaith interaction was a good idea. Chicago and other police departments I visited were warm in their hospitality. The bonds of the uniform seemed strong there. This enabled my visits to different state police organizations across the US, which included two long-term internships, surprising Humphrey Fellows working in other sectors.

Most American police officers would initially feel a bit confused on meeting me as I did not look like a police officer to them – I do not have the height and demeanour of a conventional police officer. That I had a university degree further amazed them. Some of them thought that Indian women are still in *purdah*!

Many of the officers I interacted with were unhappy with the US attorneys. They were of the opinion that their cases often do not go for trial as the reviewing attorney may not consider the evidence collected to be strong enough. In the US, an attorney has more say, unlike in India, where a police officer generally takes the final decision whether to chargesheet a case or not. This has resulted in even weak cases ending up in the courts and clogging our system.

Another noticeable feature was the police officer's forty-hour work week. This is true for other US civil servants as well. They work in all seriousness during these hours and some later on take up other private assignments. Many police officers, post duty hours, work as bouncers in restaurants. For this, they do not need the permission of the department; they only need to keep their offices informed. In India a police officer works for about eighty hours a week on average. There is no time for post-duty work, nor does the government permit it.

Though I enjoyed my mid-career year of learning in the US, I greatly missed my family. Therefore, during the winter break, I dashed home for a month. The Humphrey School of Public Affairs used to assign local families to its Fellows who would help them settle in and expose them to American culture. I was very fortunate to have Jerry and Ardie Lindhal, a sexagenarian couple of Swedish origin. They not only hosted me for my initial ten days, but also helped me settle into a studio apartment near the institute. I enjoyed meeting their children and grandchildren, decorating a Christmas tree, carving Halloween pumpkins, visiting the annual Minnesota State Fair and going for barbeques in public parks. As I am a vegetarian, the couple had to put in extra effort to cook for me, which Ardie did ever so cheerfully. Jerry, a good cook himself, spent as much time working in kitchen as Ardie, and the coffee he made was the best in the world. I have visited them four times since my fellowship programme and they have always been most welcoming. Many Indians believe that Americans mainly eat fast food, but at their place I always got a home-cooked meal with lots of greens. The American perception that Indians do not have fine-dining places is just as ignorant! The Humphrey's School's 'Host Families for Fellows' turned out to be a great initiative to the mutual advantage of the Fellows and their hosts.

I also formed a lasting friendship with a Fellow from South Africa by the name of Marie Storm, and went on to attend her wedding with Professor Harry C. Boyte at Johannesburg in 2002. Marie is very fond of Indian tea and we would talk for hours over chai. Both husband and wife are keenly interested in the working of democracy in India and visited me in Delhi in 2017.

During my Fellowship year, I had the option of choosing my subjects at the university. Along with Law, Leadership, Project Management, Research Methodology and a basic computer course, I also undertook a semester in Creative Writing. And here I am using my learnings to write this book!

When I decided to go to Minnesota, I had this intense feeling of guilt about leaving my family behind. I am sure many women experience it. Earlier in 1991, I had been offered admission into a one-year MBA course in an Australian university through a central government-sponsored training programme. My son being only five at the time, I had instead opted for the four-month-long International Executive Development Programme at the University of New England in Australia. The Maharashtra DG, V. K. Saraf, had felt disappointed that I had not accepted the

MBA offer, as it was he who had recommended my name. The executive programme was very useful as it involved taking classes at the university as well as interacting with various state police organizations in Australia. But I had missed home terribly.

Later in 2001, when I was in two minds about the Humphrey Fellowship, I had sought the advice of a friend significantly older to me. 'Don't be silly,' she said. 'If this Fellowship had been awarded to a man, he would have gone on one leg. Children will adjust – do not miss this opportunity.' In retrospect, her advice was quite sound and I gained immensely from the Fellowship programme. It may have been grudgingly, but my family did adjust to the temporary changes. My flying back for a month during the December break is an example of an act many working women perform on the tightrope of work-life balance.

21

YASHADA

'Cultivation of mind should be the ultimate aim of human existence.'

– B. R. AMBEDKAR

On returning from the Humphrey Fellowship Programme, I was posted to the Anti-Corruption Wing at the CBI in New Delhi, despite the post of Deputy Inspector General at the Mumbai office's Economic Offences Wing being vacant. I knew I was paying the price for exposing the UTI scam and there was an apprehension that I may release more worms from the can. The case had not yet been chargesheeted.

At the Delhi office, I was quick to make it clear that I would like to return to my cadre, Maharashtra. My elder son was in the twelfth standard and I had already been away from him and the family for ten months because of the Fellowship. I now wanted to pay more attention to his studies as it would be crucial for him to secure admission in a good college. Maybe he did not need me, but I felt very strongly that my presence would comfort him and thus persisted with the director of the CBI. He tried to persuade me to stay in Delhi, giving me an assurance that I would be posted to Mumbai after being promoted later in the year. But I was needed in Pune and at that critical juncture my family came first. I was relieved after about three months and I promptly reported to the police headquarters in Mumbai.

Calling on the director general of police, I sought any posting in Pune, where my family lived. He asked me if I had met the home minister of Maharashtra. I had not and told him frankly that 'I thought the buck stopped at DG's desk.' He got very annoyed at my remark. A senior officer sitting next to the DG at that time tried to placate him by saying, 'She is coming to the cadre after a long time and may not be aware of the protocol.' In a terse voice, the DG advised me to call on the home minister and dismissed me from his office.

From there I went to the chamber of Addl. DG, who looked after 'Establishment', that is, the posting of senior police officers, and told him about the DG's instructions. I added that I had no intention to call on the home minister who was notoriously corrupt. After quietly hearing me out, the ADG asked if I was ready to work at a training institute called the Yashwantrao Chavan Academy of Developmental Administration or YASHADA. The YASHADA director was seeking an IPS officer who could offer police-related inputs to trainees. I was happy to learn about the opportunity and told him that I would readily accept any post in Pune. 'As there is no money in the YASHADA posting, the minister cannot ask for it. And since there is no money, your file will not be cleared immediately and will take about a month,' he informed me candidly. Taking money for postings of all ranks had become a norm in Maharashtra by then. Files of those who pay up move very fast. 'Go relax in Pune with your family until then' was his advice. 'I will let you know when the Home Department has cleared your file.' So I returned to Pune without calling on the home minister and received my posting orders about three weeks later.

In our bleak world of corruption, one does come across aberrations. The officer whose advice I had sought was not known to be honest either and I have no idea why he decided to help me out. Later on, I met him occasionally, but he never broached the topic, and neither did I.

YASHADA traces its origin to the Administrative Staff College of Mumbai, which was established in 1963. It was relocated to Pune in 1984 and renamed the Maharashtra Institute of Development Administration (MIDA) as an autonomous unit meant to serve as the apex body for developing and promoting modern management practices and to function as a nodal state-level training institute in the field of development administration. It was rechristened Yashwantrao Chavan Academy of Development Administration in 1990, as a tribute to late Y. B. Chavan, former Chief Minister of Maharashtra and former Deputy Prime Minister of India.

I found working in YASHADA very interesting. Along with looking after the administration of the institute, as Director of the Centre for Good Governance, I travelled to different parts of the country, picking up on good governance initiatives and studying them carefully. At YASHADA, I got a lot of time to think, read and write. I designed the in-service training courses and conducted them with great enthusiasm. The trainee officers were usually an intriguing lot and would participate wholeheartedly in all activities. I would earmark a special session for them to share their individual talent with other participants. Poems and short stories written by these trainee officers were very sensitive and meaningful. I would often wonder how and why they become insensitive to citizens in the field.

Since they were from different government departments, I found my interactions with them enriching. Many of them were not fluent in English, but their thought processes and keenness to learn about national and international best practices and good governance initiatives were impressive.

There was a small pond at YASHADA next to which the faculty would meet during tea breaks to exchange ideas and discuss a whole host of topics. I loved standing and chatting by the pond, which was incidentally home to pink lotuses. This was an extremely creative space for me. As the cartoonist Frank Tyger once said, 'Doing what you like is freedom, liking what you do is happiness.'

During my YASHADA days, I also witnessed caste consciousness among the faculty from close quarters. I had observed it in the police too. But here it was quite brazen. The institute's theme colour was purple, so its entrance gate, logo, posters, stationery, publications would carry the name YASHADA in that colour. In all their wisdom, the institute's first director and his team must have made this choice. One of the later directors, however, replaced purple with blue to represent a particular caste. The original purple was finally reinstated many years after I left YASHADA. This was a director who would favour faculty members belonging to his own caste and be hostile to the rest, irrespective of their good performance. I have come across both subtle and virulent forms of such caste alliances. It can be found in all levels of government and administration, from the panchayat to the most sophisticated echelons. Caste and communal hostilities are the bane of good governance and the more we practice such animosity, the more we regress as a society.

My posting at YASHADA was an opportunity for me to not only share my learnings acquired through the Humphrey Fellowship Programme but also gain new ones. Soon I enrolled at Pune University's Management Faculty to study organizational management as a theme for my doctorate. The idea was to compare the Indian system of policing with that of the US. Professor Schuh of the Humphrey School visited YASHADA and conducted a formal session with faculty. The director was highly impressed with him. Dr Schuh, however, was more impressed by the variety of grains he got to eat in Pune. He was served rotis made of wheat, bajra, jowar, ragi, corn, barley, along with different kinds of rice and vegetables. Though an expert on agriculture, he had never seen such a great assortment of grains and cereals being served together.

We also invited many thinkers and social activists to interact with both faculty and trainees. I particularly remember the civil servant B. G. Deshmukh's talk, 'Vision for YASHADA', which was precise and meaningful. Erudite yet keeping a low profile, he was one of the institute's well-wishers and a strong believer in good governance.

About a year and a half into my YASHADA tenure, I received a call from the Mumbai police commissioner, A. N. Roy, who wanted to know if I would join his team as Joint Commissioner (Crime). Meanwhile, the corrupt minister had been replaced by one known to be straightforward and honest. My elder son had completed his twelfth standard exams by then and joined an engineering college. I thus readily agreed, even though it would mean moving back to Mumbai. I enjoyed investigation and was keenly aware that Mumbai's crime branch dealt with serious organized crime and criminal gangs. But it took nearly two months for the orders to be issued by the government.

The Mumbai crime branch has a tough macho image. I gathered that after I was considered for the post, there were second thoughts at the government level. The home minister is said to have consulted many officers as he was concerned as to how I would handle police encounters. When an officer asked him why he was considering me at all if he had doubts, it seems the minister had replied: 'To control the encounter specialists!'

While waiting for my transfer orders, I participated in a training workshop at the Lal Bahadur Shastri National Academy of Administration in Mussoorie. One day after the session ended, I went for a walk with two senior IAS officers. During our long discussion, I was surprised to note that both felt that we needed to align ourselves to a political party of our choice, at this stage in our careers, or we would suffer. Thirty years ago, the advice during the basic training used to be that civil servants should remain neutral, maintaining equal distance from all political parties. But by 2004, things seemed to have changed. I could see that the basic values of the civil services had been compromised. I was left wondering if I had been living in an ivory tower.

One fine day, the home minister decided to take the plunge and issued my transfer orders for Mumbai. I proceeded to join the crime branch, blissfully unaware of the media hype this posting would generate.

22

CRIME BRANCH, MUMBAI

'The purpose of life after all is, to live it, to taste experience to the utmost, to reach out eagerly and without fear for newer and richer experiences.'

– ELEANOR ROOSEVELT

My mobile phone would not stop ringing.

After completing my handover at YASHADA, I was on my way from Pune to Mumbai. All along, I was inundated with congratulatory messages and calls. The posting of a lady officer at Mumbai's crime branch had made headlines in local newspapers and TV channels. No one could believe that a unit with an extremely masculine image could have a woman as its chief. On reaching the headquarters in Crawford Market, I found a sea of reporters waiting for me. But the commissioner seemed unhappy and wondered aloud if it was me who had generated the media hype!

During the nineties, the Mumbai police department's crime branch, with its encounter specialists, had won over the public by delivering instant justice through the killing of notorious murderers, kidnappers and gangsters. Movies like *Ab Tak Chhappan* had immortalized them. From film stars to political bigwigs, everyone was enthralled by their daredevil acts. Somewhere along the way, however, these officers lost the plot. They started settling scores on behalf of builders, rival criminal gangs and politicians from Mumbai and its surrounding areas. They also started aligning with gangsters, and many police 'encounters' came to be seen as retaliation by one gang against the other. The officers in their 'encounter specialist' avatars became larger-than-life figures and the police leadership found it difficult to decipher the logic of many of their actions. It was also getting difficult to control and regulate some of them who seemed to have become a law unto themselves. Rivalries among these officers were as dangerous as those between criminal gangs.

It was during this phase that the home minister R. R. Patil started looking for a non-controversial officer who would work in a professional manner instead of taking sides. Mine was one of the names under consideration. But due to the pull of various lobbies, encounter specialists and many ambitious IPS officers, it took a long while for my appointment to come through. It turned out that an officer whom I thought of as a friend had told the home minister, 'She is too straight,' in an attempt to dissuade him. The truth was that he would have very much liked to head the crime branch himself. Sometime later, when I had settled into my new role, I confronted him. He did not deny the charge; instead he counter-questioned me: 'Did I say anything wrong?'

It is true that being upstanding and straightforward can sometimes become a liability in the police and civil services. At the top echelons, various kinds of compromises are made by politicians, civil servants and the police leadership. Not all compromises are bad; certain give-and-takes are unavoidable for the smooth running of the government. The reality, however, is that most acts of compromise are self-serving than for the good of the nation and its citizens. Honest officers are considered obstacles in this labyrinth. Many a time, just as I would enter a room, officers in the middle of a conversation would awkwardly go silent. This was a consequence of both gender-based discomfort and a phenomenon called 'too straight'. Instead of a badge of honour, it becomes an albatross around one's neck.

The excitement that my posting generated had many repercussions. A paparazzi chased me one evening when I had gone out for a movie with a friend, and published my photograph in a popular daily. I rang him up and said that I was a police officer, not a film celebrity, and that the kind of exposure he had given me would harm my career. To their credit, the message was well received by the media and, after that incident, I was no longer hounded while engaged in private activities. But then came a legal notice that made front-page news. The Bombay High Court had asked me for a progress report about the investigation of an undetected case of a child's kidnapping and murder. After going through the case papers, I submitted my opinion through a brief eight-page report which concluded that the investigation should continue under section 173(8) of the CrPC, which allows for further investigation in criminal cases. To my utter shock, the bench issued me with a 'contempt notice'. I learnt from the government prosecutor that he could not appear for me as it was a personal notice. Instead, he recommended a renowned lawyer, whom I rang up immediately as I was deeply disturbed. The lawyer readily agreed to represent me and, when I asked about his fees, said, 'The royal sum of one rupee.' It was a pleasant surprise and I felt hugely relieved.

Soon he came to my office, went through all the case papers and my report. In all gravity, he said, 'Madam, instead of eight pages, please make it a thirty-eight-page report, and the notice will be withdrawn. It should not have been issued in the first place. You have committed no contempt.' As per his advice, I redrafted my report, making it more elaborate. Then he presented my case in court, while I stood like a criminal in the dock. 'No contempt has been made out, my Lord,' he said, as he furnished the fresh report. And just like that, the notice was withdrawn. It left me wondering if this had been a case of judicial overreach! I will never know but when I discussed the incident with other lawyers, they also endorsed my advocate's opinion that submitting a report which may not be to the satisfaction of a judge does not in any way constitute 'contempt of court'. At one point, I had also discussed the contempt notice with the commissioner, Mr Roy, and whether I should challenge it, but he had advised against it. I have witnessed many similar incidents where I felt that the judiciary may have acted in an arbitrary manner. This is what ultimately motivated me to secure a law degree at the earliest.

In the meanwhile, I had familiarized myself with my new job and visited various units of the crime branch all across Mumbai. I made it absolutely clear that I did not belong to any lobby and that indiscipline and fake killings were totally unacceptable to me. Luckily, I had an excellent team. I did meet a few officers who had 'managed' their postings through some sources. Getting a posting of one's choice through political connections, as I've pointed out earlier, has become deep-rooted in our system. Hardly any eyebrows are raised at such occurrences. Even when the commissioner of police and the home minister were honest and professional, some police officers would find their way into the highly prestigious and often very lucrative Mumbai Police Commissionerate.

The additional commissioner of the crime branch's Economic Offences Wing, K. L. Bishnoi, had been handpicked by the commissioner, and he soon started on a mission to expedite investigations. He was succeeded by another brilliant officer, Sadanand Date. The focus of the crime branch had shifted so heavily to organized crime that the EOW, with about a hundred investigating officers, had an unaccounted number of ongoing investigations. Trials of EOW cases are also generally very long-drawn-out. Many judicial officers take up simpler cases for disposal as opposed to intricate ones involving economic offences. In such circumstances, police officers become lax, knowing that the trials can sometimes last seven to ten years. After making countless trips to the EOW offices and the courts, aggrieved citizens also tend to give up – an extremely unfortunate scenario.

Many Ponzi schemes – fraudulent investment scams that promise high rates of return to investors – were pending with investigating officers at the time. The Maharashtra Protection of Interest of Depositors (in Financial Establishments) Act had been passed, raising the hopes of small investors. They would approach my office expecting us to return their money – if not the interest, then at least the principal amount. Special courts set up under this act appointed administrators who took possession of the fraudsters' properties. But their value was insignificant compared to the amounts due to citizens, many of whom were daily-wage workers and slum dwellers. In Mumbai's flashy world of power and money, these cases often escape the attention of the media and the public. The additional CP pursued them with vigour and enthusiasm while ensuring that the quality of investigation wasn't compromised.

'Enforcement' is another sensitive unit of the crime branch and deals with various social laws and their implementation. Its mandate is to conduct raids against any illegal activity across the metropolis. It recently got into controversy due to former home minister of Maharashtra's alleged demand for money from bar owners. There is no doubt that this unit sits on a gold mine and is one of the most sought-after departments in the Mumbai Police.

In 1991, when I was DCP Crime Branch (Preventive), the Mumbai commissioner had assigned the Social Service branch of the Enforcement unit to me. I had studied its workings and conducted many operations against illicit liquor brewing and gambling. I had also organized a massive raid in Kamathipura as part of a well-meant move to rescue women forced into prostitution. During this operation, I was extremely distressed to witness the nefarious exploitation of young girls and women. Very few of the rescued women were willing to go back to their families, as they felt they wouldn't find any acceptance.

Having learnt important lessons on this front as a young officer, I decided now, as Joint Commissioner, to concentrate on the rescue of minors before it was too late. And on the extensive deployment of the Juvenile Aid and Protection Unit to rescue children. Trafficking of children has become a grave issue that requires far more attention than is currently given. Law enforcement agencies alone cannot prevent it.

To deter the youth from crime, we initiated a programme called Rehabilitation of First-time Offenders with the help of Yuva Parivartan, a local NGO. They would impart skills like driving, electrical wiring and repairing of air conditioners and refrigerators. Young boys who had strayed into the world of crime and wanted to get out were trained to become vehicle mechanics, drivers and so on.

The Mumbai crime branch deals with serious cases of crimes against women and also runs a Special Cell for Women.

In collaboration with the Tata Institute of Social Sciences, it counsels domestic violence victims and looks into their cases. We successfully opened two new counselling units in the eastern and western suburbs of the city, which aided women who found it difficult to visit the head office at Crawford Market, where the special cell was located.

The Maharashtra Police has taken a conscious decision to appoint women in all police stations so that women victims of crime would feel comfortable lodging their complaints at the nearest station. The crime branch, however, specializes in investigating heinous cases of sexual assault, gangrapes and complex cases of interstate human trafficking.

I made two personal rules during this period. One was to always be in uniform, even though the crime branch permits officers to wear civilian clothes while on duty – as a result they rarely don the uniform. Since we dealt with the most dangerous criminals and gangsters, I believed they needed to focus on my rank and not on my gender. The commissioner once wondered aloud why I was always in khaki but did not pursue the subject.

The second rule was that all minor girls rescued by police officers should be brought to me. I wanted to understand what had driven them to prostitution. I would ask the officers to wait outside while I talked to the girls. Listening to them, I would feel so disturbed that often I had to pray for strength and equanimity.

Dealing with the most ferocious gangster is much easier than carrying the burden of innocence lost!

23

A CACHE OF ARMS

'... the first requirement in the country was external and internal security. You cannot have any plan unless there is security.'

– SARDAR VALLABHBHAI PATEL

It was the hot, muggy May of 2005 and I was ardently waiting for the arrival of the monsoon, a season I love. We had just completed a review of actionable information: weapons seizures, the movements of gangsters and the threats they posed. It had been a rather exhaustive discussion. Reaching my home on the fourth floor of an apartment building in south Mumbai, I soon picked up a book on Jainism for my nighttime reading. Before long, the contents had made me feel at peace and in harmony with my inner self. I went into a deep sleep.

I woke up with a start to the sound of my mobile phone ringing. It was one of our encounter specialists, an officer who would disturb you only if he had some high-quality information. It was no different this time. A source of his had learnt of a big consignment of sophisticated weapons sent by the notorious Chhota Rajan's gang to Jawaharlal Nehru Port, which was also known as Nhava Sheva Port. I was told that the deputy commissioner was indisposed and that the officer was himself proceeding to the port. This news was too important to be left unattended, so I immediately decided to go to the spot as well. The officer was going to pick up his informant and additional staff along the way. Police officers are required to have '*panchas*', or respectable civilians, witness seizures of weapons and other articles from the scene of crime. He would be organizing that too, I thought to myself and put on my uniform in a hurry.

My official car and an escort vehicle were in the parking lot downstairs. Without wasting any time, we started for Nhava Sheva Port. Looking out of the car window, I noticed a strange-looking moon. I realized it was the only time in my life I had not enjoyed gazing at the moon, which gave me an eerie feeling. That's when my driver announced that he could take us to the port but he was not familiar with its interiors. This was understandable as the port was outside the jurisdiction of the Mumbai Commissionerate. Established in 1989, it is India's largest container-handling port and consists of a full-fledged customs house with thirty container freight stations. I knew that finding a specific container yard inside the port would be challenging.

But we lost our way even before we reached our destination. It was getting late and I started to feel restless when we saw a motorcycle behind us on a lonely, dark road that seemed to lead nowhere. We had already been driving for more than an hour. When we stopped the rider and asked him for directions, he offered to guide us to the port. Once on the correct road, I offered him a tip, but he refused, saying, 'Oh, you guys do so much for us.' Thanking him, we moved at top speed only to find ourselves stuck outside the gate of the container yard, where the cache of arms was supposed to have been stored. The officer, who was not in uniform, had reached before us but the port guards refused to open the gate. A heated argument was ongoing when we reached. After I got out and the guards saw me in my uniform and my official car in all its majesty, they finally allowed us in.

The officer and his team immediately went around looking for the container suspected to be carrying the arms. Port sheds are generally very large and can house hundreds of containers. Only the staff working there can find their way through what is otherwise a labyrinth. It was this maze the team of officers had to navigate on that dark, sultry night, searching for a single elusive container in a dockyard with hundreds of lookalikes. The dock workers sleeping in the shed started waking up one by one and observed the goings-on curiously.

To our good fortune, the officer's informant was able to identify the right container and we heaved a sigh of relief, but all too soon as the container bore the seal of a sister agency. This was a completely unexpected turn of events. We were wondering what to do when, out of the blue, an officer from that particular agency appeared. He told us that his agency had sealed the container about a month back as a 'suspicious consignment'. They may have termed it so, but we had exact information, which I felt carried more weight than a mere suspicion. So, when the officer objected to our plan to open the container, an argument ensued. He could not explain to us why they had not opened it for a whole month. I could see that he was junior to me in rank but was very bold and articulate. He had been stationed there to prevent any unauthorized access to the container. I could, however, prevail upon him, albeit after a heated argument.

In presence of two panchas and in full view of nearly one hundred dock workers who had gathered around by then, we opened the container. Another shock awaited us. It was packed with drums containing glue. And yet the information about hidden arms and ammunition had been quite specific. The crime branch officers thus started putting their hands deep inside the drums, but they mostly came up empty and covered in glue. It was a bizarre scene: the darkest hours of the night, hundreds of sleepy dock workers, a grumpy officer from a sister agency, crime branch officers dripping with glue as they searched the drums. Until we struck gold.

At the bottom of those glue ponds were carefully wrapped plastic cases containing revolvers, pistols and ammunition. They were impeccably packed and the cache had therefore survived very well in its hideout. As the officers brought out the compact weapons, the dock workers would move in closer for a good look at the sophisticated foreign-made pistols and revolvers. Under the moonlight, it soon started to look as if the officers were entertainers performing magic and the workers standing in a circle their audience. At one point I felt a little apprehensive about the porters being in big numbers while our team was small and by then in possession of a large quantity of arms and ammunition. So, I called out to my gunner in a loud voice. Understanding the situation, he immediately took a strategic position and pulled out his automatic weapon in clear view of all. Until then he had been busy admiring the weapons and the shiny round bullets. Slowly the port workers receded.

By morning we had recovered a substantial hoard of arms and ammunition, and thus neutralized an extremely grave threat to not only Mumbai but the entire nation. The document of recovery or 'panchnama' was started at midnight and completed in the morning. It was one of the biggest arms heists the crime branch had ever uncovered; the officer on the scene, a renowned encounter specialist, had truly lived up to his reputation.

After proper documentation of the seized weapons, I left Nhava Sheva Port for Mumbai to brief the commissioner about the night operation. To my surprise, I found in his office a senior officer from the sister agency that had sealed the container. The commissioner wanted the details of how we had broken the container seal placed by the agency. As I recounted the entire operation, I also informed him about the recovered weapons. It was an unbelievably large seizure even by our crime branch standards.

While the commissioner listened and looked thoughtful, the officer got up and walked out quietly. He was thereafter transferred out of Mumbai. I felt bad. It was said that the agency was waiting for someone to claim the suspicious container so they could apprehend him. This was why it had been left unopened. I did not see any logic in waiting when the officer had specific information involving a cache as big as it turned out to be. I shudder to think of the havoc those weapons could have wreaked in our country. In retrospect, that midnight operation feels surreal to me even today.

The magnitude of the arms seizure at Nhava Sheva Port was matched only by the great deluge caused by the Mumbai monsoon of 2005.

24

JEWEL THIEVES AT JOYALUKKAS

'Been there, done that.
Then been there several more times,
Because, apparently, I never learn.'

– A REPEAT OFFENDER

It was a hot and dry evening in May 2006. Monsoons were not in sight yet, and I had come out for a late-evening walk at the Cricket Club of India on Marine Drive. At the last crime conference with my crime branch officers, I had wondered if we too, like our city, were suffering a dry spell, as there had been no noteworthy detection for quite some time. Police officers generally do not discuss the details of any case they are working on, nor do they disclose any specifics about their informants. In fact, my officers were so possessive of them that several times in the past they had sought my intervention, alleging the poaching of one officer's informant by another. After my remark about the crime branch's 'dry days', certain officers approached me individually with some information they had gathered. Most officers of the branch were self-motivated, passionate about detection, always taking pride in their job. But I saw no harm in nudging them once a while.

During my evening walks, I preferred to be alone to mull over the day's events. That evening, my reverie was broken by a call from the Hyderabad-based IPS officer Rajiv Trivedi. He was seeking my help in investigating a daring case of robbery at a Joyalukkas jewellery showroom. It had taken place on 15 May 2006 – the previous night.

I had been following the news of this audacious burglary involving gold and diamond jewellery said to be worth nine crores. It had made national headlines in both print and electronic media. Television channels had been broadcasting scenes of the showroom after the incident, and visits by Hyderabad's senior police officers, including the commissioner and the director general of police. The police was of the opinion that 'a showroom having more than ₹500 million worth of jewellery should have a foolproof security system in place'. This was clearly a case of breach and the value of the stolen property had shaken the establishment. Earlier, the home minister had blamed the management for not providing tight security on the premises. He called a high-level meeting, wherein all participants noted that nine out of the twelve closed circuit TVs in the showroom were not working. Other security equipment, as well as the showroom's security guards, were not effective either.[1]

The huge, impressive Joyalukkas showroom was in the Panjagutta area, one of the busiest commercial hubs in the heart of the city, a stone's throw away from the police station. Besides, Panjagutta is a high-security zone, being home to several ministers and top officials, including the chief minister.[2] The area is locally known as 'Gold Street', as it boasts around twenty jewellery shops, such as Tribhovandas Zhaveri, Khazana, Tanishq and Boorugu. All of them have security guards in their employ and any suspicious movement should have been observed by someone at least.

Rajiv, the police officer who had requested my help, admitted that there had been cases in the same area previously as well, causing the police great embarrassment. Concerned about the spate of burglaries, they had been advising jewellers to take strong precautions. He suspected the involvement of an interstate gang, and was therefore coordinating with other states where similar offences had occurred. The call to me was a part of this effort. I had known Rajiv for some time and understood that he was under tremendous pressure. A keen sportsperson and fitness enthusiast, he was working as additional commissioner in Hyderabad then.

The targeted showroom had four floors and was said to be Joyalukkas' sixty-first retail outlet. In 1956, a man named Varghese Alukkas had opened the first jewellery store in Thrissur, his family's native town. In 1987, his son Joy Alukkas went to the Middle East to open their first overseas store in Abu Dhabi. Later, he broke off to launch his own brand – Joyalukkas – which, at the time of the burglary, had 130 outlets spread across India and thirteen other countries.[3]

Earlier in the day, I had discussed the sensational burglary with my crime branch officers, instructing two of them to fly to Hyderabad. We had learnt that the Joyalukkas spokesperson had informed Hyderabad Police that criminals had looted them of about forty kilograms of gold and diamond ornaments. Some of the diamonds were VVS1-type solitaires, each worth ₹800,000 to ₹1 million. Though the initial estimate of the loss was ₹9 crores, the actual worth was yet to be assessed. A Hyderabad-based source of one of my officers had confirmed that the criminals did not touch the strong room and lockers, which were connected to the alarm system and held gold ornaments weighing about 103 kilograms and diamonds worth ₹400 million.

We pondered if it might have been the work of an insider well aware of the showroom's security installations and, therefore, thinking it best to steer clear of the strong room. Located a short distance away from the Andhra Pradesh chief minister's residence on one end and the Punjagutta police station on the other, an outsider operating with impunity seemed doubtful. The Hyderabad police seemed to be thinking along similar lines. The photos of the criminals on the CCTV camera were blurry, so no conclusion could be drawn on their basis. I had ended our meeting by advising officers to tap their sources and look for known receivers of stolen jewellery. One of them pointed out that no one individual would be able to purchase such a huge amount of gold. Instead, the criminals would probably sell it in instalments over a period of time, making detection and recovery of the stolen property difficult. It sounded logical, but I felt that the need of the hour was to concentrate on detection and ignore the many reasons not to try and detect a case. The Mumbai crime branch had been cultivating informants in the city's Sarafa Bazar and we decided to tap all of them.

Units I and II alerted all jewellery shops in their areas. South Mumbai was already aware of the Hyderabad heist; most of our sources there opined that the stolen goods would not appear in the market so fast. We decided to physically check the housebreakers in our records the same night, especially those who operated outside Maharashtra too. There are some skilled burglars who exclusively target shops, while others keep watch on both houses and shops, striking wherever they find the security to be low. These criminals' photographs and addresses were available with us in the Property Cell which regularly monitors their movements. It was decided that all units would carry out nighttime checks of the burglars on record and details of the untraceable ones were to be shared among the units as they could possibly be operating outside Mumbai.

The team of crime branch officers that had flown to Hyderabad earlier that morning informed me that the criminals had used a rope to climb up the building next to the Joyalukkas showroom. They had managed to go unnoticed as there was some repair work ongoing in that building. The officers also confirmed that most of the CCTV cameras in the showroom were not working and the photos from the operational cameras were of no use. I learnt that the Panjagutta police station had registered a case vide Crime No. 407/2006 u/s 457 and section 380 of the Indian Penal Code on 16 May and constituted four special teams to hunt down the culprits.

In the meanwhile, we had zeroed in on a few habitual criminals in Mumbai, and had started checking their homes and hideouts. We received information that a particular group of burglars and robbers would be coming to south Mumbai for a hearing at Esplanade Court on the 17th.

Established in 1810, this huge judicial complex is also known as Police Courts as it houses many magistrate courts, including that of the chief metropolitan magistrate. From 1 April 1974, when the new Criminal Procedure Code became functional, these courts came to be officially known as the Chief Metropolitan Magistrates Courts, but among the police, they are still known as the Esplanade courts. The magnificent multi-storey court complex, with its numerous entrances and exits, was inaugurated on 31 December 1888.[4] Every day from 11 a.m. until lunch, one can literally witness a melee here as magistrates take up bail matters. Police officers escort arrested criminals, whose relatives, lawyers and sureties come to attend bail hearings, leading to massive crowds filling up the courtrooms and spilling over onto the lobbies and staircases.

The information we had received about suspected burglars attending an old criminal case turned out to be concrete – we had verified it through our sources working in the courts. We had plainclothes police officers and constables stationed in different courtrooms, lobbies, on the stairways, in the rickety old lifts and even the toilets of the court complex. The burglars' photographs were shown to this contingent in disguise.

We were very hopeful of a breakthrough but, to our dismay, the gang did not turn up. Either they had recognized the plainclothesmen and retreated or were still outside Mumbai. Nevertheless, the officers of the crime branch's Unit XII decided to pursue the lead further as the information had been thoroughly confirmed by independent sources. I did not intervene at this point, as I understood that some operations succeeded quickly while others remained a work-in-progress longer than one would like.

Later in the evening, Inspector Sunil Darekar and Assistant Police Inspector Satish Raorane of Unit XII obtained another piece of information about an active history-sheeter – a criminal in our records – belonging to the same group. He frequented night bars in suburban Mumbai, and our tipper had said that he would be visiting one that night. It was well known that he went to a night bar only after a successful operation, as he loved showering 'crisp currency notes' on bar girls, some of whom had been cultivated as informants by the crime branch.

Though a little demoralized by the morning's fiasco at Esplanade Court, where officers from other units had also been deployed, the Unit XII officers showed remarkable resilience.

With the help of their informants, they covered all the night bars supposed to be the gang's favourites. Finally, they traced a known criminal, Vinod Rambali Singh, at the Charwak bar in Borivali. He was busy drinking and, as expected, showering money on bar dancers. On sensing that something was amiss, he tried to exit through the side door, but the short, stout Inspector Sunil Darekar and the young, lanky Satish Raorane pounced upon him. Though they were not in uniform, the manager had recognized the police officers and would not permit other patrons to intervene in the scuffle that followed. An ugly scene was thus averted.

It took the unit all their interrogation skills to break Vinod Singh, a hardened habitual criminal with eighteen cases of robberies and house break-ins against him. He had been externed from Mumbai by the Borivali police station on 25 March the same year for his criminal activities that posed a threat to the community. An externment entails the police department putting forth a proposal to an executive magistrate, asserting that an individual, owing due to his/her criminal activities, is a grave danger to their locality. If supported by adequate data and crime records, the executive magistrate may accede to the police report and restrain such an individual from entering a specific area for a certain period of time. Such criminals are the most difficult to handle as they know the intricacies of the criminal justice system, are able to sneak in even if externed and have a set of lawyers ready to defend them. In any case, Mumbai being a veritable sea of humanity, externments are hardly effective in controlling the movement of criminals.

That day, however, luck was on the unit's side, as the officers who searched Vinod found in his pocket some jewellery which he could not explain. He was brought to the unit's office in Dahisar and asked to account for his movements in the past one week. After another round of intense interrogation and rapid-fire questioning by the Unit XII officers, Singh finally admitted that he, along with his associate Shirikant Singh, had broken into the Joyalukkas showroom in Hyderabad. But he refused to disclose the whereabouts of the loot and kept insisting that the jewellery had been divided among the gang members and that he was not aware of their location. The officers were loath to lose time as it could give the other gang members the chance to escape with the booty.

API Raorane, who was at this time going through Singh's mobile phone, observed that he had received repeated calls from a landline number. So he rang up the MTNL office, introduced himself and asked for the details of the landline number's owner. It turned out to be Hotel Ripon Palace in central Mumbai. Confronted with this information, Singh finally confessed that he and another gang member, Ajay Singh, had been staying in room 203 at the hotel.

Jumping into the two unit vehicles, the officers rushed to Hotel Ripon Palace, interrogating Vinod throughout the tense one-hour drive even as he continued to withhold information about the jewellery. At one point, the officers had supposedly wished to pick up some food on the way, but the young driver, Sandeep Daware, would not stop the vehicle. Instead, he exhorted the officers, saying, 'Sirs, this is not the time to think of dinner,' as he pressed down on the accelerator.

The Ripon Palace hotel is located near Mumbai Central Railway Station, between Byculla and Mohammed Ali Road. The distance between the Unit XII office at Dahisar and the station is approximately 40 kilometres. The tension in both the vehicles was palpable as officers were looking for stolen gold and diamond worth about nine crores.

Upon their arrival at the hotel, while Vinod Singh was reluctantly taking the team to room 203, Inspector Darekar noticed someone with two bags coming down the stairs. Maybe it was his sixth sense or his policeman's reflexes, but he asked Sub-inspector Ravindera Patil and constables Kamble and Jambhale to check the man's bags. At the same time, API Raorane, who was going through the register at the hotel reception, noticed that there had been a recent check-out from room 203. His heart sank. As he looked up, the receptionist pointed to the person with the bags. He had just checked out of room 203.

Sub-inspector Patil quietly and deftly took the bags from the man, ordering him to accompany the officers to the room. He was indeed Ajay Jawahar Singh, Vinod Singh's accomplice. The two bags he was carrying were filled with diamonds. There were two other bags in the room which belonged to Vinod. ASI Deshmane opened these bags to find them stacked with stolen gold – he nearly fainted on the spot.

The officers later told me that though their information was specific and Vinod had confessed to the burglary, leading them to Ripon Palace, they could not believe their luck when they actually saw the gold and diamonds. Most of them felt dizzy; some in jest blamed the driver Sandeep Daware for not letting them eat anything on the way.

When I reached the Unit XII office at midnight, I too was aghast at the sight of the jewellery, the like of which I had never seen in my life. Used to wearing simple pearl studs along with my uniform, I had lost track of how to be fashionable and all the accoutrements that came with it. It took us nearly six hours to prepare the seizure document – known as the 'recovery panchnama'. In the past such sensational detections and recoveries of gold and diamonds had led to allegations of embezzlement by the police. In light of that, I did not leave the unit office, nor did I get up to take a bathroom break, until the documentation had been completed and every piece accounted for.

After that, Vinod Singh was brought before me. A harmless-looking thirtysomething man of average height, he was an ace burglar. Whenever there was a jewellery shop burglary in Mumbai, the first person officers looked for was him – such was his notoriety. Vinod had been arrested so many times in the past that he was fully aware of our ranks, even though most crime branch officers did not wear the uniform. He told me that he had gone to Hyderabad ten days prior to the crime for a recce of the place. He had collected information about the Panjagutta gold street from a prisoner from Andhra Pradesh whom he had met while in Arthur Road Jail (Mumbai Central Prison), where they had both been imprisoned for previous crimes. After analyzing the security levels of the showrooms on the street, he had decided upon his target. For about ten days, Vinod went around the area, becoming familiar with it and observing the routines of the security guards deployed at the various showrooms. He revealed to me that he had conducted three dry runs in Punjagutta before actually striking at Joyalukkas around 1 a.m. on 16 May. He had noticed that the Joyalukkas guards were stationed on the front side and did not carry out patrols around the showroom at night.

There was a shutter on the second floor at the back of the building that Vinod had identified as a possible entry point. He thought he could cut open the lock without the guards noticing him. To access the shutter, he decided to go up the adjoining building using a rope. He added rather proudly that he had successfully performed a dry run of this act and no one had noticed him. On the evening of 15 May, Vinod and his associate

Shirkant Singh stationed themselves in the building next to Joyalukkas. At night, when the security guards were at the front of the showroom, they broke the lock of the second-floor shutter and entered. Knowing that switching on the lights would alert the guards, they had brought candles and matchboxes. They had also decided to remove only those items of jewellery placed in the display counters. Amit Garg, the then deputy commissioner of police of Hyderabad's west zone, who visited the scene of crime, had correctly stated that the criminals had been 'careful not to touch switches or the alarm system, when they made their way down to the first floor and the cellar'. While Shirikant held up a candle, Vinod collected gold and diamonds. They had brought along two empty bags, which they filled with the loot before quietly escaping through the back.

Vinod Singh had not only plotted the burglary but meticulously planned the exit strategy too. He told me that along with Shirikant Singh, he had travelled twice by State Road Transport buses between Hyderabad and Pune to see if the police checked baggage en route. Satisfied that they were in the clear, they took an SRT bus from Hyderabad to Pune after completing their 'mission' successfully on the night of 15–16 May. They had deliberately not taken a luxury bus. From Pune to Andheri in Mumbai, they travelled by an air-conditioned cab. Then they took an auto rickshaw. As Vinod Singh carried on with his confession, I saw that there was no remorse on his face, only exhaustion due to our intense interrogation and the loss of his precious loot.

My interrogation of Ajay Singh revealed that he worked in a jewellery shop in Surat and had been called upon by Vinod to assess the worth of the jewellery and help with its dispersal. He admitted to having known Vinod Singh for a long time and having helped him in the past too.

While we could not arrest their third associate, Shirikant Singh, we were fortunate to have been able to apprehend the other two so fast that all jewellery and diamonds were recovered intact. Such criminal gangs include members whose job is to receive and disperse stolen goods. In the case of gold jewellery, they are very quick to melt it so that it cannot be identified by the complainants, resulting in acquittal of most criminal cases of break-ins and robberies.

By now, the media had got wind of our detection and recovery of the loot and were thronging outside the Unit XII office on the morning of 18 May. I briefed them only after the recovered jewellery had been properly accounted for in the seizure panchnama and the document was sealed. It was a cumbersome task not only owing to the huge quantity, but also because none of us at the Unit XII office could properly disentangle the gold chains from the earrings. We were lucky to have the help of the government-approved valuer who had been called to evaluate and certify the purity of the gold and diamonds. If not for him, we would have been stuck inside the office until the cows came home or my desperation for the restroom became unbearable!

The Hyderabad police commissioner rang me up to congratulate me and the crime branch team. The Joyalukkas top management boarded the next flight to Mumbai in order to take stock of the loot. Relief was writ large on their faces. Rajiv Trivedi, the police officer who had sought my help, was overjoyed. His efforts towards interstate coordination for crime detection had borne positive results. He too flew to Mumbai to interrogate the accused. To our pleasant surprise, he made the Andhra Pradesh government sanction cash rewards for the Unit XII officers the same day. Not one to be left behind, the Maharashtra home minister R. R. Patil too declared cash rewards and commendation certificates.

All the evidence collected by Inspector Sunil Darekar was handed over to the Hyderabad police. As with any investigation, there was a lot of documentation work involved. The gang's preparation for the break-in until its execution, their trips to Hyderabad and back to Mumbai were all traced. The previous criminal records of the accused were obtained from different police stations and attached to the case papers. Sub-inspector Patil contacted Vinod's mobile network operator. Their report showed his location in and around Hyderabad from 6 to 16 May 2006 – the day of the burglary. It was a good piece of evidence and was also included in the case papers. But nothing speaks more forcefully than recovered property.

The trial finally took place in Hyderabad; Inspector Darekar went twice to provide evidence in court, explaining the minute details of the case to the magistrate. His team's detection and recovery of the jewellery was highly appreciated, while the main accused Vinod Rambali Singh and his accomplice Ajay Jawahar Singh were convicted and sentenced by the court for three years. In my opinion, these short sentences often encourage professional criminals to commit more such burglaries. It is a travesty of the criminal justice system. As a society, we must take a firm approach towards habitual criminals, whose surveillance and regular monitoring is not a violation of their human rights but essential for our community's safety.

25

EXTORTION CALLS AND TWO-AND-A-HALF ARRESTS

'If we don't tell strange stories, when something strange happens, we won't believe it.'

– SHANNON HALE

'I will teach you a lesson,' he threatened.

The officers of X project who mount and maintain electronic surveillance on the movements, activities and tactics of gangsters had been reporting an alarming increase in extortion calls in Mumbai. Many experts of the city's crime branch put their heads together to try and study the pattern. After a few days of comprehensive analysis, they concluded that most of the extortion calls originated from Kolkata and could be the work of the Chhota Rajan gang.

A team of experienced officers was rushed to Kolkata to trace the suspected caller, Vicky Malhotra. Vicky was affiliated to Chhota Rajan's gang. He had a powerful voice, quite similar to that of Abu Salem from Dawood Ibrahim's D-Company. He too had become proficient in making threats and coercive calls. Most builders and businessmen, when threatened, do not approach the police and pay up quietly. This has encouraged criminal gangs to continue extorting them.

We soon started reaching out to the people who had been receiving these threats, assuring them that we were working on tracing the callers. While surveilling Vicky Malhotra's phone within our legal limits, we noticed a strange phenomenon. He was frequently heard talking very respectfully with an unknown person, whom he would call 'sir'. We could not identify this 'sir', even though the crime branch officers can identify the voices of most gangsters. This intrigued us further.

The officers deployed in Kolkata stayed there for more than a week, following the leads that the X project team would provide, but returned without being able to apprehend Vicky. While mobile tower locations often help us reach criminals, we could not succeed in this case.

After a few days, Vicky was located in New Delhi. He was still making chilling threats and calls to the rich and powerful of Mumbai – all from his own mobile. This time, officers identified another voice as that of Farid Tanasha, who belonged to the same gang. They had become a real menace. Realizing the seriousness of these threatening calls, I advised the DCP to proceed to Delhi along with his team and arrest both the gangsters. A detailed plan was put in place as officers were going out of Maharashtra with members of one of the most dangerous criminal gangs as our targets.

But the DCP missed his flight for reasons unknown at the time. However, Inspector Patil and other officers went ahead on the same flight and gave me a call upon reaching the capital. During all sensitive operations, we follow the strict procedure of keeping our seniors informed. Since his DCP was not available, Patil was in direct touch with me to seek instructions. Immediately on arrival, his team had located Vicky in an upscale hotel in Lutyens' Delhi but did not feel comfortable accosting him there. I understood their unease. The operation was very delicate, and this crime branch team was not familiar with Delhi.

Patil, using his mobile, informed me that Vicky Malhotra was in the hotel lounge, in the company of another man. Both were busy conversing and looked relaxed. In the meantime, he and the crime branch team ordered soft drinks for themselves, sitting at a distance and observing the duo discreetly. The inspector discussed and weighed all the options with his team and decided to apprehend Vicky after he left the hotel. Calling me again, he filled me in about the atmosphere in the lounge and his decision to wait and watch. By then, we had come to know that the DCP had boarded the next flight to Delhi.

After about half an hour, Inspector Patil informed me in an urgent voice that Vicky and his 'friend' had left the hotel in their car, and he was following them in his vehicle with the intention of arresting them en route.

A dramatic chase ensued. Within minutes, Patil's vehicle had overtaken Vicky's car and stopped it in its tracks. The inspector got out, introduced himself and declared that the two men were under arrest.

Suddenly I received another agitated call from Patil, who said that Vicky's partner was urging him to let them go immediately and had introduced himself as a former director of the Intelligence Bureau. Surprised, I instantly called up Mumbai's intelligence bureau chief to check if any retired director was carrying out a secret operation in Delhi. He had no such information. But Vicky's partner continued to insist that he was in fact an ex-IB director. The next time Patil called me, it was because this person was keen to talk to me. Wondering how to verify his identity, I asked him to name his batchmates from the IPS in Maharashtra as well as their last postings. He did so with full accuracy. It struck me that he might be an IPS officer and even a former IB chief, as he claimed. On his part, he told me with impatience and offence in his tone that it was me who was lying about being the joint commissioner of police, as he knew of no woman in that role. Taken aback, I reiterated my job title. Ignoring my reply, he asked me to advise Patil to leave the spot immediately. I refused point-blank. I had flown the team all the way from Mumbai to arrest dangerous gangsters and the operation had finally succeeded. How could I ask my officers to leave after making what was an extremely important arrest – that too on the verbal instructions of a person claiming to be a former IB director. It was unimaginable and unacceptable, and I told him so very clearly. Outraged, he shot back that he would teach me a lesson, to which I replied with equal terseness that I would teach *him* a lesson. No one had ever talked to me like this.

As I discussed the next course of action with Inspector Patil, TV channels in my office broke the news that a former chief of IB had been caught with a gangster. I learnt from Patil that while we were talking, the person had rung up the Delhi police control room from his mobile, introduced himself as a former IB director and asked for a PCR van to be sent to him urgently. While dispatching the vehicle, it seemed the control room had mentioned the identity of the caller to the PCR van on the wireless network. Maybe it was to ensure that help would reach the spot immediately. The information got leaked and started circulating on television.

The Delhi PCR van brought Patil, his team, Vicky Malhotra and the supposed ex-IB officer to the police station. The DCP of

Mumbai's crime branch reached around the same time. As the issue was being sorted out, I told my crime branch team that they should proceed to apprehend the other gangster, Farid Tanasha. The X-project officers were confident that Farid was complicit with Vicky Malhotra in making those threat calls. He had also been located in Delhi, but at a different spot. I was afraid that he might learn of Vicky's arrest on news channels and run away. I was very clear that, having come this far, we could not allow Tanasha to escape.

Leaving the DCP at the police station, Patil immediately proceeded with his team towards their next target. Driving on Delhi's unfamiliar roads was proving to be quite challenging and they knew they were racing against time. Tanasha was a dreaded criminal with many violent crimes to his name. But the officers were confident they would apprehend him. They were certainly the best of Mumbai's crime branch. Reaching the suspected location, the team checked the surroundings and conducted a dry recce. The area was bustling with normal daily activities. As they were neither in police uniforms nor in a police vehicle, their movements raised no eyebrows. Quietly the team surrounded the area. Patil selected one of the shortest officers, who had a small frame, to knock on the apartment door. The moment the door opened, the team rushed in and apprehended Tanasha, who was spending time with his second wife. He had not watched the news yet and was blissfully ignorant of Vicky Malhotra's arrest. I felt such relief on being informed of the smooth apprehension.

By then, higher-ups in the government seemed to have approached senior officers of the Maharashtra Police. The presence of a former IB chief during the Mumbai crime branch's Delhi operation was denied. We were thrilled about the arrest of

Vicky and Farid Tanasha, who had gone berserk making extortion calls to industrialists, builders and Mumbai's rich and mighty. It was never our intention to confront or expose any other agency. While some newspapers reported the incident, the former chief of IB denied his presence at the scene and claimed that he was at home watching a match on TV.[1]

A senior officer later told me that the former chief had initially thought that they'd been waylaid by a rival gang. But when Patil introduced himself as a police officer, he mistook the inspector for a member of the Delhi Police. This explained why he had assumed I was lying about being the joint commissioner of police – the JCP (Crime) in Delhi was a man. We had also solved the mystery of the person whom Vicky Malhotra had been addressing as 'sir'.

Had the former IB chief not called for a Delhi PCR van, the incident would not have made for a 'breaking news' piece or even an interesting media story. There are many operations and counter-operations mounted by different police organizations and sometimes we unknowingly clash, as we had in this case. This one, however, became highly controversial[2] and the media speculated about it for some time.[3]

Years later, a former home secretary of the Government of India gave an interview alluding that the Mumbai Police had deliberately botched up a plan which involved Chhota Rajan gang members being trained by a former IB chief to carry out the execution of Dawood Ibrahim in the Middle East. Nothing could be further from the truth. It was simply a case of the Mumbai crime branch chasing a gang that was wreaking havoc making threats and extortion calls. Some officers were pained at the insinuations being made about their integrity, but our conscience has always been clear.

In fact, while planning the Delhi operation, at one point I had thought of informing Neeraj Kumar, my former boss at the CBI and seeking the help of ACP R. Singh through him. A member of the Delhi crime branch, Singh was an officer with a great network of informants, but I held back in view of the secrecy of the operation. Later I found out that Vicky and Tanasha had in all probability been working as Singh's informants. This is the way gangsters operate: they get close to one organization, supplying the authorities with 'convenient' information while creating terror in other places, as they did in Mumbai in this instance.

Eventually, Vicky Malhotra was convicted in the extortion case. Farid Tanasha, while on bail, was gunned down in broad daylight in his bedroom in Mumbai. Since the overworked DCP could not make it to Delhi in time, the post of another DCP-level officer – DCP Detection-1 – was created at the crime branch in Mumbai. Inspector Patil retired as ACP and is now happily busy farming.

The former chief of IB, Ajit Doval, went on to become National Security Advisor.

Remember what Lord Byron said? 'For truth is always strange; stranger than fiction.'

26

THE TRUTH TRIUMPHS

'Never say "no", never say "I cannot", for you are infinite. All the power is within you. You can do anything.'

– SWAMI VIVEKANANDA

Once again, my phone wouldn't stop ringing and messages kept pouring in incessantly. It was the morning of 14 April 2011. I was the commissioner of police in Pune. Sitting in the lush green lawn outside the commissioner's bungalow, I was thankful that a painful chapter in my career had ended and I had been vindicated, albeit four years down the line.

From 2004 to 2007, as Joint Commissioner of the crime division in Mumbai, my team and I had mounted several operations against organized crime gangs. Since our policy had been to go in for documentation and evidence-based processes, our fight was relatively slow and long-drawn-out. However, the Mumbai of the late nineties and early 2000s had become enamoured of 'police encounters', thanks to our trigger-happy, at times irresponsible, officers. Some of them would bump off gangsters at the behest of rival gangs or people with vested interests. Many such officers had fallen prey like Midas, the legendary king of Phrygia, known for his foolishness and greed. They were being exploited by mercenary politicians and cunning real estate developers for settling personal scores, resolving ugly disputes and making quick money.

Wild and reckless, a few of these sharp shooters would share information about 'impending encounters' with their favourite journalists, who would faithfully record their daring action, bringing these officers immense publicity. Bollywood was equally besotted with these fake daredevils, churning out gangster movies and helping officers win unwarranted laurels in the process. Since my team had put a stop to unjustified false encounters, not only were some officers unhappy, but so were certain journalists, as they had gained fame by reporting about these 'encounter specialists'.

These men had had begun to enjoy lavish lifestyles no different from those of Bollywood stars. They had lost touch with professional police work, which involved collecting evidence, seeking forensic opinion, documenting relevant material and attending courts for successful prosecution. Many of them believed that trials dragged on for years and 'encounters' were therefore an apt method for keeping the dreadfully dangerous criminal gangs of Mumbai in check. Most citizens supported the officers in those days and many continue to do so even today.

It is true that criminal trials take a long time and the conviction rate in India is indeed poor. At the Mumbai crime branch, we would often have debates on the subject. More than 90 per cent of the officers supported evidence-based policing. But we had become unpopular with the 'famous' ones as well as a very significant chunk of the media, in particular some crime reporters who had tasted blood.

As we were trudging along, looking for information about criminal gangs, we came across a serious case of extortion by Haseena Parkar, the sister of the notorious gangster Dawood Ibrahim Kaskar. Of course we pursued it but no one dared to lodge a formal complaint against her, such is the fear of Dawood. To their credit, the crime branch officers managed to secure a formal complaint and an FIR of extortion was eventually lodged against Haseena.

As soon as she came to know of it, Haseena absconded. We immediately fanned out teams to trace and arrest her, even as we gathered evidence with which to pin her down. We also put her phone number under electronic surveillance, following due procedure.

One day, the officer heading the electronic surveillance unit entered my office wearing an expression of both amusement and distress. He made me listen to an intercepted call wherein Haseena Parkar was advising her friends to organize a 'special namaz for ousting Meera Borwankar'. 'We must get her transferred,' was her instruction. It showed her desperation.

I too was at my wits' end. We had formed special squads to nab her and they were pursuing Haseena with help from their informants and checking all possible hideouts. The case had been widely reported in the media. I was aware that I was spending a disproportionate amount of my own time on it. But I also knew that cracking just one such case could send a strong message to organized crime gangs in general. Haseena Parkar's extortion case therefore became my priority.

While in the thick of investigation, on the morning of 17 May 2007 I opened the *Times of India* to find a front-page report with my photo and the headline 'Top Cop to be shunted'.[1] It had been authored by S. Balakrishnan, giving an impression that I had deliberately been going slow on the arrest of Haseena Parkar. And then, on page three, the same news was carried under the headline 'Failure to nab Haseena, Meeran pays'. A similar news piece appeared in *Mumbai Mirror*, a sister publication of the *Times*. The reporter was C. Unnikrishnan.[2]

Appalled, I wrote to the newspapers the same day, requesting that they demand an explanation from their correspondents for their 'highly objectionable, defamatory and derogatory' reporting. I also requested that clarification be published the next day on the front pages of both newspapers. The *Times of India* did publish my comments with my photo the following day, but it was on the third rather than the front page. At the end it stated, 'Our correspondent S. Balakrishnan says that he stands by the report.'

I also approached the Press Council of India and was informed that I could either pursue action by the council or lodge a criminal case of defamation. I decided on the latter. Many officers counselled me not to lodge a case against the most powerful media house of the country, but it was a question of my honour and credibility.

The state home minister R. R. Patil had, in the interim, rubbished the news report, clarifying that the government was happy with my performance and there was no move to shift me out of the crime branch. He called me up to advise me against reacting to the apocryphal new item. Like others, he was also of the opinion that the publishing house was too mighty and influential to be taken on by an officer.

Nonetheless, I persisted and lodged two defamation cases

against the *Times of India* and *Mumbai Mirror* under sections 499 and 500 of the Indian Penal Code. I knew the road ahead would be rough but I was prepared for it. Though I had nothing personal against the media houses, I wanted to flag the concern that unethical and irresponsible reporting demoralizes officers. Most honest officers do not have the resources to take on the almighty media and thus suffer in silence – this is not in the interest of the community and the nation.

In July 2007, I was posted to the Pune branch of the CID, as I wanted to be with my family. Over the next four years I travelled from Pune to Mumbai to attend each and every case hearing in the court of the city's additional chief metropolitan magistrate. I would wait for hours outside the overcrowded courtroom for the case to be called out – standing there not as an officer but as a complainant. And my resolve remained absolutely firm throughout. On many occasions, police officers attending hearings at the Esplanade courts in south Mumbai would recognize me and wonder what I was doing standing outside the courtroom. A few times the court staff offered me a bench to sit on, but almost always I suffered a gruelling wait. A number of magistrates, court clerks and staff were transferred in those four years and I faced many embarrassing moments as the case plodded along. It was the tough training I had undergone at the Hyderabad police academy that helped me withstand those testing times and all accompanying humiliations.

I am told that the home minister was approached to authenticate the news item against me, but he refused. The correspondents are said to have visited offices of the director general of police and Home Department Mantralaya, but no one provided any information against me with regards to Haseena Parkar's case.

The criminal case proceeded at a snail's pace. In my complaints I had cited the publisher, editors and correspondents of the two newspapers as the accused. During the hearings, the magistrates would ask them to attend court, but many sought exemptions from personal presence. I would invariably turn up for every hearing. Advocate Raja Thakare, now a senior counsel at Bombay High Court, stood by me through my travails, representing me and arguing my case pro bono.

Realizing that I was quite serious about pursuing my complaint and that no government or police officer was backing their news reports about my 'going slow on the arrest of Haseena Bano', the newspapers approached me and Raja Thakare for a compromise. My only condition was that both publications should apologize on the front page of their newspapers, and publish my photo alongside. I also stipulated that I would myself draft the apology.

After dithering for about six months, both newspapers published the following apology:

> An article was published in the *Times of India/Mumbai Mirror*, by S. Balakrishnan/C. Unnikrishnan, along with the photograph of Meeran Chadha Borwankar, under the title, 'Top Cop to be shunted/Borwankar wanted to go slow on Haseena.' We realise that her reputation has been damaged due to the publication of the said article which was based on erroneous inputs from sources. We apologise for the agony caused to Meeran Chadha Borwankar.

It was on 14 April 2011 that my phone began to ring without pause. That was the day front-page apology had been issued, leading to innumerable congratulatory calls and messages, even from those who had exhorted me not to lodge defamation cases, assuming I would be fighting a lost battle. As I felt relieved and vindicated, I also wondered if it was an 'erroneous input' or an attempt by organized crime syndicates to dislodge me. Or was it our own 'encounter specialists', who had sponsored the damaging front-page articles in the city's most prominent papers? Could it be that the print media bored of evidence-based policing was looking for some action? Perhaps it was a joint effort carried out by organized crime gangs, unscrupulous journalists and greedy police officers working in tandem? After all, it is not often that a baseless and highly damaging news item about a police officer appears in two prominent newspapers on the same day!

It was Mahatma Gandhi's words that had kept me going through the years that followed: 'When I despair, I remember that all through history, the way of truth and love has always won. There have been tyrants and murderers and for a time they seem invincible, but in the end, they always fall ... think of it, always.'

27

STALKING

> Stalking is 'the crime of following and watching somebody over a long period of time in a way that is annoying or frightening'.
>
> – *OXFORD ENGLISH DICTIONARY*

All through my three years at the Mumbai crime branch, I had kept aside an hour for walk-in visitors, a practice I had started at the beginning of my career. I gained a lot during these free and frank interactions with citizens. Many times, sensitive and important information was passed on to me over the course of these sessions.

A woman of about thirty years approached me one day during this open hour, and later started visiting my office regularly. The crime branch staff, fed up with her after some time, would not allow her to meet me. My office being on the first floor, she would be sent away from the ground floor itself. The officers had realized that there was something amiss with her, though she pretended to be well educated and adjusted. She wore Western clothes and spoke English, often claiming that she drove a Honda car.

After my transfer to the Pune branch of the CID in 2007, she became bolder and started sending me amorous messages, love letters and ringing me up on my landline and mobile. I notified my personal assistant, who stopped putting her calls through to me. I also blocked her number on my mobile.

Then one day she travelled from Mumbai to visit me in my office with a bouquet of flowers. I was shocked at her audacity and asked her to stop harassing me. The Pune CID's control room was instructed to prevent her from entering the office premises. But she continued to send her love letters, some of which included amorous poems, and would call me from different numbers after I blocked her original one. She also started ringing up my friends and family. We would often wonder how she had accessed their contact details. This prolonged nuisance disturbed us enormously, my younger son in particular, as he was appearing for his board exams that year.

One evening I reached home to find her having tea with my mother. She had falsely claimed to be my friend. Aghast, it struck me that she could indeed be very dangerous. So, I called the local police station and they sent their staff to my residence. Though she tried to run away, the woman was caught and produced before a magistrate. The local station's officer-on-duty found in her bag a number of poems and love letters addressed to me and produced them before the magistrate. On learning that the woman had been harassing a senior police officer for over a year, the magistrate directed that she be made to undergo a medical check-up at the local government hospital.

After two days' observation, the doctor found her to be suffering from a psychiatric disorder and opined that she required further evaluation and treatment at the psychiatric hospital. He had noted that her speech was irrational and illogical; she also occasionally threatened to commit suicide. The magistrate thus referred her to the mental health institute in Yerawada, Pune.

I had not followed the case ever since she'd been picked by the local police station, but was later told that she had run away from the institute. For some time, she stopped sending me her love letters, poems and messages and I heaved a sigh of relief.

But my peace was short-lived, as she, Asha Shamandas Bajaj, filed a criminal writ petition No. 1353 of 2008[1] against me and seven others in the Bombay High Court. She sought the quashing of the court's order of 16 June 2008, which contained the magistrate's recommendation that she be treated at the Yerawada mental hospital. She also falsely claimed that she was interested in marrying my son, and went on to insist that I had called the local police as I did not approve of her wish. It boggled my mind that after sending me more than a hundred romantic missives, she claimed that she was in fact interested in my son, who was about twenty years younger than her in age!

The advocate general Ravi Kadam, appearing for me at Bombay High Court, produced some of the amorous letters and messages that I had attached with my affidavit. He pointed out that I was a victim of this female stalker who, owing to her psychiatric condition, was causing me and my family enormous distress.

The high court bench, consisting of Justices Bilal Nazki and A. A. Kumbhakoni, mentioned that 'The letters and the SMSs which have been placed on record by respondent No.1 [me], if are true, could have been a reason for anybody to feel harassed and embarrassed ... We agree with the learned Advocate General that if a person is continuously harassed by SMSs and letters of the nature of which the petitioner was allegedly writing to respondent No.1, there should be some law against such behavior.'

And yet the court indicted me in the following words: 'If respondent No.1 had any grievance, she could have taken recourse to law and petitioner No.1 could have been booked for the offences she might have committed. But the course taken by respondent No.1 was absolutely wrong and was not expected of an Officer of the cadre of respondent No.1.'

It shocked me to see this remark from the judges, as I had not done anything wrong or unlawful, having only followed due procedure. I thus decided to approach the Supreme Court with all the material sent to me by the stalker. With the help of Advocate Ravindra K. Adsure, I filed special leave petition No. 000155/2009 on 10 January 2009. In the moments my family and I experienced extreme stress, Advocate Adsure was a beacon of hope, readily taking on full responsibility for the petition that involved a great deal of documentation and typing work. I had never met him earlier and was deeply moved by his timely help.

I also approached senior counsels Harish Salve and Uday Lalit (who later became the Chief Justice of India) and showed them the numerous messages and letters I had received from the woman. Both of them agreed to take up my case pro bono. Filing the SLP meant making a number of visits to Delhi and seeking leave from office. Preparing documents, briefing the counsels – often late into the evening – and waiting indefinitely outside the courtroom had once again become my fate.

The bench, comprising Justices D. K. Jain and H.L. Dattu, which heard the matter over the course of a few months, finally passed their order on 11 September 2009:

> Aggrieved by certain observations by the High Court of Judicature at Bombay in para 11 of its order dated 22nd October, 2008 made in Crl. Writ Petition No.1353 of 2008, the petitioner,

> a Senior Indian Police Service Officer of the Maharashtra Cadre has preferred this special leave petition.
>
> We have heard Mr. U.U. Lalit, learned senior counsel appearing on behalf of the Petitioner and respondent No.1, who appears in person.
>
> Having carefully gone through the said order in light of the material on record, including the SMS messages, we are of the considered opinion that the observations made by the High Court on the conduct of the petitioner, particularly in Para 11 of its order were clearly uncalled for ... We feel that having observed that the letters and the SMSs placed on record, if true, could have been a reason for anybody to feel harassed and embarrassed, the High Court should have refrained from making adverse comments on the conduct of the petitioner for allegedly misusing her official position.
>
> Accordingly, we direct that all observations in the impugned order, particularly in Para 11 thereof, in regard to the conduct of the petitioner shall stand expunged. The special leave petition stands disposed of accordingly.[2]

My stalker had also filed a special leave petition in 2009. But thankfully the court dismissed it with remarks at the same time they cleared my name: 'We do not find any ground to interfere with the impugned order. The special leave petition is dismissed.'

This hugely troubling and strange case of stalking by a woman tested my patience to its limits. My family also went through a harrowing time as the episode, lasting more than a year, had made many embarrassing headlines in Pune and Mumbai newspapers. The stalker still sends me messages and letters, but the frequency is now much less. Thank God for small mercies!

28

'DISOBEDIENCE'

'Above all, be the heroine of your life, not the victim.'

– NORA EPHRON

My mother was repeatedly advising me to return to duty. It had been more than eight months. Initially I had taken leave to undergo a surgery and then prolonged it based on my doctor's suggestion. Later, as I would mention in my leave application, I kept extending my time away due to a 'sensitive' reason. Ma was very apprehensive that I would get so used to staying at home that I wouldn't ever feel like returning to work again. She marshalled my siblings who, in their own ways, exhorted me to rejoin my duty. I did not.

Let me explain why. I had joined the CID after completing my stint as joint commissioner in Mumbai. As the inspector general I was supposed to lead the State Crime Record Bureau. Since I had a keen interest in computerized systems, I was interested to learn the bureau's processes. The post came with the additional responsibility of being ex-officio secretary of the Centre for Police Research in Pune. Having nearly completed my doctorate in organizational management, I could appreciate the need for research on police-related subjects and issues. So I started my new assignments with full enthusiasm.

For some strange reason, my boss at the CID would keep telling me that I had been entrusted the crime branch thanks to the then home minister, not because the Mumbai commissioner of police had sought my services. It was grating, but I learnt to ignore his comments. The crime branch was now in the past; I wanted to fully focus on the CID. I had very fond memories of my earlier tenure there, from 1993 to 1996, and had specifically requested a Pune posting so that I could live with my family.

I settled down happily in the office, especially as my old stenographer Vaidya was around and many officers from my earlier stint had welcomed me back with open hearts. The peons Bhosle and Mrs Deshmukh were ever-smiling and beating frothy cups of coffee for me once again. In this pleasing atmosphere, I began to review my units' performance when one day the boss called. His office was about a kilometre away from our CID headquarters in Sangam Bridge.

He started holding meetings with me, which I thought would extend well beyond a reasonable length of time. Therefore, whenever he asked to discuss a file, I would bring the dealing officer along. After some brief deliberations, he would dismiss the officer, offer me tea and continue with what felt to me like a waste of time. Around this time, he made two remarks about my looks, which I felt were objectionable. I decided to mention it to a senior lady officer and zeroed in on the one heading the committee against sexual harassment at Mantralaya in Mumbai. She listened to me patiently and said that she would support me in whatever action I resolved to take. The third time my boss made a similar comment, I told him sternly that I did not appreciate these remarks and he should desist from such behaviour. He turned red in the face and apologized to me. It must be mentioned that he is married to a working wife – a well-qualified professional.

The next day I reached the office to find my personal assistant in an agitated state, waiting for me impatiently. She informed me that the boss had withdrawn all my powers as Inspector General the previous evening – that is after I had confronted him. I was stunned. The news travelled fast and reached a senior officer visiting Pune that day. He rang me up and enquired about 'sacking of the powers of IG SCRB'. Since we were on great terms, I shared with him the reasons why my powers had been curtailed. He heard me without making a comment. The following day he called me up and asked, 'Meeranji, is what you told me yesterday true?' The question stung me hard. I used to think that this officer knew me well and here he was feeling unsure about something I had told him in complete confidence – a far cry from the support the lady officer at Mantralaya had shown me.

Determined to reclaim my powers, I embarked on a path of struggle. Two director generals of police tried to help me but in vain, as my boss had by then portrayed me as a 'disobedient' officer. I have always been known to hold strong views and thus it wasn't difficult to depict me as someone who didn't listen to her seniors. It was a very painful period for me but the officers and staff at the CID, probably unaware of the real reason behind the dispute between two seniors, supported me throughout.

Meanwhile, things were cheery on the home front as all four of us – me, my husband and our two children – were now together. We had just moved to a new home my husband had recently purchased. I had an uncanny feeling that soon my sons would move away, especially the elder one, who was now twenty-two and working. Having undergone a surgery in Mumbai and tired of the boss's daily memos and general pettiness, I decided to extend my leave. The DG's office soon began to ask why the inspector general was not reporting back to work. I never talked about it, but am sure that some officers had come to know of the cause behind it. After all, in every leave-extension request to the DG, I would invariably use the words 'sensitive reason'. No one asked me what it was exactly. I have observed that whenever such an episode occurs, good, honest officers suddenly become nervous around the victimized women officers, while the vile ones keep going about their business shamelessly.

A few months down the line, while I was still on leave, the home secretary rang me up to say that they were considering me for the post of Commissioner of Police in Pune. I was thrilled – but then a long period of silence ensued. So, to make the most of my free time, I busied myself with writing my first book, *Leaves of Life*, and enrolled in a local law college. I divided my day into three parts: in the early hours I read newspapers and browsed the internet, then I wrote my book, before dedicating some hours studying for my law degree. In between, I would make endless cups of tea for my elder son, a software engineer, who often worked from home. Even my family wasn't aware why I had been repeatedly extending my leave.

But like my mother, I too was beginning to feel restless and impatient. Nearly three months after the home secretary's phone call, I decided to meet the home minister R. R. Patil – it had started feeling as if the department had forgotten about me. I sought a formal appointment with Mr Patil, who received me warmly in his office, offered me tea and discussed general affairs – until I asked him specifically where he was planning to post me once I returned to duty. Somewhat vaguely he said, 'Who knows – maybe you will become the Pune commissioner of police ...' I was speechless.

After a minute's silence as the minister asked, 'But why have you been extending your leave?' I looked straight into his eyes and said, 'I do not want to work with an officer who tells me that I look beautiful when I'm angry.' Mr Patil went silent – he was visibly uncomfortable. I saluted him and walked out.

The next evening, the state CID control room informed me that they had received a wireless message from Mumbai ordering me to take over as the commissioner of police in Pune. The officer at the other end sounded excited. This would make me the first woman police commissioner in Pune *and* Maharashtra. My happiness knew no bounds. Ma was very relieved that the story was ending on a happy note. As expected, my boss at the CID wrote my annual appraisal in red letters, devoting an entire paragraph to my 'undisciplined conduct'. But the DG changed the phrasing to 'outstanding'. We never discussed why he had upgraded me in the appraisal document, nor did he ever ask me about the reasons behind my extended leave.

I may have fought my battle quietly, but there are many other ways to handle such situations. If I had brought everything out in the open and taken more senior officers into confidence, submitted my complaint in writing, perhaps my suffering would have been less.

Interestingly, six years later, a journalist asked me if I had ever faced sexual harassment at the workplace. In reply, I confirmed that I had in fact experienced it as an inspector general. The next morning, on the front page of the newspaper I read these words: '[E]ven Borwankar admits facing sexual harassment when young.' It had come as a surprise to the young reporter that even a fiftysomething woman police officer could be sexually harassed by a colleague.

29

NEW COMMISSIONER IN PUNE

'A leader is best when people barely know he exists, when his work is done, his aim fulfilled, they will say: we did it ourselves.'

– LAO TZU

The first time a woman became Commissioner of Police in Maharashtra was in the year 2010. As expected, there was great rejoicement among the public, especially women since another male bastion had been scaled. My first month at the job was therefore spent responding to enthusiastic felicitations from Punekars and giving them audience. I was relieved to have returned to work after a nearly year-long leave and did not mind the balance of life tilting more towards my chosen profession.

The eighth-largest metropolis in India, Pune is the cultural capital of Maharashtra and also known as the 'Queen of the Deccan'. It has a growing industrial hinterland, replete with information technology, engineering and automotive companies.[1] The city is famous for cultural activities, classical music recitals, a vibrant theatre and literary scene. Besides being recognized as a seat of learning – some call it the 'Oxford of the East' – Pune has made a definitive mark on the world of sports too. During the Covid-19 pandemic, it gained further international recognition as the local Serum Institute of India produced and exported the much sought-after AstraZeneca 'Covishield' vaccine.

After completing the initial formalities of taking over as Commissioner, I started visiting all the police stations in Pune. Having lived there and worked at the local CID headquarters, I was well aware of the crime situation, but I thought it was important for me to be properly visible to the Pune police team. I believe that a leader has to be present and approachable to those she claims to lead. During my police station visits, we would hold regular meetings with the staff as well as local citizens in order to listen to their views on policing.

Often, I felt disappointed by the quality of police investigation I observed during these visits. A few times I even left the police stations in anguish. While CBI and Mumbai crime branch officers had time to pursue cases assiduously and without interruptions, police officers in Pune were always running around in circles attending to multifarious duties.

There were too many VIP visits, festival celebrations, agitations, protests and so on and so forth. Lethargy and corruption too had seeped in. At the same time, I appreciated the cordial citizen–police relations in the city. As with most organizations, about 20 per cent of the staff were highly motivated and efficient, another 20 per cent were shirkers, while the remaining lot preferred to sit on the fence. Our team concentrated on bringing these fence-sitters over to the mainstream motivated workforce. But I must admit that we could probably rope in only 50 per cent of the fence-sitters.

Under these circumstances, I finalized the three projects that I would undertake during my tenure. The first community police project was named 'Pune Police Vidyarathi Abhiyan'. As part of it, we offered unpaid internships to college students at all police stations. The basic aim was to familiarize students with police operations. While working on my doctorate, I had surveyed about a hundred college students and they had shown keen interest in learning how the police functioned. The additional commissoner Sanjay Lathkar and his team prepared a detailed syllabus that the student interns would have to complete. The internships were advertised on the city police website and publicized widely. Many local colleges including the management department of the University of Pune participated by sending their students to nearby police stations. The youngsters always responded enthusiastically. An intern in fact apprehended a chain snatcher in an area under the jurisdiction of the Hadapsar police station. The university's female students insisted on accompanying the Chaturshringi police officers during night rounds. These student–police collaborations yielded many interesting experiences.

After about a year of these internships and upon consultation with Dr C. M. Chitale, the head of the management department at the university, we reviewed the usefulness of the programme. Questionnaires were drafted and presented to the interns. Students of New Law College, Shri Siddhivinayak College for Women and Maharshi Karve Stree Shikshan Samstha participated in the survey. Almost 94 per cent of the students said that mutual relations between the police and the common man improve through such initiatives; 95.6 per cent stated that they no longer felt afraid of the police after their internship; 94.7 per cent said they would recommend such internship programmes to their friends.

We called the second community police initiative 'Chowki Sabalikaran', through which we intended to improve the efficacy of police chowkies. Pune is probably the only city in Maharashtra where citizens approach their chowkis to lodge FIRs. Each police station supervises the work of two or three such chowkis. Since their jurisdictions are small, the citizens and chowki police staff know one another well.

As a part of this exercise, the IndSearch Institute of Management Studies & Research was entrusted the task of training the chowki personnel in conducting meetings with citizens. The institute's faculty trained the police staff on how to draw agenda items in advance, take down meeting minutes and prepare reports of action taken. Professor Sham Wagh of the institute steered the project. After training sessions were conducted for all police chowkies in Pune, joint meetings were held to assess the implementation and impact of suggested improvements. The institute collected feedback from citizens and police officers on the usefulness of meetings and participation levels. They expressed their overall satisfaction with regards to the conduct and recording of the meetings post training sessions. Even though there were times when specified agenda items were not pursued, the faculty noted that the 'participation of citizens is more important and an encouraging factor'.

Our third project was the creation of 'Study Circles' in each police station by inviting local experts to discuss diverse topics. Many inspectors took keen interest in these sessions and reported that eminent Punekars were more than willing to share their knowledge with police officers. In my profession, people tend to get sucked into routine police work and thereby start stagnating. Study circles can help broaden our perspective and enrich us as individuals. Our endeavour therefore received a very positive response and has since been adopted by many officers.

We also revived the 'Mahila Dakshata Samitees' at all police stations in Pune. This stems from my belief that the police alone are insufficient to handle the ubiquitous issue of crimes against women and that collaboration with civil society, academicians and NGOs can improve our services.

The Mahila Dakshata Samitees in Maharashtra were constituted in the early 1980s, with local women being nominated to lead these groups and cooperate with police stations to help women victims. There were hardly any females in the police force in those days. Later on, the Maharashtra government introduced a 33 per cent reservation for women in all government departments, leading to more women joining the police. While reactivating these committees we weeded out those who were not interested in the work these groups did – many had been appointed simply on the basis of their political allegiance.

A two-day state-level conference was held to mark and celebrate twenty-five years of the 'Mahila Dakshata Samitees'. Women from far-flung corners of the state came to attend it, even though they had to fund the trips on their own as the Pune police could only make arrangements for their stay. Their sessions were highly interactive and their awareness about the latest legal amendments impressive.

I was completely focused on ensuring the conference's success until a phone call from a young woman took me by surprise. 'Madam Commissioner,' she began, 'is it a crime to have coffee in Pune late in the evening?' Feeling a bit baffled, I asked her to elaborate. Instead, she asked to see me. So, I invited her to visit my office between 4 and 5 p.m., during the one hour I used to reserve for citizen walk-ins.

The woman came along with a friend and began recounting her story. A few days back, the two of them were having coffee at a cafe near the airport when a group of boys at the adjoining table started teasing them. Initially they ignored it but when their obnoxious behaviour became unbearable, they dialled police control room, seeking help. The police operator responded promptly but asked them why they were out so late in the evening. Could they not have had coffee at home? He was arrogant and rude. The young girls were livid and decided to approach me.

Pune's police control room was on the same floor of the building as my office chamber. We had recently installed new technology that allowed us to record all our phone conversations with citizens. Since the girls had provided the exact date and time of the incident, I asked the control room officers to locate the conversation. When the recorded conversation was played to me, it became immediately clear that the police constable who had taken the call was indeed very rude. He was arguing with the girls instead of directing a nearby police vehicle to go to their aid. Without wasting any time, I transferred him out and initiated disciplinary action. Had these young women not taken the initiative to bring the control room operator's unjustified conduct to my notice, he would have continued in the same vein. Two-way communication between citizens and police is only of mutual benefit.

Though I was introducing various measures to strengthen citizen–police relations, this incident exposed the underbelly of the police as an organization. I realized that we still had miles to go.

30

A YOUNG LIFE LOST

'Violence is the last refuge of the incompetent.'

– ISAAC ASIMOV

'Why are you apologizing?' thundered the director general on the phone. That day television channels were repeatedly showing a news scroll that read: 'The Commissioner of Police (Pune) has apologized.' I realized that the DG had seen it too.

The reason I'd done it was a painful one. He listened to me, without once interrupting, and put the phone down softly. The Maharashtra director general of police at the time was the celebrated officer D. Sivanandhan.

On 20 March 2010, a young girl named Jyotsna Karbhari Bagul had approached the Chinchwad police station of the Pune commissionerate with a written complaint that her distant relative Yogesh Bachhav had been harassing her and her parents. Jyotsna was then in the third year of her computer engineering course at the D. Y. Patil College of Engineering in Akurdi. She was serious about completing her studies and pursuing a career of her choice. What better place for it than the city of Pune, one of the most progressive places in India as far as women's emancipation, education and freedom were concerned? Jyotsna was from Mulgaon in Nashik, where her father worked as a schoolteacher. She had been brought up to value education.

A smart, ambitious girl, she was totally focused on her studies, but lately Yogesh's infatuation with her had been causing her some unease. As he happened to be a distant relative, Jyotsna complained to her father who took up the issue with Yogesh's parents. He was duly warned against approaching Jyotsna and it was made clear to him that she was career-oriented rather than being interested in marriage, which Yogesh had been proposing to her.

Despite this communication, Yogesh had followed Jyotsna on a college trip to Alibag, as he was unhappy about her going out with her batchmates. Agitated by his constant stalking, she had once again complained to her parents and Yogesh was given a serious warning. But instead of gracefully accepting the circumstances, he proceeded to visit Jyotsna's parents in Nashik. An altercation ensued, with Yogesh alleging that Jyotsna's father had not only turned down his proposal of marriage but had also beaten him up. While he did not lodge a police complaint, he did not stop harassing Jyotsna either.

On 1 September, Yogesh confronted Jyotsna in Pune and proposed to her again, only to be rejected for the umpteenth time. So, he threatened her with murder and to commit suicide himself, before leaving on his motorcycle. The next day, he sent a long message to Jyotsna's father, yet again offering to marry his daughter. Turning him down, Mr Bagul notified Jyotsna of what had just transpired. And tragically, on 3 September, around 8 a.m., when Jyotsna and her friend Sadhana Godse had gone to fetch their lunchbox from a nearby eatery, Yogesh Bachhav murdered her in broad daylight.

When the case was reported to me, I felt badly shaken. What further shocked me was that Jyotsna had approached the Chinchwad police station twice, once with her father, during the period she was being harassed. They had even lodged a written complaint. It was the local police station's utter apathy and failure to call Yogesh to either warn or detain him that had led me to issue a public apology. I felt the loss of this young life so acutely that Yogesh's arrest seemed to me quite meaningless.

Jyotsna's friend Sadhana described the cold-blooded murder much later. On that fateful morning, Jyotsna was going to her college on her two-wheeler, with Sadhana riding pillion. When Sadhana got down to pick up the lunchbox, Yogesh reached the spot on his motorcycle. She saw him assaulting Jyotsna with a *koyta* – a sharp sickle. Her neck and her back were badly mauled. When Sadhana rushed to help her friend, he assaulted her too, injuring her left leg, before stabbing Jyotsna mercilessly until her body went limp and lifeless. Then he drove his weapon into his own stomach. The whole thing happened so fast that within seconds all three were lying on the ground with blood splattered everywhere. Jyotsna was most grievously injured. Passersby, including Kedar Birajdar, a friend of Sadhana's, rushed them to the hospital. Jyotsna was declared dead on arrival, while Sadhana and Yogesh slowly recovered.

The preliminary inquiry showed that two officers – an inspector and an assistant inspector – had failed to respond when Jyotsna and her father approached the police station. They were immediately transferred from the police station. A constable on duty at the time too was found negligent. He was also suspended.

The senior inspector in charge of Chinchwad police station, Mahesh Madhukar Joshi, investigated the case. Sadhana Godse's complaint was recorded while she was still in the hospital as she was both an eyewitness and a victim of assault in the case. After recording other eyewitness statements and seizing the assault weapon, Inspector Joshi filed the chargesheet against the accused in the court of the judicial magistrate in Pimpri on 4 December.

During the trial the prosecution examined eight witnesses, including Sadhana Godse, to prove the charges levelled against Yogesh. Kedar Birajdar, who carried the injured Sadhana to the hospital, was also examined. The police traced two more eyewitnesses – Sandeep Rikame and Manisha Choudhari. Inspector Joshi recorded their statements and examined them in court. These young witnesses boldly laid bare the truth before the sessions judge B. R. Patil and secured a conviction for the gruesome murder of young Jyotsna Bagul.

Yogesh Bachhav's statement of defence contained a complete fabrication: he stated that on the morning of 3 September 2010, an unknown person had assaulted Jyotsna. He and Sadhana Godse had in fact intervened and tried to help their friend. The unknown person had supposedly assaulted them too and run away. Despite these tall claims, he could not produce any witness to corroborate the facts. On 18 February 2015, Justice Patil convicted Yogesh Bachhav to life imprisonment for the murder of Jyotsna Bagul and to seven years' imprisonment for the attempt to murder Sadhana Godse. He was further convicted for his attempt to commit suicide and sentenced to six months' imprisonment.

These convictions came through nearly four and half years after the horrific event, despite the accused having been in prison. Cases wherein the accused are already in prison generally come up for trial fast. In this instance, the police had submitted the chargesheet to the court within the stipulated ninety days.

Delay in trials due to an immense pendency of court cases and witnesses not supporting prosecution are two major reasons for the collapse of India's criminal justice system. While the conviction in this case was ultimately heartening, one question has always haunted me: Could we have saved Jyotsna in the first place?

31

THE MINISTER

'Politics, as the word is commonly understood, are nothing but corruptions.'

– JONATHAN SWIFT

I was visiting the Lashkar police station. Having recently taken over as the commissioner of police in Pune, I was getting acquainted with the crime scenarios at different police stations and meeting the officers. On one of those days, I received a call from the divisional commissioner that the district minister had asked for me and I should see him the day after, in the morning. He emphasized that the minister was very punctual and I should arrive five minutes before the scheduled time. He also mentioned that the issue of the Yerawada police station land needed to be discussed.

After reaching my office, I picked up the relevant file and discussed it with the joint commissioner. He informed me that the additional commissioner had been attending all meetings relating to Yerawada in the divisional commissioner's office. I learnt that the land, measuring around three acres, had been auctioned and we had to hand it over to the highest bidder who would, in return, construct five hundred residential quarters for policemen in the existing police headquarters. The police station, he added, would be shifted to a nearby place. I remembered having heard of the decision and that the DG at the time had opposed it. Nevertheless, I carefully studied the facts on record in the file. They revealed that the auction had throughout been led and supervised by the divisional commissioner. It was very surprising as the land belonged to the police department.

As per schedule, I met the district minister in the divisional commissioner's office. He had a huge paper map of the area with him. He explained that the auction had been successfully concluded and I should proceed to hand over the land to the top bidder. I replied that as Yerawada had become literally the centre of Pune, the police would never get such prime land in future. And that we needed it to construct more offices as well as residential quarters for the police. I added that having recently taken over, giving police land to a private party would be perceived as the new police commissioner having sold herself out. But the minister simply overruled me and insisted that I complete the process, which he declared was over. Unhappy with his instructions, I asked him politely why my predecessor – the previous police commissioner – had not handed over the land if the auction had already concluded. I even said that the process, itself was flawed, in my opinion, and against the interest of the police department. It would just not be possible for me to relinquish such a prime piece of police land to a private party when we ourselves needed it, I told him gently but with finality.

The minister lost his cool and hurled the map at the glass table. He made many remarks against the then home minister

R. R. Patil in particular that are best not reproduced here. I saluted him and left the chamber, determined not to let my department down. Being the child of a police officer, I have very strong loyalties to my profession – and I felt them during this altercation.

Realizing that I had no intention to part with the land, the highest bidder filed a case in the Bombay High Court. He had already deposited ₹1 crore advance with the government. The price he quoted, however, was far below the market price and I knew this was a cartel. He must have greased very many palms and thus could not afford to see his 'dream castle' going down. To his bad fortune and my good luck, the CBI had in the meanwhile cited him as an accused in the 2G scam.

Around this time, someone from the office told me about a local police officer who was rather knowledgeable about land matters. I called and advised him to go through the file, study the issue and discuss it with me. Together, we came to understand the shady background to this deal. The officer prepared a date-wise chart, impressing me with his dedication as well as clarity of thought. A few months later, when the case came up for hearing at the high court, I naturally sent him to brief the public prosecutor in Mumbai. On his return to Pune, he informed me that the prosecutor was unhappy about the conflicting stands of the home department and the commissioner of police. While the representative from the home department had no objection to handing over the land, having accepted one crore as advance, the inspector, as the representative of the Pune police commissioner, would not let it happen. The prosecutor suggested that the matter should be internally sorted out by the commissioner and the home secretary. I therefore wrote a very strong letter to the home department against the so-called auction of police land and followed it up with equally strong reminders to nullify the whole 'deal'.

So, the home minister Mr Patil called a meeting of all concerned, wherein I pointed out that giving away police land, even if some kind of dubious procedure had been followed, would not be in the interest of the department. Though the home secretary initially defended the auction, he later agreed that the police should retain use of the land. Mr Patil, who had twice earlier advised me not to oppose the transfer of land, seemed very unhappy with my assertive stand at the meeting. In spite of this, at the end of the discussion, it was decided that we would not exchange the land for the police quarters the builder had promised to build at the Shivaji Nagar police headquarters.

Emerging from the meeting at Mantralaya, I had a feeling that I had ruffled some powerful feathers. Mr Patil had always supported my transparent policies, but this time he seemed to have his hands tied as the 'district minister' was undoubtedly more mighty. In fact, a senior police officer told me, 'No one, neither the officers nor the media, dares say no to "dada".'

I think this tendency to be yes-men has destroyed the civil services and is one of the main reasons for our country's poor governance and rampant corruption. Civil servants taking a firm stand has become as much of a rarity as politicians' ability to appreciate different viewpoints. And there is a definite scam in handing over precious government land to private players, with huge kickbacks to politicians and bureaucrats.

After some months, when riots broke out in the Bibwewadi area of Pune, the district minister took his sweet revenge by giving a short TV interview in which he mentioned that 'something will have to be done about the police commissioner'. I immediately rang up the DG, K. Subramaniam, and suggested that I proceed on leave or be transferred elsewhere. He pacified me, saying that the minister was not in charge of the home department and I should not get let his remarks disturb me. Half an hour later, the chief minister rang me up and repeated what the DG had already told me.

I soon sought an appointment with the district minister. At the government guest house in Pune, I asked him about the comment he had made on Marathi TV channels. Imagine my surprise when he denied it squarely and with a straight face!

In June 2012, I received a phone call from the chief minister's office, asking if I had any preference for my next posting. I mentioned that the post of the additional director general at CID Pune was going to be vacant and I could be considered for it as I had worked there as superintendent and inspector general. A few days later, the chief minister himself called me and said, 'I cannot post you at the CID. "They" have made it a prestige point and we have to abide by coalition dharma. If you want to continue in Pune for family reasons, please identify any other post.' I of course understood who 'they' were. Some officers told me that many cases against powerful builders under the Urban Land Ceiling and Regulation Act were pending investigation with the CID, as a result of which 'you would never be posted there'.

At senior levels, there are not many posts outside Mumbai. I was wondering what to do next when the CM's office gave me a call again to ask if I would accept the position of the chief of Maharashtra prisons, which has its headquarters in Pune. I readily agreed, little realizing the challenges that were in store.

I had only heard that 'the future is unknown and so is your potential'. Never thought it would prove true for me.

32

BEHIND THE POLITICAL CURTAIN

'Ma'am, we want to see you as the Mumbai police commissioner,' pleaded the additional commissioner of police. He was trying to persuade me to not insist on registering a criminal case against two powerful politicians who had been caught planning violent activities in Pune. It was 28 December 2010 and the case was against a member of legislative council, Neelam Gorhe, and Shiv Sena leader Uddhav Thackeray's personal assistant, Milind Narvekar.

Earlier, on 23 December, the Pune Municipal Corporation had passed a resolution to remove the statue of Dadoji Konddeo, a Brahmin, from Pune's Lal Mahal,[1] the childhood home of the Maratha warrior Chhatrapati Shivaji. Dadoji is said to be Shivaji's guru. But a section of Marathas believe it to be a falsehood concocted by Brahmins for self-glorification. The Sambhaji Brigade, an offshoot of the Maratha Seva Sang, had been agitating on the issue for some time.

The mayor of Pune had decided to form a committee of historians to unearth the facts, but this was not acceptable to many in power within the municipal corporation. They remained adamant about removing the statue. An intense caste controversy was now brewing in Pune, as protest marches and counter-agitations intensified. Party workers from the BJP, Shiv Sena and some other Hindu outfits started gathering at Lal Mahal every night and voiced their opposition to the resolution proposed by the Maratha-dominated Congress–NCP. Pune was veritably on the boil.

Sensing that the agitation could turn violent, the corporation moved the statue to one of its municipal gardens during an early morning operation on 27 December. The opposition, in particular the Shiv Sena, strongly objected to this and took out a procession from Lal Mahal to the municipal office. Some of the agitators took to violence, ransacking and vandalizing a few corporation offices, including that of the mayor. Some of them threw the mayor's chair out on the street.[2] The opposition parties then called for a Pune bandh on 28 December. Markets, offices, educational institutions and other establishments were urged to remain closed, with only essential services such as hospitals or fire brigade exempt from the bandh.

The special branch of the Pune police was sending regular alerts to local police stations and briefing me as well. As the bandh could lead to mass violence, we were monitoring the events with great vigilance. It distressed me to think that instead of working for the well-being of Pune's citizens, these political parties were diverting their attention from the plethora of potholes, water scarcity and various grave environmental issues and focusing on the past over meaningless matters. Having put in about thirty years of service, I also knew that for most politicians, personal wealth and not citizen welfare had top priority. But as the commissioner of police, I was responsible for maintaining peace in the city, so I put my personal distress aside and decided to concentrate on my professional calling.

At the meeting of deputy commissioners organized to take stock of the situation, I found the special branch DCP particularly perturbed. His job was to collect intelligence, and he didn't mince his words as he warned us about imminent violence. The same evening, he once again reviewed the law-and-order situation in the city and, in consultation with the joint commissioner, sought my permission to put certain phone numbers under surveillance. I received his formal letter seeking authorization late that evening.

Monitoring phones is a very sensitive task, and we do so only when there is considerable intelligence with regards to violence, serious crime, terrorist activity and so on. I consented only after assuring myself that both the DCP and the joint commissioner had applied their minds in recommending phone numbers for observation. As per procedure the commissioner of police has been authorized to do so for three days. I thus allowed the same, i.e., phone tapping of numbers anticipated to incite violence.

Early in the morning of 28 December, I donned my uniform and left on a patrol along with my escort vehicle. In my experience, if senior officers go out patrolling, the juniors come out with equal enthusiasm. Our uniformed presence dominates the scene, demoralizing mischief-makers. The police wireless network also alerts all police stations that senior officers are out and about, which tends to have a salutary effect.

I was crossing the Deccan area of Pune city when I received a call from the DCP of the special branch; he requested me to come to the head office. He was a highly seasoned officer, and I knew that he would not call me unless it was very important.

I immediately asked my driver Jadhav to reverse the car and we headed to the police headquarters in no time, with our surprised escort vehicle trying its best to keep up as we zipped ahead. On my arrival, the DCP asked me to listen to a phone conversation tapped the previous night at 23:56 p.m. (27 December 2010) where two Shiv Sena leaders could be heard planning road blockages, burning of buses and trucks, violence and stone-throwing in particular areas.

It was a very cold morning, but I could feel the blood rushing through my veins. Such ruthlessly planned violence with no thought to the possible loss of lives! I could hear the DCP warning the officers on his walkie-talkie about the likelihood of violence in areas he had identified through the interception of this phone conversation. Additional personnel had already been rushed to those areas and zonal DCPs had also been asked to proceed to those spots immediately.

The police are known to be at their best during emergencies and I felt it in that moment. The control room officer had taken over seamlessly, ordering the movement of special squads and directing senior officers based on information provided by the special branch. Though we could not prevent stray incidents of aggression, attacks on buses and stone-pelting, we were certainly able to save the precious lives of our citizens.

After handling the situation on the ground, late in the evening we sat down in my office for a thorough analysis of the conversation between the two political leaders. The city was quiet and the shops had slowly started opening. Police stations were registering criminal cases in connection with violence reported in areas under their jurisdiction. For my part, I sought the registration of a criminal case against Neelam Gorhe and Milind Narvekar. It seemed to me that the conspiracy hatched during the phone conversation we had tapped was the main source of all the vandalism that had taken place in the city. This is when it came as a rude shock to me that the officers were reluctant to register the case. It was the first time in my career that I felt my instructions were not being followed. And it was around this time that the additional commissioner said he would like to see me become the Mumbai commissioner of police. He was suggesting that registering a case against two powerful politicians could be harmful for my career. He was the same officer who had boldly organized the late-night relocation of Dadoji Konddeo's statue.

I decided to send the joint commissioner to the Bund Garden police station to ensure the registration of a criminal conspiracy case CR NO. 512 u/s 153, 120 r/w 34 of the Indian Penal Code against Gorhe and Narvekar. It created quite a sensation in the city and the media got busy relaying this 'unbelievable' news. People indeed found it hard to believe that all-powerful politicians could be booked in a criminal case.

Aware of the case's sensitivity, I instructed my competent staff officer Inspector S. M. Nadgauda to take over the investigation and moved the government for appointing a special prosecutor. It is very rare for a senior officer's staff officer to be asked to investigate a criminal case. But I felt that the situation called for it. I then approached eminent lawyers in Pune to take up the prosecution. But none agreed, making me realize the challenges the case would face in the future. I thought of Jadhavrao, my special prosecutor in the Jalgaon sex scandal cases. Age was now against him, so I turned to the advocate P. S. Suryavanshi, a bold, competent and straightforward lawyer whom Jadhavrao sir trusted completely. Inviting him to my office, I was pleasantly surprised when he agreed to take over the assignment as a special prosecutor. I knew that Advocate Suryavanshi and Inspector Nadgauda would make a formidable team and the case was in safe hands.

However, I had underestimated the clever politicians. Getting bail almost immediately, the duo virtually stonewalled the investigation. The investigating officer wanted to collect their voice samples and compare them with the recorded conversation available with Pune police's special branch. These comparisons are conducted by forensic laboratories, who then give their opinion to the investigating officers. Inspector Nadgauda was following standard procedure but the duo refused to provide the voice samples.

Thankfully, the judicial magistrate wouldn't accept their refusal. In his detailed order dated 23 February 2011, he pronounced that the police's request for voice samples was justified. After this, Gorhe and Narvekar appealed to the session court to have the order dismissed, but it was their appeal that got thrown out on 7 January 2012. The courts well understood and appreciated the concerns of the police in this highly sensitive case. Even the Bombay High Court, which the accused had approached, denied their petition No. 371/2012.[3] The court, in its order dated 28 March 2012, clearly mentioned that taking voice sample does not violate Article 21 of the constitution. The investigating officer, in the meanwhile, chargesheeted the case on 11 March 2011. The Supreme Court therefore held that the issue of the voice samples could be taken up 'during the trial and that will be decided by the court in accordance with Law'.[4] The recent Criminal Procedure (Identification) Bill, 2022, passed by the Parliament now formally authorizes investigating agencies to seek voice samples of accused during the course of investigation.

By a stroke of 'good fortune' for the two accused in our case, the BJP, in alliance with the Shiv Sena, came to power through the Maharashtra state assembly election in 2014. There were immediate efforts to scuttle the criminal case trial vide S.C.C.NO.5394/2011, *State vs. Nilam Gorhe etc.*, pending against Gorhe and Narvekar. The government sent a letter to the special prosecutor to withdraw the case as per section 321 of the Criminal Procedure Code. But the court did not agree to it and made strong comments in response:

> Government Resolution is in respect of agitations by social organizations, political parties where offences are registered for breach of prohibitory orders. Present case is registered for offence punishable under section 153, 120(b) of IPC i.e., criminal conspiracy for wantonly giving provocation with intent to cause riot. This case is based upon telephonic conversation to provoke riot. This is not offence of breach of prohibitory orders ... So also this case is not against Ganesh Mandal volunteers. It seems that committee has misconstrued facts of this case ... there is misconception of facts at committee level.

Faced with the 2 November 2015 court order passed by the judicial magistrate S. R. Nimse against the case's withdrawal, the government first cancelled the approval for the appointment of the special prosecutor P. S. Suryavanshi. This was followed by another letter recommending the withdrawal of the case.

In October 2017, Gorhe and Narvekar finally succeeded in getting the criminal case (S.C.C.NO.5394/2011) withdrawn. The judicial magistrate P. T. Gotey passed his order on 26 October 2017, accepting the application made by the Maharashtra government's law and judiciary department through the district government pleader. It said: '... the second application for seeking withdrawal is not barred ... it is related to political and social agitations. So also, the policy decision is taken by the Government to have social harmony in the society.' How ironic to find social harmony mentioned in a court order approving the withdrawal of a case that in fact had created disharmony in Pune!

With the BJP–Shiv Sena in power, many criminal cases involving their party workers were subsequently withdrawn. When in power, other political parties do very much the same, encouraging their members to indulge in violence, vandalize public and private properties, burn buses and railway bogies, knowing that cases against them will be quietly withdrawn. Citizens are either unaware or mute spectators to the play of section 321 of the Criminal Procedure Code, which empowers a prosecutor to withdraw cases with the court's consent. Prosecutors generally obey the orders of the government, that is to say, the political party in power. The judiciary, in many cases, takes a firm stand, but some magistrates and judges regrettably have feet of clay.

All the facts of this case are now before you, my readers. It is for you to consider and decide whether certain politicians are our friends or foes, and to note how violence is regularly and carefully planned in our country, with scant respect for the lives of innocent citizens.

33

PRISONS AND A CELEBRITY

'It is said that no one truly knows a nation until one has been inside its jails. A nation should not be judged by how it treats its highest citizens, but its lowest ones.'

– NELSON MANDELA

Stepping down as Commissioner of Police to become the chief of the Maharashtra state prisons department was not easy for me. It took me some time to adjust. Just before my new job began, a police officer who had worked with me twice earlier gave me a call. He was quite agitated about my decision. Knowing that he was my well-wisher, I listened to him patiently and explained that the chief minister of Maharashtra had wanted to appoint me as the chief of the CID, but it was not acceptable to his coalition partners. The officer did not argue further.

Soon after starting in my new role, I realized that the prisons in Maharashtra suffered great neglect. My predecessor, the earlier chief of prisons, had become very controversial. He had been suspended from service by the Maharashtra government on various charges, including those of corruption. I also noticed that the prison officers had high hopes from me and were looking for positive energy and fresh initiatives. This helped me emerge from my own low phase.

I noticed that the department did not even have its own website, while every district police in the state proudly displayed one. I also felt that technology could help prison administration immensely. We therefore created an E-cell with young, technology-friendly officers who would not only train grassroots-level prison officers but be responsible for computerization with help of Goa Electronics Ltd, a public-sector enterprise. We also approached Rajesh Agarwal of the Maharashtra Directorate of Information Technology and started collaborating with his team to bring state prisons on par with other departments.

I started touring and interacting with the administrative staff, officers and prison inmates at the fifty state prisons. The general impression that prisoners are dangerous is not true. Personally, I have never felt scared or threatened by the presence of any criminal. I cannot explain why.

Most convicts – about 30 per cent of the prison population – gradually reconcile to their fate. They adapt to the daily routine of their prison and, over a period of time, develop a sense of community within the high walls. Morning prayers, kitchen work, carpentry, leather work, masonry, painting, stitching, bakery, weaving and many other activities keep them busy. Looking after one another's welfare adds meaning to their lives. Since they are paid for their work, some of them even manage to send money home, while others spend it on buying daily-use items from the prison canteens. Evening prayers are enthusiastically attended before the prisoners call it a day. This is a typical day in the Maharashtra prisons.

It's a different story with undertrials. As their cases are pending in courts, they are generally restless and anticipate the day they might get bail. Some of the state's central prisons located in Pune, Aurangabad, Nashik and Nagpur are terribly overcrowded with undertrials, and Arthur Road in Mumbai is the worst. A high-security central prison was constructed and inaugurated in Taloja, Navi Mumbai, in 2008. But it takes about two and a half hours from there to the Mumbai courts, and police escorts are not readily available to accompany inmates on the journey. The issue of prisoners overcrowding continues to be a matter of graveness all over India.

I was surprised that this non-availability of police escorts had never been brought to my notice as the superintendent or commissioner, and I decided to take it up seriously. We started talking to senior police officers and seeking their intervention. In one of my presentations to the Bombay High Court, I highlighted this fact only to realize that I had offended the Maharashtra DG. It is well known that the Indian Police is understaffed and overworked, with about 20 per cent vacancies at any given time. Providing escorts to undertrials is thus not a priority; law and order and crime investigation are understandably given more importance.

In another meeting with the chief minister, I sought the same emoluments and perks for the prison staff as the state police. During the lunch break, the DG asked me if I was an 'enemy of the police'. I chose to ignore his remark as I had found the chief minister to be rather receptive. He acted very swiftly and prison officials soon got the dues we had requested.

I also proposed that more prisons and barracks should be constructed and lobbied for the early release of undertrials under section 436(A) of the CrPC. Lack of space in prisons and overcrowding pose serious health hazards to prison inmates, leading to the spread of contagious diseases, skin infections and tuberculosis. To my mind, we were violating the inmates' basic human rights. This unsalutary situation gets further compounded by the lack of even the most basic medical facilities. To my distress, I found that most politicians and their builder friends were eying prison land because of their prime locations, instead of constructing more barracks or improving prison facilities.

So, we sought government approval for declaring some of the prisons or at least some portion within them as 'open prisons' where the inmates could be in the open air, till the land and undertake other agricultural activities. Working outside the prisons' concrete confines can be a great stressbuster and therapeutic for prisoners. Soon we had ten new open prisons in the state. And agriculture officer Sanjay R. Phadtare and his team introduced modern technology and innovation in farming.

There were many dedicated officers in our team. Sunil Dhamal looked after court procedures; Umesh R. Deshmukh ensured transparent procurement while Shahu B. Darade made the E-cell hub of information technology of Maharashtra prisons.

We collaborated with Pune University, Karve Institute of Social Service and Tilak Maharashtra Vidyapeeth, accepting interns from the institutes to work at the Yerawada prison and encouraged law colleges all over the state to work in partnership with district prisons. We also involved NGOs in upskilling prisoners and introduced them to motor mechanics, electrical repairs, circuit wiring and similar work with the help of reputed companies. I found our association with 'Prayas', a field action project of the Tata Institute of Social Sciences to be most systematic and meaningful.

But, despite my best intentions, I must admit that I could not control the corruption in the department or the nuisance caused by mobiles that would get sneaked into the prisons. Often, the prison staff were complicit with the prisoners in these misdeeds. Even though hand-held metal detectors had been introduced, mobiles and other contraband would make their way in. One can gauge the degree of corruption by the fact that the then superintendent of Mumbai Central Prison (Arthur Road Jail) was arrested by the Anti-Corruption Bureau with about forty lakhs of unaccounted cash at his official residence. While corruption within the police force is an open secret, the same rot inside prisons is not as well known. Sometimes I think that we need a National Correctional Service along the lines of the Indian Police Service to deal exclusively with prisons. But then, it's not as if the IPS has been able to tame the police's corruption. In fact at times it has worsened it by its example! A truly frustrating situation.

During a part of my tenure as the chief of Maharashtra prisons, the film star Sanjay Dutt was in jail. He had first been arrested in April 1993 and was alleged to have accepted a consignment of three AK-56 rifles and related ammunition, one 9mm pistol and cartridges, as well as a batch of hand grenades, a completely illegal act. These weapons were part of a larger consignment smuggled into the country by Dawood Ibrahim Kaskar and his associates, who had planned bomb blasts in Mumbai.[1] Dutt claimed ignorance about these plans and is said to have told the investigators that he had received the guns and ammunition to protect his family after receiving threats following the post-Babri-Masjid-demolition riots in December 1992.

He had been imprisoned earlier but was released on bail as the case was pending trial. In 2006, after the trial concluded, the Terrorist and Disruptive Activities (Prevention) Act court sentenced him to six years in prison under the Arms Act. But he had been acquitted of terrorism-related charges. Dutt had appealed against the verdict, but the Supreme Court upheld his conviction in 2013. It was only then that Dutt, one of Bollywood's most prominent stars, surrendered to the remaining period of his sentence.

He was first confined at Arthur Road Jail and later shifted to Yerawada Prison in Pune. The transfer had to be kept confidential as the media was always sniffing around for Sanjay Dutt-related developments and tended to overpublicize the issue. In the past, a huge crowd of journalists had chased the official vehicle in which he was being moved to a new location. This time I tasked a senior prison officer for Dutt's transfer from Mumbai to Pune at night in order to avoid undue publicity. But this turned out to be impossible as Dutt was afraid that he would be killed in an encounter on the way! His fear was so real that he started sweating and complained of having a fever. Meanwhile, news of his move out of Arthur Road Jail was leaked and a huge crowd started to gather outside the prison gates.

So, we decided to postpone the transfer and withdrew the team that had been deployed. Dutt was counselled against making his shift to Yerawada an issue and it was impressed upon him that his apprehension about an 'encounter' was misplaced. Sometime later we were able to quietly and successfully move him and prevented the sober work of judicial custody from becoming a public farce.

Shortly after, in a bizarre development, Dutt secured a court order that allowed him to enjoy home-cooked food in prison. This facility is available to undertrials – whose cases are pending in the courts. But Dutt had now been convicted, which made it surprising that the court had given him this concession. We decided to challenge the order. Dutt was soon informed that we had initiated the process of getting the order modified. I was told that he made no fuss and took to eating what his fellow inmates ate. We did get the home food order of the court reversed. We were very clear that no special treatment should be meted out to Dutt simply because he was a celebrity. The prison superintendent and deputy inspector general would take extra care on this account. I would often carry out counter-verifications through my own sources within Yerawada Prison. Even so, all kinds of rumours about the actor enjoying 'VIP treatment' would regularly surface, making headlines in the media.

Once when newspapers started reporting that drugs were being supplied to Dutt, I decided to check the facts myself. After a scheduled visit to the Yerawada women's prison, I asked my driver Mahesh Hirwae to take the official car to the men's prison, which is located just opposite. He was taken aback but took me there nonetheless. Certain protocols need to be followed when a senior officer visits a prison; however, I decided the situation demanded otherwise. Getting out of my car, I asked the jail guards to open the main gate and hurried inside. I was in full uniform that day. While my escort officer entered our details in the register at the entrance, I headed to the small barracks where I knew Sanjay Dutt was kept. I was walking fast and the security officer and guards made long strides to catch up.

When the prison constable opened the door to the barracks, he was shocked to see me – it took him a good minute to grasp what was going on. We ran a thorough search of the barracks, checking every nook and cranny, but did not find any drug or objectionable item.

At the time, Dutt was sharing his cell with Yusuf Mohsin Nulwalla, a co-accused in the Mumbai blast of 1993. Inside, we found piles of papers and numerous books. But what surprised me the most was a huge number of *bidis* as well as high-quality cigarettes. The prison superintendent Yogesh Desai had, in the meantime, reached the barracks and told me that Dutt was a habitual smoker who regularly bought bidis from the prison canteen. Every prison inmate can buy canteen items worth a fixed amount each month. The upper limit of these purchases is revised from time to time.

I noticed that Dutt seemed rather happy to see me. He had found out from his sources that I hailed from Punjab and had studied in Fazilka – earlier a taluka, now a district. It was my turn to feel surprised and embarrassed. As he enthusiastically shared information about my background, I tried to change the subject by enquiring about the mattress in the barracks. The superintendent explained that it had been provided on the basis of formal medical advice – given in writing –as Dutt suffered from backaches. The actor said that he had been exercising regularly to keep his back in good shape. Indeed, he looked lean and healthy and had no bags under his eyes.

During his incarceration, the cine star would often interact with his fellow inmates. He had been active on the Yerawada FM programmes ever since the superintendent had introduced the radio into the prison. I was told that Dutt would hold counselling sessions on air for prisoners and was generally following all prison rules and regulations. He was also taking part in various cultural activities. He had realized that the chances of his parole, furlough and early release were dependent on his good behaviour in prison. The inmates had supposedly become fond of him and appreciated his 'therapy' sessions.

After a detailed discussion with local prison officers, it was decided that an entertainment event would be held in Pune to raise resources for a prison welfare fund. It followed the template of *Umang*, the annual show held by the Mumbai Police for their welfare fund. We knew that Dutt's presence would ensure a good citizen turnout. When Superintendent Desai mentioned the plans to him, Dutt agreed and actively involved himself in the preparations. There were many other inmates who were either talented or had experience in singing and acting. They participated with equal enthusiasm. After rehearsals for the show started in earnest, we gave exclusive broadcast rights to Doordarshan. Balgandharva Rangmandir, the most popular auditorium in Pune, was booked. The tickets sold out within a few days of the announcement.

I would ask for frequent status updates about the arrangements, as this was one of those rare events which involve bringing inmates out into the public. I watched one of the final rehearsals and was impressed with how well the show had been planned.

Serious about following due legal process, we had consulted local legal luminaries, as prison inmates are considered to be in judicial custody.

At some point during the event preparations, I realized that the Yerawada prison officers were ignoring the basic rules of prison security; they were getting carried away by their excitement. My sources within the prison informed me that the famous film director Rajkumar Hirani had been permitted inside during a rehearsal. I was indignant, and the officers tried to assuage my anger, saying that he was giving a 'professional touch' to the show.

A day before the event, I learnt from an old Mumbai crime branch informant that a group of gangsters were planning to serve breakfast to the prisoners at Balgandharva Rangmandir prior to the show. I asked a resourceful and experienced police officer from Mumbai to get the information verified. He confirmed that it was indeed correct, adding that the bulk of the tickets had been bought by either the same gang or Dutt's friends. On the other hand, the Doordarshan team, very happy with their exclusive rights, had reached Pune and recorded parts of the final rehearsal.

My informant's insistence that a criminal gang had got involved with the programme was bothering me. I had also noticed that my own prison officers were getting swayed and becoming unprofessional. After some serious thought, I decided to cancel the show at the last minute.[2]

There were requests from different quarters, including some from senior Mumbai government officers, asking me to reconsider. But with things not going according to plan and protocol, I was firmly of the opinion that the show could create serious security issues.[3] Therefore I stuck to my decision and we returned the ticket amounts to the buyers. Many people, within the prison and without, were disappointed of course.

A while later, another crime branch officer confirmed that gangsters were planning to bring the showmen breakfast, which may have contained narcotics too. Slowly but surely, life in Yerawada Prison returned to its normal pace. The enthusiasm that the show had generated withered away and the media got busy alleging favouritism in Sanjay Dutt being granted parole and furlough. We reopened the prison manual, counting and re-counting the number of 'leave' days allowed to the actor, replying to innumerable questions raised about the life of the celebrity in prison.

I wish citizens and the media, instead of being obsessed with incarcerated celebrities, would take as much interest in the working of Indian prisons and the skills that should be imparted to inmates for their rehabilitation.

34

THE HANGING

> 'The impact of terrorism, not merely on individual nations, but on humanity as a whole, is intrinsically evil, necessarily evil and wholly evil.'
>
> – BENJAMIN NETANYAHU

Two events etched in my mind and in public memory are the hangings of Ajmal Kasab and Yakub Memon. When I took over the prison department, the thought that I would one day supervise and actually witness hangings had never crossed my mind.

On taking over as the additional director general of prisons in mid-2012, I started receiving legal correspondence about the capital punishment of Mohammed Ajmal Amir Kasab, whom the Mumbai Police had captured in the early hours of 27 November 2008. He along with nine other Pakistan-trained terrorists had attacked the Chhatrapati Shivaji Terminus, the Oberoi Trident and Taj Mahal Palace hotels, Leopold Cafe, Cama Hospital and the Nariman House Jewish community centre in Mumbai on 26 November, killing 166 and injuring more than 300. The terrorists had carried out coordinated attacks across Mumbai, which lasted four days and shook India and the world.

After the police investigation was completed, Ajmal Kasab was imprisoned in Arthur Road Jail. His trial began shortly afterwards. Kasab was convicted on 3 May 2010 and sentenced to capital punishment by hanging on 6 May.

Whenever I would go to the Arthur Road prison, I would invariably visit him in his highly secure barracks. I would also do a round to assess the security provided to him by the Indo-Tibetan Border Police – the Central Armed Police Forces are more professional than state police in security-related matters. Kasab's security was indeed an extremely sensitive issue. Thus, while the outer cordon of security was the ITBP's responsibility, the inner cordon had been secured with the most efficient prison officers. I always found them alert and vigilant.

Prison staff, including the doctors, were very careful about Kasab's diet and health. He was, however, never served any 'special' dish such as biryani and the like as publicized. I was told that initially he would keep himself busy with physical exercises, but as time passed, he became quiet and impervious to what was happening around him. When I questioned him during my visits, he would either keep quiet or just smile. The prison officers, though, had many stories about his violent, aggressive behaviour when he was first brought in. It was after only a few months of his trial in court that he became subdued.

Kasab hailed from the village of Faridkot in the Okara district of Punjab, Pakistan. He and nine other members of the Lashkar-e-Taiba, an Islamist terrorist organization founded in Pakistan, are said to have been trained at a remote camp in Muzaffarabad and later at Pakistan-occupied Kashmir. Indian forces killed nine of them during the Mumbai attacks, while Kasab was the only terrorist to have been captured alive. His trial was keenly watched around the world.

After a special court convicted Kasab and sentenced him to death by hanging, his lawyers appealed first to the Bombay High Court before going to the Supreme Court. On both appeals being rejected, mercy petitions were filed with the governor of Maharashtra and subsequently with the president. In other words, despite intense public fury against Ajmal Kasab, India was following the due process of law.

Sometime in October 2012, R. R. Patil, the home minister of Maharashtra, visited Pune and called me to the circuit house. I had not seen him in a long time and was surprised at being summoned. When I entered his chamber, I noticed that he looked somewhat grim. After exchanging pleasantries, he asked me about the course of action we should take if the president turned down Kasab's mercy petition. I had not expected him to bring up this topic, so I quickly composed myself and briefed him about what I knew of the process that would follow. After a long pause, Mr Patil confided that there was reliable information that some hostile countries might interfere with the legal process and we would therefore need to take great precautions around the time of the execution. He insisted that a minimal number of officials should be involved to maintain secrecy.

The following day, I briefed the prison officials who had been tracking the various stages of Kasab's appeals and mercy petitions. The superintendent of Yerawada prison, Yogesh Desai, and Sunil Dhamal from my office seemed most knowledgeable about the goings-on. They had prepared a detailed chart of responsibilities in case we had to go ahead with the hanging. I also took up the issue with the principal secretary of the home department in Mumbai and it was decided that this particular file would be handled by select officials only, who would personally hand it over to the next officer concerned. Each point of decision-making was identified and officers briefed. We were soon informed that the president had rejected Kasab's mercy petition. The court issued a black warrant immediately thereafter.

While documentation and legal processes were being undertaken in Mumbai and Pune, we began our own preparations at Yerawada Prison. The last hanging in Maharashtra had taken place more than thirty years ago. We had to dig up old information to brush up our knowledge. The Maharashtra prison manual was dusted and each line read and re-read to ensure we would not make any procedural mistake. Superintendent Desai selected men in whom he had complete confidence to execute the death warrant. His wish to involve a few officers from outside Pune was granted, given that we were dealing with an extremely sensitive operation of national significance.

During the home minister's next visit, I was once again summoned to the circuit house. My driver Amrut Patil, an experienced and shrewd prison officer, remarked while driving me to the location, 'I think you are all finally going to hang Kasab.' I was startled by his observation but kept quiet. Seated in his chamber, the minister looked even graver than last time. His wide, round eyes reflected his feelings. I had great respect for Mr Patil, one of those rare honest ministers. He wanted the minute details of our preparations and I briefed him accordingly. Despite convincing him that we had taken utmost precautions about the mission's secrecy and due procedures, the minister seemed anxious and uneasy. His eyes reflected his discomfort more strongly than his words.

I conveyed all of this to my team. Desai, the Yerawada superintendent, was a man of experience. He assured me that he had assembled the best team possible and the execution process would not be leaked as he had shared it with only the highly trustworthy people involved. I visited Yerawada Prison thrice to keep an eye on the arrangements. Fearing that the prison staff might find my frequent unscheduled visits strange, I would drop in at the prison bakery where a new bread oven had recently been installed. I am not sure whether this was deceptive enough, but I could tell that the officers and staff were not aware of the mission. The usual routine of prison administration continued at its slow, lumbering pace.

Meanwhile, the principal secretary home department was personally taking the black warrant file to senior officials as it had to ultimately be delivered to the chief minister of Maharashtra. Once the exhausting paperwork was completed, it was re-verified at both Mumbai and Pune before we could move Kasab from Arthur Road to Yerawada, where the hanging was to take place.

I deliberately attended an official police function at the State Reserve Police Force grounds in Pune – which I knew would be well covered by the media – just to gauge if they had any inkling of the upcoming event. Reporters from both English and regional-language media houses came up to me to talk about various issues, but no one asked about Kasab. Nor did any police officer present there raise any query about him.

About thirty-six hours before D-day, an inspector general escorted Kasab from Mumbai to Pune at night in a highly fortified convoy. Full secrecy was maintained. The escort team too had been handpicked and consisted of Mumbai crime branch officials. Once they handed Kasab over to Yerawada prison officials, the escort team was quarantined in Pune's prison premises; their mobiles were confiscated. They were quite shocked, as they had expected to return to Mumbai after completing their task.

Since most of them had worked with me earlier, they expressed their strong displeasure to me, requesting that their phones be returned, as their families would get worried if they couldn't reach them. They complained about not having a change of clothes either. I had too much on my mind at the time to assuage their feelings and concerns. The mission's secrecy was paramount and I was feeling anxious.

The next day Kasab's mandatory medical examination was conducted and he was found to be fit. As per the prison manual, a medically unfit person cannot be hanged. We completed the legal formalities that included seeking the presence of a magistrate and a doctor at the execution to be carried out the following morning. There were only about ten of us who were aware that Kasab had been brought from Mumbai to Yerawada Prison in Pune. While the atmosphere in the prison was normal, its daily routine proceeding uninterrupted, we were very much on edge. It was one of the most stressful moments of my career, no doubt – not because of the actual operation but the state government's demand that all information was to remain confidential.

That night, however, a Mumbai reporter got wind that Kasab had been shifted from Arthur Road to Yerawada. In order to verify this, he rang a senior Mumbai police officer, who told the reporter that he was not aware of any such transfer. But the man persisted and called up Mr Patil, who also denied any knowledge. Both of them alerted me immediately. When the same reporter called me, in the coolest possible manner, I told him that his source was wrong.

But the reporter's call had unsettled me. We had come this far and now barely ten hours before the hanging, the information seemed to have leaked out. Taking Ajmal Kasab out of the Indo-Tibetan Border Police's custody, driving him from Mumbai to

Pune and assuming that no one would talk about it to an outsider was probably too much to expect, I thought to myself.

I had originally decided to go to Yerawada Prison at midnight on 20 November. The court had scheduled the hanging for the early morning of 21 November 2012. But after receiving those phone calls, I decided to leave for Yerawada immediately. It was around 9 p.m. and that part of Pune is quite lively around this time. I was apprehensive that my car with its amber beacon would attract undue attention. So I asked my security officer if he would let me ride pillion to Yerawada on his motor cycle. The officer was most perplexed, but I guess he had no choice but to agree!

I wore my official blazer over the uniform, picked up my laptop and we sped towards Yerawada Prison. My aim was to hide my uniform and my identity. Reaching the main gate, I took off the blazer, introduced myself to the man in-charge, who opened the gate with some surprise. As soon as I reached the superintendent's office, I turned on my laptop looked on the internet for any information about Kasab. There was none. Highly relieved, I sat back and took stock of the day's events and our preparations for the execution.

After completing more legal formalities, the next morning, Ajmal Kasab was brought out from his barracks. The magistrate, medical officer, DIG and Yerawada superintendent were present along with a small group of carefully selected staff. The atmosphere was very grim. None of us had ever witnessed a hanging and were feeling quite apprehensive. Having lost a lot of weight, Kasab looked like a child terrorist, in total contrast to his demeanour on the day he had recklessly fired his automatic weapon at civilians at the Chhatrapati Shivaji Terminus on 26 November 2008. Now here he was, finally paying for his unforgivable cruel deeds.

At the dong of the clock, Kasab was hanged. All of us standing around were too numb, after days of gruelling work, to even notice our reaction. Our silence was profound. Not even a bird chirped on that early morning of 21 November 2012.

Kasab was buried and his last rites were conducted solemnly, as per his religion. It was an austere ceremony, performed with respect and courtesy.

I sent a message to R. R. Patil from my mobile, informing him of the execution. It was then that he broke the news to the media, and the world woke up to justice having finally been served to a heinous terrorist.

Feeling completely spent, I walked out of Yerawada prison and suddenly the thought of the Mumbai crime branch team I had quarantined the day before crossed my mind. I asked my driver Patil to take me to their barracks, bracing myself to face their wrath. To my utter surprise, they came out grinning, with ACP Ramesh Mahale at the helm. He was the chief investigator of the 26/11 terrorist attacks. Even though he and his team had escorted Kasab from Arthur Road to Yerawada, they had no idea that his execution was so imminent. The news had just reached them. They felt proud of having played a crucial role in the execution of a terrorist responsible for the death of 166 innocent citizens.

Completing this secret and sensitive mission while following due process was a remarkable feat on the part of Maharashtra prison department. The teamwork and coordination displayed by various divisions of state and the central government were exemplary. A painful chapter in the history of Mumbai and indeed the nation had been successfully closed. At last.

35

MY TWO EYES

> 'We live in a time of terror ... the real goal of terror is not to kill people but to kill thought; to so demoralize a society that it implodes from within.'
>
> – JOHN LAHR

One of the jails I visited as the chief of Maharashtra prisons was Nagpur Central Prison. There I had met Yakub Memon, the serial bomb blast convict who had been sentenced to death. His various appeals were pending at different levels and my office had been diligently keeping track of them. Yakub always looked fit and energetic to me. He was a chartered accountant by profession. While in Nagpur Jail, he had enrolled himself for an MA in English Literature and Political Science through the Indira Gandhi National Open University, or IGNOU. He had also been pursuing his case closely and had become quite well versed with legal procedures.

During my visits to the separate areas where death-row prisoners are kept in the Pune and Nagpur prisons, I had noticed that the atmosphere would be subdued, with the inmates having resigned themselves to their fate for the most part. While monitoring their appeals, we could not understand the many delays they suffered, and it bothered us greatly. Each file was in its own state of limbo: there would be appeals with the high courts and Supreme Court, mercy petitions with the governor, the President of India, curative petitions waiting to be listed and so on. A desk at my office would routinely correspond with different agencies and had succeeded in concluding only Ajmal Kasab's case.

Then one fine day we received Yakub Memon's death warrant. He was the brother of Tiger Memon, one of the prime accused in the 1993 Mumbai blasts of 12 March 1993. On that 'Black Friday', between 1:29 p.m. and 3:40 p.m., twelve well-planned simultaneous blasts were carried out at Bombay Stock Exchange, the Air India building, Hotel Sea Rock, Hotel Centaur Juhu, Zaveri Bazaar, Katha Bazaar and Century Bazaar. They were masterminded by the known criminal Dawood Ibrahim, with Tiger Memon and Yakub Memon, among others playing accomplice, allegedly to avenge the December 1992 demolition of Babri Masjid. As many as 257 citizens lost their lives and more than a thousand were injured in the blasts.

During the trial, the special court convicted Yakub Memon under the TADA and IPC on 27 July 2007. Since all avenues of appeal and mercy had been exhausted by 2015, the news of Yakub's death warrant made headlines in the media. It was in complete contrast to the secrecy surrounding the execution of Ajmal Kasab in 2012.

The Maharashtra chief minister, who was also responsible for the home department, took a meeting in Mumbai and reviewed the preparations for Memon's hanging. Being new to the job, he had many officers in attendance, some of whom had nothing to do with the process. They simply wanted to be in the new CM's good books and showed a kind of enthusiasm that seemed to me rather unprofessional. After the meeting, a few officers hung around giving suggestions to the chief minister that contradicted the decisions taken in the meeting that had just concluded. This is the dark underbelly of the civil services – one finds so many bending backwards to please their political bosses. The CM had never held any ministerial portfolios earlier and the rush to impress him was glaring.

Meanwhile, the Nagpur prison officials got busy with making the necessary arrangements. They discussed the legal procedure with Yogesh Desai and his team who had earlier executed Kasab. Since there was no need for secrecy this time, I felt less anxious, but moved from Pune to Nagpur nevertheless.

Once again, we went through the legal steps involved and refreshed our knowledge. The process of hanging is very sensitive and delicate. Preparing for it was time-consuming and exhausting. I wondered how officers were handling the pressure but decided against discussing it as everyone seemed preoccupied. After taking stock of the situation, we decided to commission the same team that had executed Kasab.

Yakub's friends and family rallied around him and filed another curative petition in the Supreme Court. They met me in Nagpur Jail and requested that they be allowed to pursue the petition. 'Of course,' I replied and assured them that we would not take any hasty step. As execution is the culmination of years of legal process, I had no intention of committing any procedural mistake at this advanced stage. A senior police officer called and advised me 'to finish it off for once and all'. The government machinery seemed tired, especially as the terrorist attack had taken place in 1993 and we were yet to see any closure in 2015. There is no doubt that in India we stretch our due procedures so much that they sometimes become meaningless.

While supervising the arrangements for the execution, I visited the high-security area inside the Nagpur prison, where Yakub had been shifted. During my earlier visits, I had always found lots of books and files in his cell. It was bare this time. The atmosphere was quiet and grim. I asked him if he had written his will. He said that he had. Previously, he had lamented to me that he had never held his daughter in his arms. I remembered our conversation that day and hoped that he had willed in favour of her as well as his wife. Had he done so, I asked him. 'Ma'am, they are like my two eyes. Yes, indeed I have willed everything to them,' he told me with great emphasis and a smile. Yakub was aware that his family was trying to approach the Supreme Court again.

The media had gone ballistic by then over the imminent capital punishment to be meted out twenty-two years after the crime. Journalists were following our every move in Nagpur. Many of them had come from different parts of the country to cover the execution. The Nagpur Police had to impose section 144 around the jail as the prison security could not be compromised at any cost. Some journalists would tail me from the police guest house to the prison and back. So, I decided to move into the jail itself.

The stress of having to follow the exact procedure was palpable, with dummy executions being carried out within the prison premise. Despite us bringing in the old team and having the same old desk doing the paperwork, we were all tense. The night before the hanging, the DIG came to me twice as he had certain doubts about the procedure followed for the mercy petition. I decided to clarify it with the home department in Mumbai and sent them a fax. I found that the concerned desk officer and the additional chief secretary of the home department were working late and monitoring the whole process. It was midnight by then and law books were being consulted at Mantralaya to find a suitable answer to the query.

While waiting for clarification, I received a phone call from a senior police officer who asked if I had seen the news on TV. I wondered what was wrong with him when he hastened to add that the Supreme Court had initiated a midnight hearing of the curative petition filed by Yakub's family. A three-judge bench comprising Chief Justice H. L. Dattu, Justices T. S. Thakur and Anil R. Dave took cognizance of the petition. This was quite unheard of. Tired to the bone, we waited for instructions from Delhi and Mumbai. In the wee hours, Mumbai finally came back with a reply to our query. Meanwhile, the Supreme Court turned down the petition and we got a go-ahead at last.

Early in the morning on 30 July 2015, Yakub Memon walked confidently towards the noose. I could not see his face as it was covered but could sense the tension in the air. As opposed to the quietude around Kasab's execution, in Nagpur, all the prison inmates knew about Yakub's fate, yet there was an eerie silence that day. We could only hear the birds chirping.

After the magistrate and medical officer present completed their lawful duties, Yakub Abdul Razak Memon was hanged. His body was to be handed over to his family. I left the place after ensuring that legal procedures were being followed to a tee. While on the way to the jail superintendent's office, I found a senior prison official rushing towards me. In an extremely disturbed voice, he told me that there was a call from the chief minister office that the execution had been videotaped by an unknown person and it was being broadcast. I was stunned. It was unbelievable that the whole operation had been recorded. We had taken all precautions, including checking the rooftops of neighbouring buildings beforehand.

I turned back immediately. As I entered the execution space, the DIG arrived as well. He was frowning furiously and had clearly received the same information. Together, we verified each and every spot and talked to all officials involved. Though we concluded that there was no breach, we couldn't discount the faint possibility that the process had been captured through a hidden camera or mobile phone.

To our tremendous relief, we were soon informed that the news was wrong and a scene from a film about 26/11 showing Kasab's hanging had been used to mislead viewers. It featured a lady police officer (presumably based on me) supervising the hanging. This was the recording sent to the CM's office and it was wrongly assumed that Yakub Memon's hanging had been recorded. This unpleasant incident made me and my team go through some extremely stressful moments.

I found the legal process to be very taxing as well, especially the delays in capital punishments and the paperwork that the prison department has to pursue until the end. The dummy executions, not to mention the actual hangings, are extremely demanding operations. The fear that one wrong step and the judiciary would pounce on us always gnawed at us. The gravity of an execution as the finale of justice feels heavy and enormous.

While in the case of Kasab, the principal secretary of the home department was closely associated throughout, the new one at the time of Memon's hanging had proceeded on a foreign training programme. However, the additional chief secretary stepped in – this is the strength of the bureaucracy. Maharashtra prison officials too stood strong, not only completing enormous amounts of paperwork with meticulousness but also following the law to the hilt. It deserves a salute from the entire nation.

A few months after the hanging, Yakub Memon's wife sought my help to secure a passport for their daughter. I was undoubtedly taken aback but I gladly helped her. In her I met a graceful, cultured lady and a deeply caring mother. I visited the Mumbai passport office and the office of the ministry of home affairs' foreigners' division in New Delhi to ensure that the child got her legal right, which she ultimately did.

In my mind, there was never any contradiction in my two roles.

36

THE BLACK AND WHITE COATS

Injustice anywhere is a threat to justice everywhere.

– MARTIN LUTHER KING, JR.

'We can meet socially but I shall not attend meetings called by your office,' said the director of prosecution. I was taken aback. And we know that our prosecutors wear black coats in courts.

Recently promoted to the post of Director General of the legal and technical division, my assignment included supervising the prosecution wing of the state and forensic laboratories of Maharashtra. Having worked in both police and prison departments, I saw it as an excellent opportunity to work with the other two crucial wings of the criminal justice system.

I had never seen prosecution from close quarters and had a tendency to recommend the appointment of special prosecutors for sensitive cases. As police officers we appreciate that prosecutors are very important for presenting our cases in courts, but it is a division that needs more focus and strength. Though the director of prosecution did not welcome me, I tried understanding the issues plaguing the department and realized that prosecutors are as overworked as police officers. They typically run from one court to another throughout the day.

I had experienced this recently, after sanctioning a case to be prosecuted under the Maharashtra Control of Organized Crime Act as Pune Police Commissioner. While a police officer can register an FIR under the IPC, he requires a senior officer's permission for prosecuting under the stringent MCOC. This is to ensure that such an act, which can lead to severe punishments, is not misused. I was called to the court to give evidence for this particular case of organized crime in Pune. The prosecutor who soon turned up seemed ill-prepared. The special judge hearing the case twice rebuked him for wrongly quoting the number of accused involved in the crime.

In another case I was being examined in the court when defence advocate became very aggressive. The courtroom, which was empty when my cross-examination started, was soon overflowing with curious onlookers. I requested the judge to restrain the advocate, to which he quipped, 'But why is your prosecutor not objecting?'

Some prosecutors do not take the trouble to read and understand their cases. Instead of accepting their own accountability, they tend to blame witnesses for their weak memory and the police for poor quality of investigation. This is another reason for a low rate of conviction in the country.

Before Independence, prosecutors were part of the police department. In 1973, the Code of Criminal Procedure was amended and the prosecution and police were separated. There were some attempts to keep them together. But, in August 1975 in the case of *Jai Pal Singh vs the State of Uttar Pradesh*,

Justice K. Singh of the Allahabad High Court, quashed the UP government's order wherein the assistant public prosecutors were put under the administrative and disciplinary control of the superintendent of police and the inspector general.

> It is ultimately, suggested in unequivocal terms that ... there should be complete separation between them ... the officers of the Police Department who will have investigated the cases to be prosecuted in courts shall have no manner of control or influence over the prosecutors who conduct the cases in courts based on the investigations made by the Police Department.[1]

Similarly, the Supreme Court in *S.B. Shahane and Others vs the State of Maharashtra*, the bench consisting of Justices Kuldip Singh & N. Venkatachala in April 1995 upheld the separation of police and prosecution, remarking:

> In the result, we ... direct the Government of Maharashtra to constitute a separate cadre of Assistant Public Prosecutors either on district-wise basis or on state-wise basis, by creating a separate Prosecution Department for them and making the head to be appointed for such Department directly responsible to the State Government for their discipline and the conduct of all prosecutions by them before the Magistrates' courts and further free such Prosecutors fully from the administrative and disciplinary control of the Police Department or its officers ...[2]

As a result of this separation, the conviction of criminal cases has gone down drastically in Maharashtra and other states. The Malimath Committee, on the subject of criminal justice system reform, has, however, recommended bringing the prosecution and police together again.

Besides prosecutors in magistrate courts, there are public prosecutors in session courts who try serious cases like murders and dacoities. Section 24(4) of the CrPC details their appointment: 'The District Magistrate shall, in consultation with the Sessions Judge, prepare a panel of names of persons, who are, in his opinion fit to be appointed as Public Prosecutors or Additional Public Prosecutors for the district.'

Consultation with the sessions judge is mandatory, but many states have amended this section and deleted the provision that lists this requirement. As a result, these appointments are now made entirely on a political basis, and merit has suffered immensely. Officers like me thus seek special prosecutors for all our sensitive cases under section 24(8) of the CrPC: 'The Central Government or the State Government may appoint, for the purposes of any case or class of cases, a person who has been in practice as an advocate for not less than ten years as a Special Public Prosecutor.'

Special prosecutors generally perform better but are more expensive to engage. Sections 301 and 302 of the CrPC envisage victims engaging their own lawyers, but their role is very limited. In November 2019 the bench of Supreme Court Justices M. M. Shanthanagoudar and Deepak Gupta clarified that 'a victim can engage a lawyer to represent him or her in a criminal trial, but the lawyer wouldn't have the right to examine a witness or advance arguments in court'.[3]

Since the director of prosecution had strong objections to reporting to a police officer – the officer being me – I paid more attention to the other facet of my job profile, that is, forensics – the white coats of our science laboratories. To my utter amazement, like Maharashtra prisons, the Directorate of Forensic Sciences too did not have their own website, and we were at the end of 2015. I set remedying this as my first target. After a great deal of efforts and data collection, we could launch a website with the help of the Department of Information and Technology. We hoped that besides bridging the gap between citizens and forensic laboratories, it would enable active interaction between the police and the experts. Many times, police officers would be waiting for forensic reports, unaware that the expert had dispatched them by post. Now, the website could be accessed by both parties for communication; it also enabled the online dispatch of forensic opinion without compromising confidentiality.

Forensics, which the public comes face to face with during the trials of sensational cases, is a highly specialized field and citizens must take keen interest in the way it works. The Maharashtra forensic labs have various wings: Toxicology; Biology; Serology; DNA; General Analytical and Instrumentation; Prohibition and Excise; Ballistics; Physics; Cyber Forensics; Tape Authentication and Speaker Identification; and Psychology.[4]

The Toxicology, Serology, DNA and Biology wings receive the maximum number of samples from the police for forensic opinion. Ballistics, Tape Authentication and Psychology are also accessed by different investigating agencies, though not as frequently, compared to the former set.[5]

Modern-day investigation is exceedingly dependent on technology. On the other hand, witnesses can be unreliable. They may forget fine details, get confused due to the defence lawyer's tactics, can be bought over, or simply remain untraceable. Technology in the form of forensic analysis of the crime scene, as well as samples of blood, hair, sweat, wash from stomach, viscera, saliva, poison can help identify the victim as well as the accused.

Besides, the seizure of narcotics under the Narcotics Drugs and Psychotropic Substances Act, 1985, can only be proved through forensic analysis of the impounded drug.

Forensic reports are thus crucial for securing conviction and proved extremely useful in the high-profile Sheena Bora murder case in Mumbai, for example. The forensic analysis of the bones and skeletal remains found in Raigad district, where her body was allegedly dumped and burnt by her mother Indrani Mukerjea and mother's former husband Sanjeev Khanna three years before the murder came to light, helped the case move forward. Forensic examination of the bones would prove the victim's gender and age. A keenly watched case like this can collapse if the dead body recovered by police is not properly identified. Such is the importance of forensics, a wing of the criminal justice system that I feel has been callously ignored.

Once during my visit to the forensic lab in Nagpur, I found an internationally published paper by an expert pasted on the walls outside his room. When I asked about it, he told me that no one acknowledged his expertise, so he thought he would paste his article on the wall. To get a paper published in a reputed international journal is a significant achievement. But our forensic experts are unsung heroes. If we want criminals to be convicted, we must invest in the latest forensics equipment and encourage forensic experts to upgrade their skills and knowledge regularly. Establishing forensic universities, as was done in Gujarat, is a good step in this direction.

Many readers would recollect the infamous 'tandoor murder case' in New Delhi. The conviction of Sushil Sharma in this case too was based primarily on forensic evidence. Sushil had objected to his wife Naina Sahni's friendship with a man named Matloob Karim, who had been her classmate. On the night of

2 July 1995, Sushil came home and found Naina talking to Matloob on the phone. Furious, he shot Naina dead. Later he took her body to the Bagiya Bar-Be-Que restaurant in Hotel Ashok Yatri Niwas and tried to dispose of it with the help of the restaurant manager, Keshav Kumar. Together they stuffed the body in a tandoor. The police arrested Kumar but Sharma escaped. Finally, he surrendered on 10 July 1995. Forensic DNA evidence was used to establish the identity of the victim. However, Maxwell Pereira, the renowned IPS officer supervising the investigation, recently revealed that the first forensic analyst in the case 'jumped the gun' and told the media that the body had been chopped up. 'In the post-mortem report he ruled out the use of firearms and we were totally aghast, because we had already recovered the bullets. We had gone to the house, we had stumbled on the information from the accomplice and our theory of the use of firearms was being washed out,' Pereira said.[6]

Wrong forensic reports can thus damage a case, though, in this instance, a second autopsy was ordered. The investigation could prove that Naina Sahni had been shot dead and, thereafter, the accused put her body in a tandoor. However the theory that her body was chopped up before the pieces were placed in a tandoor became entrenched in people's minds as a result of the initial false impression created by faulty forensic opinion.

A chargesheet was filed in the court on 27 July 1995. After more than eight years, on 7 November 2003, Sushil Sharma was sentenced to death and Keshav Kumar given seven years' rigorous imprisonment. Sharma appealed the verdict at the Delhi High Court, which upheld the lower court's decision. On 8 October 2013, a three-judge bench of the Supreme Court upheld Sharma's conviction but commuted his death sentence to life imprisonment. This timeline shows how long it takes for an appeal to be heard in the Supreme Court – eighteen years in this case. The 'tandoor murder case' later became a landmark case with regards to the use of DNA evidence and a second autopsy to establish the guilt of the accused.[7]

The importance of forensic analysis can also be understood through this highly publicized case of narcotic seizure by the Mumbai Police. On 9 March 2015, about 112 kilograms of a substance suspected to be mephedrone (popularly known as Meow Meow) was seized from the Satara residence of police constable Dharmaraj Kalokhe, who was posted at the Marine Drive police station in Mumbai. Another approximately twelve kilos of suspected mephedrone, a small quantity of hash and a fake voter ID card were seized from his locker at the police station. Along with him, five officers of the Anti-Narcotic Cell, as well as Shashikala Patankar, a drug peddler on record, were arrested. Constable Kalokhe was later dismissed from service. However, the same year, Mumbai's Forensic Science Laboratory sent a report certifying the seized substances as monosodium glutamate, commonly known as Ajinomoto – a food additive.[8] Even so, the police sought a second forensic opinion.

When I was Director General of the legal and technical division, the experts protested against the police seeking a second opinion. I could understand the Mumbai Police's position in this case. The forensic analysis of the seized material turning out to be MSG had caused them great embarrassment. They sought the Bombay High Court's permission for carrying out a forensic analysis outside Maharashtra. Naturally, this miffed the experts at Maharashtra labs.

The Chandigarh Forensic Science Laboratory also identified the substance as MSG. With forensic laboratories all over India facing a lack of resources and manpower, the police's requests for second opinions increase their workload. The Supreme Court of India[9] has in fact taken note of this and ordered that 'any requests as to re-testing/re-sampling shall not be entertained under the NDPS Act as a matter of course. These may, however, be permitted, in extremely exceptional circumstances, for cogent reasons to be recorded by the Presiding Judge ... in the absence of any compelling circumstances, any form of re-testing/re-sampling is strictly prohibited under the NDPS Act.'

Keenly aware of the importance of forensic sciences, we commissioned joint training programmes for police, prosecutors, magistrates, medical doctors and forensic experts. Initially the Bombay High Court was reluctant to send their magistrates for training, but by personally coordinating with the registrar, we could get the judiciary on board. These joint training sessions proved very beneficial for all the wings, which they would mention to us in their feedback.

Awareness weeks, when the general public can access these laboratories to learn about forensics, have become very popular in Maharashtra. We also started internships for students who are curious about the way the labs operate. New regional forensic laboratories were started in Nanded and Kolhapur. Now most states have mobile forensic labs that can reach crime scenes at the earliest so that samples can be collected immediately and before there is a chance for them to get contaminated.

Maharashtra has three colleges where the forensic sciences are taught as a degree course. However, the basic qualification required for recruitment in government forensic laboratories was a degree in the 'pure sciences'. Graduates from these three colleges in Mumbai, Aurangabad and Nagpur could not take the exams held for government posts. After some effort, we could persuade the Maharashtra Public Service Commission to change the recruitment rules and allow students from these three institutes to compete along with pure science graduates.

My tenure as Director General was a very interesting phase in my career – one that taught me a lot. When I think of that time, I remember Albert Einstein's words: 'Commit yourself to lifelong learning. The most valuable asset you'll ever have is your mind and what you put into it.'

37

HUMAN TRAFFICKING

> 'Human trafficking is a multi-billion-dollar growth industry because, unlike drugs, which are gone as soon as they are used, humans can be recycled. Because they can continue to be exploited, they're a better investment for traffickers.'
>
> – TERRY COONAN

Human trafficking is the 'forced exploitation of individuals by those in the position to exert power over them'.[1] It destroys human lives. It affects all countries, especially poor ones like ours. According to Ruth Dearnley, 'Whether the place we live is a source, destination or transit point for trafficking, none of us can claim to be wholly unaffected by this crime.'[2]

Since I have been involved in action against trafficking from my very first posting in Nashik, I want to draw attention to young girls and women being forced to sell their bodies either through deceit or due to abject poverty. There are powerful organized gangs consisting of both men and women to whom young girls *and* boys, sell their bodies or labour. Nearly half the victims of human trafficking are under eighteen years of age.

Coming from a middle-class family, I did not have much idea about prostitution and the gravity of the issue. Prostitutes for me were 'bad women'; they were to be arrested and punished. In the 1980s, even the police did not look at them as victims. So, while conducting raids on dens of prostitutes at Nashik during my first posting in 1985, we would arrest them under section 110 of the Bombay Police Act. It was well known that they would pay their fine and return to the flesh trade again. Policemen were in any case not very comfortable conducting such raids and even more uncomfortable in my presence. I was shaken out of my complacency when, during a raid on a roadside dhaba on the Nashik–Mumbai Highway, I found a prostitute with one leg climbing into the police van on crutches after she was arrested by my team.

Slowly, NGOs, especially those working for women, started highlighting the serious issue of forced prostitution and how women were being exploited. Often dire poverty led them to flesh trade. In many cases they were pushed into it by male or female agents who would lure them by promising employment. Most were illiterate and from rural areas or small towns. Once in the trade they had no opportunity to go back as the community and family would not accept them.

In 1991 I gained some understanding of the issue when, as DCP of Preventive Crime in Mumbai, I organized a big police raid in Kamathipura, Mumbai's red-light area. A day prior to our raid, I visited it street by street, with an officer of my unit feeling very awkward all along. We were in civil clothes; I was wearing a salwar kameez. Women of all ages were standing, sitting, peeping from roofs, balconies, making all kinds of gestures to solicit customers. Kamathipura is an extremely congested low-income area, where people are constantly on the move. No one seemed to consider these women's behaviour strange. The neighbourhood shops were busy and crowded. Unperturbed, street hawkers sold sundry goods, among them fruits and vegetables.

We planned the details of our raid and sought extra help from the police commissioner. My officers were not enthusiastic and told me in clear terms that 'these women' would return to prostitution in a few days after getting bailed out. I was also told that they do not consider the police their friends. Instead, they were loyal to their '*dhandewalis*' and would not provide evidence in court against these 'bosses'. The officers' cold and staid response unnerved me as much as my youthful enthusiasm irked them for its naivety.

Ultimately, we went ahead and conducted a massive raid. Officers and policemen entered a number of identified buildings simultaneously. In one of the rooms, we were surprised to hear disparate knocks from below the floor and discovered a hidden chamber where some girls had been kept concealed. We found curtains dividing small rooms into smaller ones – beds separated like in a hospital ward, with up to ten women entertaining their clients at the same time. It was nauseating and claustrophobic to say the least.

My officers were right. Only nine out of more than two hundred women rescued wanted to go back to their families. They were hostile to me when I talked to them, encouraging them to go back. They were also blunt. Many asked, 'Where was your police when we were forced into prostitution?'; 'Do you think our families will take us back?'; 'We are regularly sending money to our families and children; please spare us your sympathy.' The nine who were willing to return were moved to the 'protection home' from where they would be sent back to their villages or towns, after their families had been informed.

Meanwhile, the Bombay High Court came across a racket wherein the same agents and 'dhandewalis' would approach the protection home staff claiming to be the parents of the rescued girls and take them into custody. Soon thereafter, the girls would again be driven into prostitution. It was thus decided that proper verification would be carried out before handing over the rescued girls to their families.

This process of verification is quite cumbersome, especially if the victim is not from Maharashtra. The police, while corresponding with their counterparts in other states, also take the help of NGOs. This NGO–police collaboration has proved to be very useful. Rescued girls are sometimes very impatient to go back to the trade and are known to have escaped from the custody of the protection homes, which most of the girls find constricting. They are generally in a disturbed and distressed state of mind. NGOs coming forward to expedite their return to their families has proved to be quite a positive contribution, though I was appalled by a few such organizations holding conferences on human trafficking in five-star hotels. It seemed farcical to me.

The issue of forced prostitution has slowly been taken up at national and international levels as 'human trafficking'. Governments everywhere have become serious about handling this menace. The United Nations started giving funds and training to police officers in India during the late nineties. Resources in the form of officers as well as offices earmarked for fighting human trafficking were provided, as were vehicles and equipment; funds for NGOs to rehabilitate rescued women began pouring in. State governments too were now matching the grants, though some states continue to be in denial about trafficking-related exploitation. The fact is that all states in India are affected by it. Sometimes the information may not reach the police, or they have other urgent priorities, like recurring public order issues and heinous crime. The role of civil society and NGOs thus becomes very crucial for information-sharing and rehabilitation of rescued victims.

During my tenure as joint commissioner of Crime in Mumbai, wiser now with age, I decided to focus on the rescue of minor girls. I had limited resources and my past experience had shown that all women do not want to be rescued, as they had either reconciled to their fate or their families were unwilling to accept them. It has been established through various field-research papers that a girl who has been removed from the environment initially thinks of the police and administration as her enemies. It takes about two weeks of counselling at protection homes for them to realize that it is the agents and dhandewalis or gharwalis who are the real enemies. After tying up with various NGOs, we began our raids and rescue operations in earnest. The commissioner started sealing brothels based on our reports. Officers and staff therefore took to rescuing minors with enthusiasm. Yet, after every conversation with these minors, I would feel depressed. Tales of cheating, fraud and poverty which forced parents to sell their daughters were so painful that I thought I would lose my mental balance. I prayed to God to give me strength to continue. I would remember William Wilberforce's words: 'You may choose to look the other way but you can never again say you did not know.'

As the police commissioner in Pune from 2010 to 2012, I once again resolved to rescue minors forced into prostitution. I had seen the Mumbai commissioner exercising his powers under section 18 of the Immoral Traffic Prevention Act in order to seal the brothels. The Pune commissioner until then had not used this power, and I decided to do so. I handpicked a team of competent police officers – Inspector Bhanupratap Barge,

H. C. Ashok Takalkar, Naik Datta Jadhav and the lady officers APIs Vimal Bidwe and Ashwini Jagptap, who are known to be sincere and dedicated. After they selected their own teams, we embarked on our mission, rescuing minors and sealing brothels as per the provisions in the act. We brought a great deal of attention in particular to Budhwar Peth, the red-light area of Pune. Many minors sent discreet messages and letters to the police teams and, acting on the information provided by them, we were able to remove the girls from brothels.

Soon lawyers started filing cases against the police's sealing and closure of brothels. They even went up to the Bombay High Court. Our teams had to present their cases in court and carry out rescue operations simultaneously. Their paperwork and documentation increased fourfold. But we persisted. Until an inspector challenged me at our monthly meeting, pointing out that the brothels we thought we had closed down had simply shifted to the suburbs. So much for our efforts!

Sometime later, a team from Bollywood approached me, wanting to know about the police action against prostitutes. I had by then been transferred to the Maharashtra prisons department. Still, I shared my experiences with them as they seemed serious about the theme and its cinematic portrayal. Busy with office work, I forgot about it until one day I was informed that the film star Rani Mukerji wanted to visit my office in Pune. My staff was very excited, but she was not happy that I had not seen her movie *Mardaani*, which she was promoting at the time.

So I went with a friend to a cinema hall, as incognito as possible, getting out of my police car some distance away from the theatre. While watching the movie, I found a guy moving around with a torch in hand, searching for someone. Arriving at my row, he exclaimed on recognizing me, 'Madam

Commissioner, this movie is based on you – I hope you are aware of that!' He was the manager of the cinema hall. I squirmed in my seat, while the viewers nearby laughed on hearing his sudden loud announcement.

The sad truth is that we have failed to make a dent in the flesh trade, as is evident from the increasing number of missing young girls in India today. One reason is that corruption has made deep inroads in governance as well as in the police force.

When I was the joint commissioner in Mumbai, we received a letter in February 2007, written originally in Hindi by an offender named R. Prakash. He had been arrested in a case of human trafficking, and his letter was addressed to the Mumbai commissioner of police:

> The police officer asked me to get ₹3 lakh transferred on the account of his friend R. Shetty, one lakh for the advocate the officer had hired for me and two lakhs for the four police officers, including himself. During the enquiry, Shetty's mobile number can be found in the officer's mobile to verify the amount I organized to be sent to him. Once I reached the prison in judicial custody, other prisoners advised me not to send any more money to police officers as the case would at any rate be charge-sheeted in ninety days. But now I have been booked under the MCOC[1]. In lock-up, I went on hunger strike and did not eat for two days. On the third day, an assistant inspector asked me why I was not eating. I started crying and told him everything. He suggested that I fight in court instead of starving. He asked why I had not explained everything to 'Borwankar Madam' when I was put before her as an MCOC accused. The API rang up the unit in-charge, as the actual unit head was on leave, and advised

him to take me to Borwankar Madam so that I could break my fast. He added that he was recording it in the diary.

But instead of taking me to the joint commissioner's office, I was taken to JJ hospital. One of the police officers met me there and told me I should organize some money; they would thereafter enable me to run away from the hospital. He assured me that there would be an enquiry for fifteen–twenty days and then everything would go into cold storage. When the SI and head constable in charge of the escort had gone to make copies of hospital papers, he gave me a phone. I used it to contact my friends and got four transfers done for ₹49,900 – one in my name and three in the names given to me by the officer.

After the money transfer, the officer told me that he would put an alcoholic staff on night duty and that I should bribe them and escape. These constables came for night shifts on 26th, 27th and 28th. They would not handcuff me at night in the hospital. On the 28th we all went to Banjara Bar and Restaurant opposite JJ hospital. We had our dinner. I called for a bottle of Misty whisky. The policemen drank it, while I had Foster's beer. Had chicken tandoori and paid the bill of ₹895. Around 11:30, they went off in a drunken stupor and I fled the hospital. By the time you receive this letter I would have run away ...

Today the situation is no better, with politicians leading the band of corruption in governance. It is only well-informed, vigilant citizens who can hold the administration accountable and make corrupt practices less attractive. Ultimately, we need a criminal justice system wherein a trial concludes within a year of the offence having taken place. Is it asking for the moon, I wonder.

I put up a struggle against human trafficking throughout my career, even though initially my own understanding of it was not too clear. I am happy that my name and position have been associated with fighting one of the gravest challenges facing us – the trafficking of vulnerable women and innocent children. The uniform is one of the most powerful tools for social change and justice. I am grateful that I got to don it and use the powers vested in it to the best of my ability.

38

WHEELS OF CHANGE

'You must be the change you wish to see in the world.'

– MAHATMA GANDHI

'Ma'am, we have done it!' exclaimed the young officer of the Indo-Tibetan Border Police (ITBP) who had accompanied me during my Ladakh tour. He was referring to a marathon one-day jeep trip we took to visit the border outposts at Lukung, Phograng and Chartse. Lukung is located 142 kilometres east of Leh and is known as the 'Gateway'. At an elevation of 4,378 metres (14,364 feet), it is awe-inspiring to the first-time visitor and quite tough for our men who keep the borders secure. Phobrang lies on the Indo–China border on the Lukung–Phobrang–Chartse road, with Chartse being at an elevation of 4,442 metres (14573.49 feet). And despite rough weather, we had covered it all in one day: talking to the men in uniform, understanding their daily challenges, admiring their grit and determination.

Little did the officer know that as the director general of the Bureau of Police Research and Development and later as DG of the National Crime Records Bureau, I was on tour across the country. I had been visiting various police organizations, training academies, prison-related institutes, central armed police forces, forensic laboratories and universities specializing in law, the criminal justice system and forensics. Both bureaus have an all-India jurisdiction.

The Bureau of Police Research and Development, popularly known as BPR&D, is the only one in the country dedicated to the study and research of issues related to the police, prisons and the Central Armed Police Forces. In fact, it studies the entire gamut of the criminal justice system and makes recommendations to the central and state governments. It also holds national workshops, seminars and conclaves. Officers are generally keen to participate in the training programmes organized by the BPR&D. It has five detective-training institutes in Jaipur, Kolkata, Hyderabad, Ghaziabad and Chandigarh and a Central Academy of Police Training in Bhopal. Its active collaboration with universities, academic institutes, law schools and NGOs has given it an edge in policy-making. *Data on Police Organizations* is the bureau's eagerly awaited premier annual publication. It profiles all state police organizations and much more.

The National Crime Records Bureau is a repository of information on crimes and criminals. It monitors, coordinates and implements the Crime and Criminal Tracking Network & Systems (CCTNS) connecting 15,000-plus police stations and 6,000 higher offices of the police in the country. It also maintains a 'National Digital Police Portal', which caters to the police and to citizens. It allows police personnel to search for criminals and suspects on the CCTNS database. Citizens can file online complaints here and seek antecedent verification of tenants, domestic workers, drivers, search for missing persons, procure no-objection certificates for the purchase of second-hand vehicles and information on proclaimed offenders. The bureau controls the Crime Multi Agency Centre or Cri-MAC and also maintains the National Database on Sexual Offenders (NDSO). It is the national repository of all fingerprints in the country and has a databank of more than one million ten-digit fingerprints of criminals – both convicted and arrested. Actively involved in training at national and international levels, the bureau is replete with state-of-the-art technology. *Crime in India,* also published by the bureau, is the only reliable and most-referenced crime data analysis report in the country.

Hundreds of training courses for the police, prisons and CAPF officers from all over India are conducted by the bureaus I was heading. They are also closely associated with the National Police Academy in Hyderabad. Visiting the North Eastern Police Academy in Shillong, the Police Academy in Punjab, the Jodhpur Police University, Rashtriya Raksha University in Gandhinagar and many other such institutes meant that I was travelling and interacting with officers from different states and learning from the faculty, students and trainees. Life was in the fast lane during my last year in the Indian Police Service.

Around this time, strangely an episode in China took me back to my childhood in Punjab and Fazilka. I had gone to China to participate in an international conference on prison administration. The Indian ambassador to China was my batchmate from the Foreign Service and I decided to say hello to him. The protocol officer was as formal as the decorum demanded. The Indian embassy itself was huge and formidable. As I entered the formal world of diplomacy, I was taken aback by the eerie silence all around. It was daunting and overwhelming. However, the ambassador's personal assistant greeted me with a broad smile, breaking down the walls of silence and exclaiming, 'Oh ma'am, I wish I had known that you are a "Chadha from Fazilka"!' He had just Googled me and was mighty pleased with his discovery. And I heaved a sigh of relief that life in the embassy could be normal after all!

Earlier during the same conference, when we were suddenly asked to explain an Indian viewpoint, our delegation turned to me for an answer. One of the delegates mentioned that such sudden interventions are best replied to in English by those who have studied in English-medium convents. After explaining the national perspective to the best of my ability, I told him that I was not a product of any convent but from a government school in Fazilka. It was a most basic institute with not even chairs or benches for its students. We sat on mats on the floor and learnt through the school years.

Another interesting incident took place on one of these visits. The faculties of our detective-training schools insisted that I meet all of them together. They were police officers of diverse ranks from different states. Their demand was simple, but I was quite surprised. Due to the detective-training school nomenclature, the faculty there thought of themselves as school teachers, which, though a venerated profession, made them feel 'inadequate'. I promised to look into it and took up the issue with the home secretary in Delhi. A highly professional and well-travelled officer, he laughed the request off, saying that Harvard too has a 'business school', besides medicine and law 'schools' and there was no need to change the name of our training institutes. When I conveyed this to the faculty, they were disappointed, pointing out that Indian and American cultures were different. No matter which detective school I visited, I heard the same complaint.

In the meanwhile, we were moving the Ghaziabad detective-training school to a new and impressive building. The then home minister of India Rajnath Singh had agreed to inaugurate it. While presenting the invitation card to him personally, I requested if he could kindly declare it detective-training 'institute' instead of a 'school'. I explained the demand of the faculty and staff and their logic behind it. Mr Singh listened to me patiently and responded with a smile, 'I will declare not only this one an institute but the other "schools" too.' I was pleasantly surprised but kept his decision to myself, not sure if it would be implemented as the home secretary had turned it down earlier.

The inaugural function started in full solemnity. I was holding my breath when the chief guest stood up to deliver his speech. Mr Singh did remember his promise and, with a flourish, declared that all BPR&D detective-training schools would henceforth be called detective-training institutes. The loud applause his announcement received from the audience was deafening.

It is indeed said that names or titles don't mean much, but if a particular title hurts the self-esteem of an organization, there is no harm in considering a change. Change, however, is not all that easy. Management programmes often dedicate a full course on change management. Many bestselling books have been written on this subject alone. An experience I underwent bears the same testimony as well.

I was sitting alone in a huge building on an impressive modern campus that had been constructed for both the bureaus. The new campus is in the Mahipalpur area of southwest Delhi, on the border with Gurgaon. The structure – imposing and inspiring – with a well-laid-out green belt around had been under construction for some eight years. Being used to the old office on Delhi's Lodhi Road, the bureau officers and staff were reluctant to shift to the new place which was not well connected by bus or metro at that time. They would come up with innumerable excuses and keep stalling the move on one pretext or the other. I had been trying to persuade them, while also persisting with the National Building Construction Corporation Ltd. to complete construction of the campus. After about ten months of following up and numerous meetings, I concluded that the situation demanded an autocratic and perhaps an unpopular action on my part. After giving a month's advance notice and specifying a move date, I shifted to the new campus alone, despite requests by senior officers to defer it further. The lady inspector general of the Training division, Sundari Nanda, however, was the only officer who openly and strongly supported my action. According to her, moving to the beautiful, modern campus would improve the image of the BPR&D, besides being very good for the officers' and staff's self-esteem.

Working alone in the magnificent new premises for nearly a month, I suddenly found that the NBCC had speeded up the final touches to the campus. The embarrassment caused by my sitting alone had worked like a potent weapon. The bureau officers and staff started trickling in. The first to move was of course the lady IPS officer, her entire department in tow, who brought along three truck-loads of training material!

By the time we took up the task of decorating the BPR&D lounge and the officers' mess, our enthusiasm had become infectious. Everyone chipped in and worked beyond office hours, picking up decor items, wall clocks, carpets and paintings. Despite the government policy against serving liquor, a beautiful bar was created by an officer who said, 'Nothing stops us from having soft drinks in style.' The librarian worked overtime in order to discard old books and thoughtfully stack the new ones. The gardener whom I had warned against his continuous absence from the Lodhi Road office purchased new plants and flowers for the campus. Each staff member was provided with a green indoor plant which they nurtured with great care. The canteen staff, already famous for their delicious food, started serving the dishes with panache, which was refreshing for a government set-up.

By the time I left the bureaus, the collective resistance to shift had turned into an immeasurable enthusiasm to make it the best campus in Delhi. It was my turn now to veer them back to our core mission of conducting research and training. And to make the Crime and Criminal Tracking Network & Systems truly operational. The pride with which they would show our new campus to the visiting academicians and national and international police officers demonstrates that success lies in having your team with you. I certainly had mine, albeit after a few initial hiccups and the usual resistance to change.

And then the wheels came to a stop. One knows about retirement and its precise date at the time of joining the service. Yet it is hard to accept when the day finally arrives. I had been winding up over the last few months and had released my first book *Leaves of Life* just in time. It was most heartening to see the response of the youth for whom I had penned it.

The teams of the Bureau of Police Research and Development and the National Crime Records Bureau bid me farewell from the Indian Police Service on 30 September 2017, as I completed thirty-six years of uniformed service.

As Maya Angelou would say:

> My mission in life has not been
> ... merely to survive but to thrive
> and to do so with some passion,
> some compassion, some humor
> and some style.

I had it all and I dare say enjoyed every minute of my career. There is no competition to the uniform when it comes to passion, compassion, humour and style: passion for living life to the fullest, compassion towards citizens, humour as a constant through even the most difficult investigations, and the uniform itself, which, in all that it encompasses, is the greatest style statement one can ever make.

NOTES

2. Ganeshi

1. physical training

5. The Tough Police Training

1. First Report of National Police Commission (1977), I.1.2.

6. New Learnings in Nashik

1. District Nashik, Government of Maharashtra. https://nashik.gov.in/about-district/ (accessed 9 May 2020 and 21 April 2022).

7. Mom-Cop

1. District Kolhapur, Government of Maharashtra. https://kolhapur.gov.in/en/about-district/ (accessed 10 and 11 May 2020).

8. The Long Road to Justice

1. *Rajendra Gandhi vs State Of Maharashtra And Shrikant Yeshwant Deshpande,* No. 1856 (Bombay High Court, 14 October 1988).
2. https://indiankanoon.org/docfragment/1029589/?formInput=reporter%20%20%20%20filter%3A%20%20%20%20editors%20defamation%20civil%20suits
3. *Rajendra Gandhi vs State of Maharashtra and Another,* Sessions Case No. 6 (Bombay high Court, 17 October 1988).
4. Upendra Baxi, "The 'Ultimate Violation of Self': Reflections on Judicial Discourse on Attempted Rape," Eastern Book Company,

India. https://www.ebc-india.com/lawyer/articles/98v6a1.htm (accessed 27 May 2020 and 15 June 2022).

5. https://main.sci.gov.in/jonew/judis/13789.pdf.
6. Baxi, Upendra, "The 'Ultimate Violation of Self' : Reflections on Judicial Discourse on Attempted Rape," Eastern Book Company, India. https://www.ebc-india.com/lawyer/articles/98v6a1.htm (accessed 27 May 2020 and 15 June 2022).

9. Bombay Port Thefts

1. https://mumbaiport.gov.in/writereaddata/linkimages/7268201644.pdf (accessed 5 and 7 August 2021).

13. The BDD Chawl Riot

1. "History of B.D.D. Chawls", *MeMumbai* (blog), 25 December 2018. https://memumbai.com/bdd-chawls/.

14. The First Woman District Police Chief of Maharashtra

1. District Aurangabad, Government of Maharashtra. https://aurangabad.gov.in/history/ (accessed 11 April 2020).

16. The Jalgaon Sex Scandal

1. District Jalgaon, Government of Maharashtra. https://jalgaon.gov.in/history/ (accessed 12 May 2020).
2. "Banana republic Jalgaon bears fruit," *Indian Express,* 18 June 2004.
3. Lekha Rattanani, "Role of influential men in blackmail and forced sex rocks Jalgaon in Maharashtra, " *India Today,* 31 July 1994. https://www.indiatoday.in/magazine/special-report/story/19940731-role-of-influential-men-in-blackmail-and-forced-sex-rocks-jalgaon-in-maharashtra-809457-1994-07-31.
4. "Reference to Advisory Boards," National Security Act, 1980.
5. Lekha Rattanani, "Probe in Jalgaon's sex scandal case gathers pace, 35 arrested," *India Today,* 15 August 1994. https://www.indiatoday.in/magazine/indiascope/story/19940815-probe-in-jalgaons-sex-scandal-case-gathers-pace-35-arrested-809537-1994-08-15.

6. CR No.73/1994 registered in Kotwali Police Station and CR No.81/1994 registered in New Mondha Police Station, Parbhani district, Maharashtra.
7. *Munna alias Ravindrasingh Dilipsingh Parihar vs. State of Maharashtra,* Special Leave Petition (Cr.I) No (s) 5048/2018, Court No.7 (Supreme Court of India, 27 November 2018).
8. *Kalyan v/s State of Maharashtra,* Review petition No 255 of 2019 in Special Leave Petition (CRL) No.4201 of 2018 (Supreme Court of India, 16 July 2019).

17. Highway Dacoits

1. District Satara, Government of Maharashtra. https://www.satara.gov.in/en/history/ (accessed 12 August 2021).

19. White Collar Crimes

1. Dr A. P. J. Abdul Kalam, "The Effects of Corruption on Good Governance and Human Rights," 9 May, 2006, address during the inauguration of the seminar, Vigyan Bhavan, New Delhi. http://abdulkalam.nic.in/sp090506.html.

20. The Hubert H. Humphrey Fellowship

1. Source World of Statistics
2. https://www.pib.gov.in/PressReleasePage.aspx?PRID=1873307
3. Source World Statistics.

24. Jewel Thieves at Joyalukkas

1. "Three held in Mumbai for Hyderabad heist," *Live India,* 18 May 2006. https://www.liveindia.com/news/zzv.html.
2. "Police get vital clues in Hyderabad jewellery theft case," *Web India* 123, 18 May 2006. https://news.webindiaXII3.com/news/articles/India/20060518/337343.html.
3. "Joy Alukkas," *Forbes.* https://www.forbes.com/profile/joy-alukkas/#5eee97e048aa.

4. "Chief Metropolitan Magistrate's Court, Mumbai," *E-Courts Mission Mode Project*. https://districts.ecourts.gov.in/mumbai-cmm-court (accessed 18 and 22 May 2020).

25. Extortion Calls and Two-and-a-half Arrests

1. Vappala Balachandran, "Chhota Rajan's Victims May Have Cause to File Suit Against the Government," *Wire*, 4 May 2018. https://thewire.in/security/troubled-times-may-lurk-before-the-nda-vis-a-vis-chhota-rajan. Chhota Rajan's Victims May Have Cause to File Suit Against the Government (thewire.in)
2. "Doval part of covert op to kill Dawood in 2005: Shocking revelations by BJP MP put Modi government in fix," *Firstpost*, 25 August 2015. https://www.firstpost.com/politics/doval-part-of-covert-op-to-kill-dawood-in-2005-shocking-revelations-by-bjp-mp-put-modi-government-in-fix-2406788.html.
3. "Chhota Rajan arrest planned by NSA Ajit Doval in attempt to get info on Dawood," *Firstpost*, 28 October 2015. https://www.firstpost.com/politics/chhota-rajan-surrender-op-was-planned-by-nsa-ajit-doval-whos-been-trying-to-get-evidence-on-dawood-from-his-most-bitter-rival-2483414.html.

26. The Truth Triumphs

1. S. Balakrishnan, "Failure to nab Haseena, Meeran pays," *Times of India*, 17 May 2007. https://timesofindia.indiatimes.com/city/mumbai/failure-to-nab-haseena-meeran-pays/articleshow/2055874.cms.
2. "Borwankar wanted to go slow on Haseena," *Mumbai Mirror*, 18 May 2007. https://mumbaimirror.indiatimes.com/mumbai/other/borwankar-wanted-to-go-slow-on-haseena/articleshow/15708552.cms.

27. Stalking

1. https://indiankanoon.org/doc/50347/
2. https://main.sci.gov.in/case-status

29. New Commissioner in Pune

1. District Pune, Government of Maharashtra, accessed [18th August 2021]. https://pune.gov.in/.

32. Behind the Political Curtain

1. Imtiaz Jaleel, "Statue's removal creates controversy, violence in Pune," *NDTV*, 27 December 2010. https://www.ndtv.com/india-news20/statues-removal-creates-controversy-violence-in-pune-443121.
2. "Senas protest Shivaji guru's statue shift," *Business Standard*, 20 January 2013. https://www.business-standard.com/article/economy-policy/senas-protest-shivaji-guru-s-statue-shift-110122800115_1.html.
3. *Dr Smt Neelam Gohre vs. State of Maharashtra*, WPCRL 371/2012 (Bombay High Court, 28 March 2012). ANR in Law means another
4. *Neelam Gohre vs. State of Maharashtra*, Cri 4814/2012 (Supreme Court of India, 28 August 2012).

33. Prisons and a Celebrity

1. *Sanjay Dutt vs State Of Maharashtra*, Criminal Appeal No. 1060 of 2007 (The Supreme Court of India, 21 March 2013).
2. Aditi Pai, "Pune misses Munnabhai's magic as police call off Sanjay Dutt's show," *India Today*, 26 September 2013. https://www.indiatoday.in/featured/story/sanjay-dutts-show-cancelled-in-pune-212371-2013-09-26.
3. "Yerawada jail show put off, reason not clear," *Indian Express*, 27 September 2013. https://indianexpress.com/article/cities/pune/yerawada-jail-show-put-off-reason-not-clear/.

36. The Black and White Coats

1. https://indiankanoon.org/doc/1569030/
2. *S.B. Shahane & Others v. State Of Maharashtra & AN*, Case no.: Appeal (civil) 676 of 1982 (Supreme Court of India, 21 April 1995).
3. *Rekha Murarka v. The State of West Bengal and ANR, Criminal Appeal No. 1727 of 2019* (Supreme Court of India, 20 November 2019).

https://main.sci.gov.in/supremecourt/2019/30637/30637_2019_13_1501_18457_Judgement_20-Nov-2019.pdf.

4. Directorate of Forensic Scientific Laboratories Home, Government of Maharashtra. https://dfsl.maharashtra.gov.in/1035/Home (accessed 30 April 2020 and 21 July 2021).
5. Ibid.
6. Divya Narayanan, "The wrong theory that survives 23 years after Delhi's infamous 'tandoor murder case'," *Print*, 7 March 2018. https://theprint.in/defence/the-wrong-theory-that-survives-23-years-after-delhis-infamous-tandoor-murder-case/39927/.
7. Ibid.
8. Mengle, Gautam, "Anti Narcotics Cell still lacks testing kits for mephedrone," *Hindu*, 19 February 2019. https://www.thehindu.com/news/cities/mumbai/anti-narcotics-cell-still-lacks-testing-kits-for-mephedrone/article26306767.ece.
9. *Thana Singh v. Central Bureau Of Narcotics* (Supreme Court of India, 23 January 2013). https://indiankanoon.org/doc/63332651/.

37. Human Trafficking

1. Ruth Dearnley, "Prevention, Prosecution and Protection – Human Trafficking," *UN Chronicle* by United Nations. https://www.un.org/en/chronicle/article/prevention-prosection-and-protection-human-trafficking#:~:text=In%202000%2C%20the%20United%20Nations,been%20signed%20by%20177%20countries.
2. Ibid.
3. Maharashtra Control of Organized Crime Act

LIST OF ABBREVIATIONS

ACP: Assistant Commissioner of Police
Add CP: Additional Commissioner of Police
API: Assistant Police Inspector
ASI: Assistant Sub-Inspector
ASP: Assistant Superintendent of Police
BARC: Bhabha Atomic Research Centre
BDD: Bombay Development Department
BJP: Bharatiya Janata Party
BMC: Brihanmumbai Municipal Corporation
BPR&D: Bureau of Police Research and Development
BPT: Bombay Port Trust
BSF: Border Security Force
CAPF: Central Armed Police Forces
CBI: Central Bureau of Investigation
CCTNS: Crime and Criminal Tracking Network & Systems
CID: Crime Investigation Department
CM: Chief Minister
CP: Commissioner of Police
Cri-MAC: Crime Multi Agency Centre
CRO: Chief Risk Officer
CrPC: Code of Criminal Procedure
CVO: Chief Vigilance Officer
DCC: District Cooperative Credit Bank

DCP: Deputy Commissioner of Police
DG: Director General of Police
DIG: Deputy Inspector General of Police
DSB: District Special Branch
DSPE: Delhi Special Police Establishment
EOW: Economic Offences Wing
FIR: First Information Report
FSL: Forensic Science Laboratory
IA&AS: Indian Audits and Accounts Service
IAS: Indian Administrative Service
IB: Intelligence Bureau
IFS: Indian Foreign Service
IG: Inspector General of Police
IGNOU: Indira Gandhi National Open University
IL&FS: Infrastructure Leasing & Financial Services
IPC: Indian Penal Code
IPS: Indian Police Service
ITBP: Indo-Tibetan Border Police
JAPU: Juvenile Aid and Protection Unit
JCP: Joint Commissioner of Police
JNPT: Jawaharlal Nehru Port Trust
LBSNAA: Lal Bahadur Shastri National Academy of Administration
LCB: Local Crime Branch
LeT: Lashkar-e-Taiba
MCOC Act: Maharashtra Control of Organised Crime Act
MIDA: Maharashtra Institute of Development Administration
MLA: Member of Legislative Assembly
MP: Member of Parliament
MT: Motor Transport
MTNL: Mahanagar Telephone Nigam Limited
NBCC: National Buildings Construction Corporation

NC: Non-cognizable Case
NCDC: National Civil Defence College
NDPS Act: Narcotic Drugs and Psychotropic Substances Act
NDSO: National Database on Sexual Offenders
NGO: Non-governmental Organization
NPA: Non-Performing Assets
NSA: National Security Act
PAP: Punjab Armed Police
PCR: Police Control Room
PD: Police Department
PIL: Public Interest Litigation
POCSO Act: Protection of Children from Sexual Offences Act
PT: Physical Training
PTC: Police Training College
RBI: Reserve Bank of India
RCF: Rashtriya Chemicals and Fertilizers Limited
RTO: Road Transport Office
SCRB: State Crime Record Bureau
SHO: Station House Officer
SI: Sub-Inspector
SIT: Special Investigation Team
SP: Superintendent of Police
SVPNPA: Sardar Vallabhbhai Patel National Police Academy
TADA: Terrorist and Disruptive Activities (Prevention) Act
TIP: Test Identification Parade
UN: United Nations
UNESCO: United Nations Educational, Scientific and Cultural Organization
UPSC: Union Public Service Commission
UTI: Unit Trust of India
YASHADA: Yashwantrao Chavan Academy of Development Administration

ACKNOWLEDGEMENTS

In the making of this book I must acknowledge the contribution of my family and friends who have, over the years, patiently listened to my stories in uniform and encouraged me to share them widely. And Sunanda Mehta who introduced me to Teesta Guha Sarkar at Pan Macmillan India. Teesta worked on the book with me closely. Her colleagues Shreya Gupta and Isha Banerji helped with the finishing touches, while Haitenlo Semy prepared the cover.

My grateful thanks to officers of all ranks of the Maharashtra Police, prisons and other departments who made my thirty-six-year-long career in uniformed service unforgettable. I hope my story will inspire readers to stay strong and upright in their own professions and value the importance of social justice and a responsible civil society.